GW00670524

GERARD RONAN

'The Irish Zorro'

The extraordinary adventures
of William Lamport (1615-1659)

First published in Britain and Ireland in 2004 by Brandon
an imprint of Mount Eagle Publications
Dingle, Co. Kerry, Ireland and
Unit 3, Olympia Trading Estate, Coburg Road, London N22 6TZ, England

ISBN 0 86322 329

2 4 6 8 10 9 7 5 3 1

Cover design by id communications, Tralee
Typesetting by Red Barn Publishing, Skeagh, Skibbereen
Printed and bound in the United Kingdom

For Cliona and Eleanor

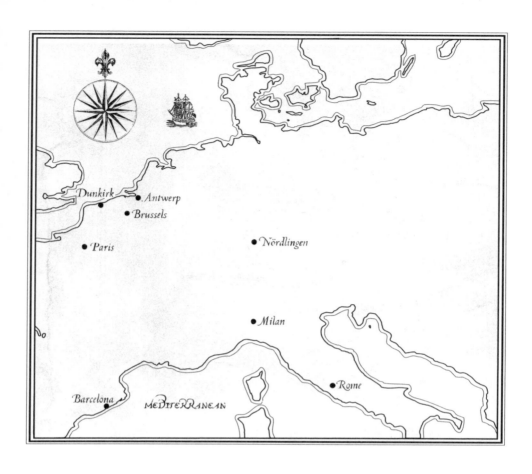

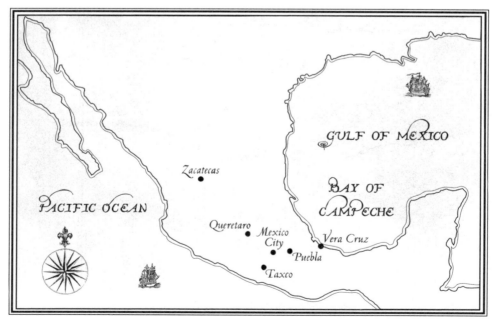

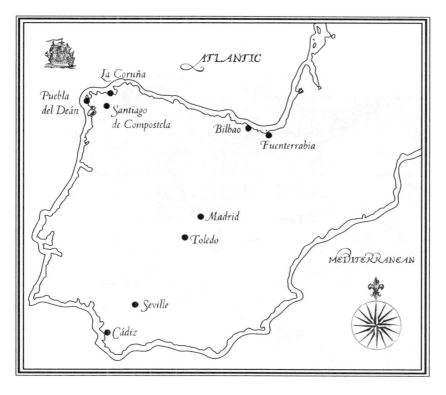

List of Illustrations

between pages 158 and 159

PREFACE

O<small>N</small> 6 A<small>PRIL</small> 1999, in her address to the Mexican Senate, the Irish President, Mary McAleese, called her audience's attention to a fact known to only a handful of Mexicans and Irish alike. Not too far away, she noted, in the vestibule of the capital's Column of Independence, there stood a statue erected in memory of an Irishman, Don Guillén de Lampart (or plain William Lamport as he would have been known in his native Wexford), a man 'recognised as one of the first precursors of Mexican independence'.

Her Excellency, had she been aware of the fact, could also have noted that in nearby Coyoacán the young students of Guillén de Lampart Elementary School occasionally sang an anthem in his honour, or that his story, obscured by cliché and surmise, and misted by the passage of time, had inspired the work of several Mexican novelists and playwrights. His life in Mexico, or rather a romantic and fictionalised version of it, may also have played a part in the creation of Johnston McCully's Zorro—an iconic figure that in its turn inspired the creation of Bob Kane's Batman.

The primary purpose of this book, however, is not just to explore whether or not William was deserving of his title of 'Precursor of Mexican Independence' or to determine the extent to which he may or may not have merited his more recent incarnation as 'Zorro the Irishman', 'The Irish Zorro', 'Paddy O'Zorro', etc., but to tell the story of a talented young man fated always to be an outsider and of the adventures that brought him to Mexico in the first place. It is the reality of his life with which this book seeks to concern itself: a reality as strange, if not stranger, than the fiction it is said by some to have inspired.

By the time he had celebrated his thirteenth birthday, William Lamport had already been arrested in London on a charge of high treason.

Following his escape, he spent two years or more aboard a pirate vessel, on which he helped to defeat the English navy at the siege of La Rochelle (1628). By twenty-five, at a time when Europe was soaked in the blood of religious wars, he had already travelled most of the continent, was claiming proficiency in no less than fourteen languages and boasting a curriculum vitae that included various episodes as a scholar, pamphleteer, engineer and military tactician. He may also have played a pivotal part in altering the course of European history at the Battle of Nördlingen (1634).

Sent to Mexico as a spy following a scandalous affair with a young noblewoman at the court of Felipe IV of Spain, he was arrested by the Inquisition in October of 1642 for plotting a rebellion—the stated aims of which were to abolish slavery and establish an independent Mexican state. On the night of 25 December 1650, he broke out of his cell in a manner so daring and brilliantly conceived that rumours immediately began to circulate that he had been assisted by demons. That escape, and the pamphlets he posted throughout the city as he fled, made him something of a local legend: a legend that endures to this day.

When starting out on this journey I had originally intended William's adventures to form no more than a part of an anthology of similar stories I had collected over the years. But the more I delved into the facts of his life and evaluated what had thus far been written about the man, the more I came round to the opinion that he deserved a far better epitaph than to be dismissed as 'one of those exuberant Irishmen who are so typical that they appear caricatures of themselves' (C. Roth, *The Spanish Inquisition*, 1964). That Roth was not the only historian to use the words 'typical' and 'Irish' in his description of William Lamport only added to my determination to dig deeper. There was nothing 'typical' about William Lamport.

Attempting to strip away the myths, embellishments and prejudices that surrounded the adventures of this controversial son of Wexford, and to thread together what remained into a coherent story that might begin to bring him to life as a person, has been a difficult task: rather like trying to reconstruct a window from shards of broken glass. The window, of course, can never look the same; especially when some pieces remain missing and others have been warped beyond all recognition.

The best one can hope for is a credible approximation of what it appeared like once.

For that reason alone, this book makes no pretensions to being a scholarly study. Nor does it purport to be a biography: there are just too few threads to be able to weave such a tapestry. Indeed such was the mythology that had already accumulated, and continues to accumulate about the man, that at times it seemed as though the present had deformed the past to a far greater degree than the past could ever inform the present.

Related to all this was the fact that while the last nineteen years of William's life had already received significant attention from historians, the previous twenty-five had received hardly any at all. In this respect much of what is written here is entirely new, especially with regard to the formative years prior to his arrival in Madrid. Also new is the discovery of his business dealings with Doña Inés Maldonado and the placing of such dealings in the crucial context of the great drought of 1641–1642: pivotal events totally overlooked by previous biographers.

There was also the considerable problem of not being able, for the greater part of his story, to allow William to speak with his own voice: so much of what was recorded having come from the last years of his life and a time when he was not in the best of mental health. To quote him at length on any aspect of his early life, therefore, was to risk pre-judging him: to draw him from the start as the man he became.

In an effort to address this problem, I have strived to link his accounts of the major events of his life to the known facts and, where possible, to sift out the obvious exaggerations. In the few instances where I was faced with a complete absence of proof, I had little option but to resort to reasonable conjecture; but where I have done so it has been clearly signposted. As for those occasions where dialogue has been used, these have been carefully reconstructed by transposing the testimony of witnesses from the third person into the first: they are not of my own invention.

Despite the limitations of what could be achieved without resorting to fiction, I felt that William's story, or rather what little of it remains, still deserved to be told, and the following reconstruction has been founded entirely upon reliable authorities, manuscript as well as printed, literary as well as political, the most important of which are listed amongst the sources at the end of this book. Nevertheless this is still, essentially speaking, William's story, and more or less as he told it himself, even to the point of referring to his elder brother by the name of 'Fray Juan' (Friar John). As this brother was never mentioned by any other name, I too have called him 'John', although this may simply have been a religious name he took upon entering the Franciscan order at Wexford.

It had also been my original intention to provide footnotes to the text, but the detailed and difficult nature of the detective work meant that these soon became so copious, lengthy and repetitive, that they almost doubled the size of the book. Given the style and nature of what I was attempting to write, I felt compelled to remove them. I recognise, however, that the absence of footnotes will increase the difficulty of relating the source material to the appropriate sections of the book and, in an effort to address this problem, I have departed from conventional protocol and listed the sources by title rather than by author, and grouped them according to their greatest relevance to the various phases of William's life. I hope this does not detract from your enjoyment of the book, and that it goes some way towards assisting those who wish to delve further into the depths of this rather remarkable and complex story.

(1)

*I*N THE EARLY summer of 1628, en route to the French port of St.
Malo, the captain of a Scottish merchantman spotted the sails of five
armed galleons on the horizon. Close-hauled and gaining fast, they flew
black ensigns at their mastheads and offered quarter for immediate surrender. Unable to outrun them, he struck his colours and came up into
the wind.

By the time the pirates had stripped their prey of her cargo and fittings, her disconsolate captain found himself with little option but to set
back to London. For one of his passengers, the realisation came as something of a blow. A callow youth of slim build, milky skin and a thick mane
of auburn hair, he came from the tiny port of Wexford in the south-east
corner of Ireland. His name was William Lamport. Before him lay a reputation as one of the precursors of Mexican independence, a colourful
chain of careers as a scholar, war hero and spy, and a scandalous love
affair with a young noblewoman at the court of Felipe IV of Spain.
Behind him, already, lay a classical education, a seditious Latin pamphlet, and a charge of high treason. He was thirteen years old.

What happened next is unclear. Having just escaped from prison, a
return to London was obviously out of the question: he had no wish to
imperil further the lives of those who had so recently helped to smuggle him out of England, or indeed his own. But whether he was taken
captive—as he himself would later claim—or whether he actively sought
sanctuary, the upshot of it all was that he bade farewell to his Jesuit
guardian, placed his trust in his family motto ('*Deus Providebit* . . . God
will provide'), and boarded one of the pirate vessels. It was to be the
beginning of one of the most extraordinary adventures ever recorded.

(2)

*J*UST TWENTY-SEVEN YEARS had passed since the day William's father, Richard Lamport, helped to pilot a Spanish armada into the southern Irish port of Kinsale. The Spanish had come to support a rebellion by the native Irish against their English overlords: a rebellion that was being led by the Gaelic chieftain, Hugh O'Neill.

It was the autumn of 1601. Elizabeth I sat on the English throne and was struggling to gain total control of Ireland. As the subjects of a Protestant queen, the Irish were expected to conform to Elizabeth's religious beliefs. The Catholic faith, therefore, was outlawed in Ireland, though conformity to the official religion could not really be enforced except in those areas where the English were completely in control, and sometimes not even there.

As fellow Catholics, one might have expected Richard Lamport's friends and neighbours in Wexford to have enthusiastically supported a rebellion that aimed at ensuring their religious freedom, but there were few who did. They may have been Catholics, but as the descendants of Anglo-Norman knights who had invaded Ireland in 1170, they also considered themselves to be English. Called 'Old English'—to distinguish them from the more recently arrived, and exclusively Protestant, New English settlers—they professed temporal allegiance to the King and spiritual allegiance to the Pope. It was a difficult game to play, but necessity had made them masters of ambiguity.

Richard, however, was a stubborn and devout Catholic for whom matters spiritual always took precedence over matters temporal. A survivor of the worst of the Elizabethan persecutions and land settlements, he had lived to see his beliefs become synonymous with treason, his neighbours executed for carrying priests to France, and both friends and family forsake the true faith to hold on to their lands and titles. He had also lived to see a distant cousin raised to the position of Catholic primate of

Ireland, and when Peter Lombard promised a 'crusade indulgence' to all Catholics who took part in the rebellion, Richard was amongst the few in Wexford to respond.

The reluctance of his friends and neighbours was understandable. Were O'Neill to win, they stood to lose everything to the native Irish: were he to be defeated, they could lose everything, in the subsequent purges and confiscations, to the Crown. So fearful, in fact, were the Old English clergy of the consequences, that not only did they lobby against O'Neill in Rome, they even preached against him from the pulpit. In his excommunication of Elizabeth I, they argued, the Holy Father had not deprived her of Ireland. There was no legal or religious impediment, therefore, to their acceptance of the Queen as their 'temporal' head. Such sermons, however, cut little ice with Richard, and on 2 October 1601, he helped to steer the armada of Don Juan del Águila into the harbour at Kinsale.

What followed was nothing less than a disaster. The impatience of the Hiberno-Spanish leadership allowed the English to snatch an unlikely victory from the jaws of almost certain defeat, and effectively gifted control of Ireland to Elizabeth. The English conquest was now complete, and serious damage had been done to the cause of religious tolerance. Even Peter Lombard was forced to admit it was time to 'render unto Caesar' and focus on the struggle for religious rather than political liberty.

In the aftermath of battle, Richard Lamport ended up helping to transport defeated and disillusioned Irish troops to the Spanish armies in La Coruña and Flanders. It was a lucrative enterprise—the exodus being so great that the Spanish were soon able to consolidate the exiles into one entirely Irish regiment—but it was also a dangerous one, and sometime between 1608 and 1610 his ship was lost. Thankful for small mercies, he returned to Wexford where, at the height of a boom in the local herring fishing industry, he proceeded to reinvent himself as a merchant.

The girl who was to become William's mother was called Allison (variously hispanicised as *Aldonsa* or *Alonssa* in the Spanish records), and she was the second daughter of Leonard Sutton of Rahayle—a local nobleman who appears to have shared at least some of Richard's ties to

Spain. In 1598, Sutton not only survived an attack by English pirates on a Spanish ship sailing from Cádiz to London, but also a brief spell as a captive in a North African prison. His ship, *Le Handymayde de Villa Wexford*, was also known to be actively engaged in smuggling. It is not beyond the bounds of possibility, therefore, that Richard Lamport had at some time worked for, or with, his new father-in-law.

Allison was just a girl in her late teens at the time she was taken from the country manor in which she had been reared to the Wexford town house where her new husband, a man old enough to be her father, had recently installed her marriage bed. It was to prove a difficult transition. Compared to the idyllic surrounds of her upbringing, Wexford, like most other towns of the period, was noisy and unhealthy. Faction fights were not uncommon outside the local brothels and alehouses, and the saline bite of the fresh sea air was frequently tempered by the malodorous effusions of the local tanning pits and curing houses, not to mention the raw sewage that was tossed each morning into the feculent and verminous alleys that ran steeply downhill to the docks. Within the quarter moon of the town's defensive wall, a little over a thousand souls shared living conditions so cramped that disease, when it deigned to strike, spread quicker than a piece of salacious gossip.

Allison's adaptation to urban living was not helped either by her husband's continued absences. Unable to forsake the sea for long, Richard had no sooner wed than he had resumed his 'commercial' voyages to France and Spain. Nevertheless, over the course of the next eight years, she bore him three sons and a daughter. William, the second born, or rather the second to survive the perils of childbirth and infancy, entered the world on 25 February 1615.

William's birth marked a watershed in the family's fortunes, as it more or less coincided with the sudden re-enforcement by an Irish parliament—dominated now by 'New English' Protestants—of a body of anti-Catholic legislation that up to now had been largely ignored. Catholic lawyers were disqualified, Catholics were purged from the county commissions of the peace, and a group of Wexford landowners who dared to take their grievances to London found themselves transported to Virginia for their trouble. No longer considered fully English, and unwilling to consider themselves fully Irish, the Old English were forced to construct for themselves a separate and unique identity in which race, nationality and religion squabbled like jealous siblings.

Just six years later, at about the time that William was cutting his second teeth, the bloody sport of bull-baiting arrived in Wexford from Spain. Trailing in its wake came a renewed interest in all things Spanish and an expectation that the coronation of Felipe IV would yield a fresh initiative in their attempts to find a remedy to the discriminatory policies of the English administration. Hopes were raised even further by the news of the proposed marriage of England's Prince Charles to Spain's Infanta María. A Catholic queen on the English throne, it was thought, would bide well for a relaxation of anti-Catholic legislation and there were many in Ireland who were anxious to ensure that a guarantee was woven into the marriage contract.

Against this tapestry of international political intrigue, Richard Lamport set sail for Spain on a 'business' trip, the extended duration of which suggested rather more than simple commerce (in later years, William would seek to remind the Spanish King of 'the many and illustrious services performed on behalf of Your Majesty and your predecessors, by my Catholic parents and antecedents'). Whatever the nature of Richard's business, while he was absent from Wexford his young wife was gathered to God.

Allison's death was sudden, unexpected, and to this day unexplained. But like so much of what happened about this time, it was not beyond William's comprehension. He was old enough by now to understand that death was not reversible: that it could happen to anyone, even himself. He was also at that age when children can so easily fall into holding themselves accountable, through their own actions or omissions, for all manner of family tragedies for which they bear no responsibility whatsoever. Whatever the reason, after his mother's corpse had been lowered into the earth and the emotional tide of solicitude and condolences had finally turned, he became an unusually angry and unruly child.

Along with John (the eldest), and Gerald and Catherine (younger by one and two years respectively), William was shepherded from the family home and into the care of relatives. It was a trying time for them all, but most especially, it seemed, for William. Finding little consolation in the well-meaning efforts of his new guardians, he seemed possessed by some devilish compunction to push everything to its limit. His relatives were tolerant—he was only eight—but in John's eyes he was being let away with murder.

The five-year gap between John and William might as well have been twenty at this juncture, for it not only affected the way in which each interpreted their very personal tragedy, but also the manner in which each was consoled. By the norms of the day, William was still a child: John, on the other hand, was on the threshold of manhood and expected to provide his younger siblings with a manly example of fortitude and composure. It was just one more example of allowances being made for the younger brother; another brick in the wall that was slowly being raised between them.

A year later, about the time the royal marriage negotiations collapsed, Richard Lamport returned to Wexford to hear for the first time of his wife's untimely demise. With grief and remorse pulling down on him like a pair of roped millstones that could be unbound only by an unselfish act of atonement, he took a sudden mind to enter the priesthood. He was growing old. It was time to think of his eternal salvation. To begin his preparations, he moved out of the family home and into the house of Father William Devereux; a renowned schoolmaster in his mid-forties. The children were left where they were—with one exception.

It is not known for certain why Richard chose to bring William with him to Devereux's (according to John just 'father and son' moved in). Perhaps it had been on account of his precocity; perhaps he was seen as a potential priest, bishop or cardinal; perhaps he had simply become too troublesome for his aunt and uncle to cope with. Whatever the reason, the fact was that William was yet again being singled out for special treatment.

For many years previous to this William Devereux had been a fugitive from English justice, never spending too long in any one town or more than a couple of nights under any one roof. In 1623, however, as England's Prince Charles was setting out for Spain, the Irish government was ordered to suspend the enforcement of anti-Catholic legislation lest it prove to be a hindrance to Charles' proposed marriage to the Infanta María—who at that time was digging in her heels and threatening to enter a convent rather than marry a heretic.

When Charles eventually returned from Madrid, embarrassed, empty-handed and calling for war with Spain, it looked as though the suspension would be lifted. His subsequent marriage to another Catholic princess, Henrietta Maria of France, however, more or less cemented the arrangement. Just how relaxed things had become in Wexford in the meantime was evidenced by the fact that Devereux could now openly lodge himself within the town; for not only was Devereux a Catholic priest, he was the Parish Priest of Wexford.

Richard was not the first Lamport that Devereux had prepared for the priesthood, and he would probably not be the last; but between his tutoring of Richard and his efforts to draft a catechism for the local children, he had little time for William and the primary responsibility for his education was delegated to Thomas Furlong, a local Augustinian from whom William received daily instruction in reading, writing and the rudiments of Latin.

After Furlong died, in 1625, responsibility for William's education passed to a brace of Franciscan friars who operated out of a private residence on High Street. Their names were Anthony Turner and Walter Cheevers, and he studied with them until the autumn of 1626, when his father was finally accepted into the Order of Saint Augustine at Selskar Abbey. Kissing William goodbye, he told him what life expected of a man and put him aboard a ship bound for Dublin. They would exchange the occasional letter, but they would never meet again.

(3)

BELIEVED BY NOW to be a something of a prodigy, William might, under different circumstances, have been heading to Dublin's Trinity College. But the hindrance of the oath of supremacy—which involved recognising the King of England as the 'supreme head on earth of the whole Church of Ireland'—meant that devout Catholics could no more attend a university than they could practise law or hold public office. So when the next best thing, a Jesuit college on Dublin's Back Lane, finally opened its doors, Richard saw to it that William was one of the first pupils to be enrolled.

Situated on the brow of Cork Hill, just a stone's throw from the city's fish market, the Back Lane seminary (these days 'The Taylor's Hall') was essentially a converted red-bricked townhouse that shielded a school, a chapel and twenty-six rooms—just twelve of which were at the disposal of the students. A gated arch led, by way of a flagstone path, to an oak-panelled main door where new arrivals were customarily received by the rector, Henry Cusack, and introduced to the rest of the students and faculty.

Restless, imaginative and somewhat impulsive, William was in many respects like every other eleven-year-old of his generation. But at Back Lane his new classmates were not children, they were young men (the youngest being some four years his senior). With precocity offering scant protection from the sensitivities and jealousies of the seminary, it was a lonely and difficult time, especially in the quietest hours of the night when, doors bolted and candles doused, it could not have been easy to suppress the feeling of abandonment.

And yet opportunities like this were as rare as horses on the streets of Venice. With the Jesuits being so highly dependent upon patronage, William's acceptance as a pupil is unlikely to have been entirely a matter of ability: in fact it speaks volumes for Richard's wealth and influence that his son was enrolled, not as a seminarian, but as a *lay* student. No matter how difficult the transition, William was now honour-bound to make the most of the privilege and to grow up fast. The problem with accelerated paths of development, however, is that not all of life's lessons are learnt as thoroughly as they might be and the trappings of childhood are not always exhausted and left behind.

One of only eleven students, of whom eight were seminarians, William shared the top floor cloisters with his Jesuit mentors, whose daily routine followed the monastic model and began, after morning ablutions and meditation, with Mass in the first floor chapel.

A wood-panelled room about seventy-five feet long and twenty-seven feet wide, the chapel boasted a high roof, a railed gallery, a raised altar and a pulpit. There were no fixed pews, save for those around the wall between the four confessionals, and the room had 'neither chimney, table nor window that any may look out of'. The absence of windows provided a certain degree of privacy, but the drone of Father Nicholas Nugent accompanying his self-composed hymns on the organ would have left passers-by in little doubt as to what was taking place within. More accustomed to secret prayers in cramped living rooms, William would have found the experience both novel and spiritually uplifting— an act of blatant defiance almost, given the proximity of Dublin Castle (the epicentre of English administration in Ireland).

Breakfast followed Mass each morning, after which a brief period was spent helping with household chores or reading some carefully selected books. There then followed the first of two classes, which were followed by a further period of private study before dinner (always taken at midday). An hour of recreation was allowed between 1 p.m. and 2 p.m., after which the remainder of the afternoon would be devoted to further classes and study periods, an hour of which also followed supper. It was a strict regime; but nobody laboured under the illusion that they were anything less than privileged.

In eight of the eleven city parishes at this time, Catholics were in the majority—the only exceptions being the parishes of St. Werburgh, St. John and St. Catherine. The first two, which lay adjacent to Dublin Castle, were frequented mainly by government officials and their families; the third lay in what was effectively an aristocratic suburb. Catholics outnumbered Protestants within the city walls by a factor of two to one, and a whole network of places of worship had long since been established under the auspices of the Catholic gentry who had discreetly opened their homes and estates for the celebration of the Mass. The opening of a Jesuit college, however, represented an entirely new departure.

Of all the Catholic religious orders, the Jesuits were by far the most reviled by the Protestant establishment. Leaders of the Catholic Church's attempts to counteract the spread of Protestantism, they were essentially a military order and their presence was especially feared in England, where the *Act against Jesuits, seminary priests and other such like disobedient persons* had made it a crime of high treason for them to even set foot inside the country. Though only marginally less feared in Ireland, the constraints of domestic and foreign policy had made it inadvisable to act against them with quite the same vigour as had led to the martyrdom of so many of their English brethren. No-one doubted, however, that that day would eventually come. The existence of the Back Lane seminary, therefore, was considered extremely precarious—an iron to be grasped while still hot.

For the next year or so then, Back Lane became home from home for William and, apart from daily conferences with Father George Fitzgerald, the Master of Novices, which everyone was required to attend, he spent the greater part of his time in the august company of his professors of humanities, Henry Plunkett and Thomas Quin, from whom he learnt the rudiments of the *Trivium* (grammar, rhetoric and logic). He also received lessons in Greek from a certain John Shee.

At his father's insistence, William's education was occasionally supplemented by private tuition in the arts of poetry and panegyric from Sir Nicholas White, who lived just fourteen miles outside the city in Leixlip Castle. The member of parliament for the county of Kildare, White was the son of a notorious convert to Catholicism and the grandson of a former Master of the Rolls in Ireland (a man who had once enjoyed the confidence of Elizabeth I).

In choosing White as a tutor, Richard had probably hoped to obtain for William the kind of influence that might procure for him an English education. Extraordinary political changes were taking place at this time: changes that promised new opportunities for prodigious youngsters like

William, and which could *only* be availed of in London. But though well thought of, White no longer wielded anything like the influence of his late grandfather, at least not of the kind that William needed. The good fathers, on the other hand, knew a family who did.

The architect of the aforementioned changes, Sir John Bathe, was the grandson of a Chief Baron and the son of a Chancellor of the Irish Exchequer. As a grandnephew of the ninth Earl of Kildare, through whom he was related to Elizabeth I, he was so well connected at court that he had once held the post of equerry to James I—a surprising appointment at the time, given that he was unashamedly Catholic. Religious restrictions, however, were usually only a problem for men of Bathe's pedigree when accompanied by suspicious politics and Bathe's allegiance had long since been established—or at least that's how it appeared at the time.

At the peak of his fame and influence, Bathe had been on intimate terms with the Spanish Ambassador to London, various members of the Privy Council of England, and with the court of Felipe III of Spain— where he was known as 'Don Juan of the powerful memory'. There were, however, a number of individuals in Spain who suspected him of being a double agent: suspicions that were not entirely without foundation.

During the early years of the century—at least according to a report of Andrés Velázquez, the councillor in charge of the Spanish secret service—Bathe had operated as a spy for the Spanish. But he had also been in the pay of the English: in November of 1613, in fact, he had been secretly ordered to create dissent within the ranks of the Irish regiment in Flanders, and to widen the divisions that already existed between the Old Irish and Old English communities in Spain. Five years later, prior to leaving Madrid for Flanders, a suspicious Florence Conry, one of the chief advisors to the Spanish Council on Irish Affairs, wrote to Felipe IV warning him to be wary of Bathe:

> In this Court there resides an Irishman named Juan Batheo to whom Your Majesty gives forty crowns a month, not in consideration of his own services to Your Majesty, nor those of his ancestors, all of whom served the Crown of England, for they are of the English race, but because of his good parts and

particularly because of what he calls his Art of Memory. I have learned from a secret and reliable source that, when the said Don Juan first came here, he promised the Viceroy of Ireland, called Arthur Chicester, to inform him of affairs of state which he might hear and to find out in this Court that which would be of service to the King of England and, to confirm his loyalty to the said Viceroy, when the said Don Juan landed in Lisbon, he sent back certain information concerning the navy.

Conry went on to detail Bathe's dealings with the English Ambassador, John Digby, and to advise that it would be dangerous to allow him access to the court. But Spanish bureaucracy moved with incredible lethargy and though the letter was discussed at a meeting of the Council of State on 19 May, action had yet to be taken when, on 16 July, Bathe stabbed the illustrious Donal O'Sullivan Beare to death as he attempted to intervene in a duel between Bathe and the historian Philip O'Sullivan outside the Monastery of Saint Dominic.

The 57-year-old O'Sullivan Beare, one of the most influential leaders of the Irish community in Spain, had been planning to return to Ireland to lead another rebellion there and this, at least in the opinion of some, was the true reason for his assassination. Bathe's story, however, was that he had been set upon by a group of Irish soldiers led by O'Sullivan Beare and that he would have been killed had it not been for the intervention of two passing Spanish knights. In a letter to the Spanish king, dated September 1620, he claimed that *his* version would be corroborated by the local magistrate and his officials.

Upon his release, Bathe fled to London where he received an annual pension of £500 from a grateful James I and quickly rose to a prominent position at court. His influence on all matters Irish even survived the death of James and at the time William was sent to London, Bathe was advising the government of Charles I. To all and sundry it appeared that there was no-one more loyal and royal than Sir John; but nothing was ever quite what it seemed with this enigmatic Irishman.

The primary reason for sending William to the Bathes, however, dates back to March of 1625 and the ascent of Charles I to the English throne. So determined was the new king to declare war on Spain that just three months into his reign he set in motion the plans for what was to prove a disastrous maritime raid on Cádiz. No matter what the outcome of the raid, it was a safe bet that the Spanish would seek to retaliate by invading Ireland (where they could always count on the support of the native Irish). Anxious to ensure that his back door was adequately bolted, Charles now needed the support of *all* his loyal subjects, regardless of their religious beliefs.

It was an opportunity too good to miss and Sir John Bathe was quick to spot the possibilities. He immediately took it upon himself to negotiate improved conditions for the Old English community in return for their promised support. Although pretty much a self-appointed spokesperson, he succeeded, nevertheless, in September of 1625, in obtaining various concessions from the Crown, amongst which was a promise to replace the oath of supremacy with one of allegiance. At the same time as he was attempting to force these concessions from Charles I, however, Bathe was also advising Felipe IV of Spain on the current deployment of English forces in Ireland and the best means of instigating yet another rebellion there!

The Old English were now expected to subscribe the sum of £3,000 to the government and recruit an auxiliary militia force to defend Dublin against a possible Spanish invasion. Amongst those Bathe nominated for the command of this force was his close ally, the Earl of Westmeath (to whom William claimed to be related), and amongst those nominated for subordinate positions was Sir Nicholas White the younger (William's private tutor in the 'Art of Panegyric'). It would seem then, apart from the recommendations of his Jesuit tutors, that there were other, more personal reasons why responsibility for William's education was being accepted by the Bathes.

Bathe, in fact, had already backed himself into a corner, having recently called for a return to the practice of sending the children of Ireland's Old English gentry to England to be reared and educated. Here, he believed, the study of English law and customs would make them better qualified to hold those official positions currently denied them by anti-Catholic legislation. He could hardly refuse a prodigy, especially now that the removal of the oath of supremacy was promising to open new doors to Catholics of proven ability.

For the younger sons of the 'gently born'—whose elder brothers had customarily inherited sole title to the family estates and businesses—the law offered the only profession outside of the Church or the military that was seen as 'acceptable' employment and under the new agreement Catholics would once more be admitted into the Inns of Court. Richard, it would appear, had never envisaged his son becoming a Jesuit, but a lawyer: hence the private tuition from Sir Nicholas White, himself a lawyer and the owner of a considerable swathe of land around Dunbrody in Co. Wexford.

In the summer of 1627 then, a chaperone was assigned to William— a certain 'John of Enniscorthy' (most likely the Father John Wadding he would later mention as having been amongst his tutors in Dublin but who was not listed amongst the residents at Back Lane)—and the pair were sent down to Merchants' Quay to book their passage to England. On the next high tide they began the short sea crossing to Chester, eyes abaft and fixed on dark shadows of the Dublin and Wicklow mountains as they fell away behind them. There was no family to wave them off, no tearful goodbyes: their only fanfare the plaintive cry of the herring gulls.

(4)

$\mathcal{T}$HE NATIVE ENGLISH looked upon him as something of a foreigner. In Ireland he had always been considered English, but in England he was considered Irish. His Wexford dialect was perceived as old-fashioned, quaint, and reminiscent of the poetry of Chaucer. When speaking of the city some twelve years later, William would recall that one of the primary reasons he had been sent to London was 'to learn the English language'.

But for all that, London was a wonder; with its great buildings, long broad streets, and the great *mélange* of galleys, drumblers, barques and gilded river barges that ploughed the murky waters of the Thames. Equally exciting were the crowds of booksellers that thronged Paternoster Row and the Churchyard of St. Paul's. The current passion was for works of a spiritual nature, but one could generally find something to satisfy even the most bizarre of tastes. To a curious youth, it was akin to finding Aladdin's cave.

As for his tutors, there were few more intelligent or educated Catholics in London than Sir John Bathe, and William could not have had a more powerful mentor. Primary responsibility for the direction of William's education, however, was delegated to the man who, for the duration of the youngster's stay in London, was to become his guardian—a certain 'Father Bathe' (a Jesuit priest who does not appear amongst the records of the English Jesuits). Although William never stated as much, I have always believed these two Bathes to have been related. He never said what became of the man who chaperoned him to London.

Apart from private tuition, William's education was further supplemented by the lectures of the eminent professors of the Gresham College—a charitable institution once described by Sir George Buck as 'the third universitie of England'. Created with the intention of providing advanced education for mariners and merchants who lacked either the wherewithal or the right to attend a university, the Gresham provided free weekly lectures in divinity, rhetoric, geometry, medical science, astronomy, law and music.

The chair of geometry being vacant at this time, William was also sent for private tuition to a brilliant young Oxford graduate by the name of John Greaves (later to fill the vacant chair at the Gresham, and later still the Savilian Professorship of Astronomy at Oxford). Apart from an appreciation of all things mathematical, Greaves also managed to awaken in William an insatiable curiosity about the natural world around him by introducing him to the study of 'Natural Magic' and the 'Secrets of Nature'—the disciplines of which ranged from the study of botany, alchemy and animal behaviour, to the ancient search for the *substantia vitae* (a legendary cure-all).

It was a basic tenet of 'Natural Magic' that nature abounded with hidden forces that could be understood by means of rational explanations and harnessed to the benefit of mankind. For many Catholics, however, these sciences lay much too close to pagan superstition and witchcraft for comfort: the secrets of nature being the secrets of God and beyond the permissible limits of human knowledge. Moreover, in its attempt to enforce doctrinal uniformity and protect the faithful from superstition, the Catholic Church had condemned *all* magical activity as heretical.

As a Protestant and a scientist, Greaves had little tolerance for Roman obscurantism. The boy was twelve years of age: it was time he knew of such things. For William it was just another adventure, a furtive sally into an orchard of forbidden fruit. It was to be the first of many.

In just one subject did Sir John Bathe opt to tutor William personally, and that was the equally controversial 'Art of Memory', an ancient rhetorical technique discovered about the time of Pythagoras and adapted by Cicero to become part of the standard training for orators and scholars. The art had been invented by the poet Simonides of Ceos, who, following the collapse of a banquet hall in which he had recently been dining, succeeded in identifying each and every one of the grossly disfigured corpses by picturing the banquet hall in his mind's eye and recalling where each of the guests had been sitting. Realising that human memory could recall emotionally charged images more easily than abstract ideas, and ordered chains of associations more easily than random ones, he proceeded to develop a memory technique that involved transforming large tracts of information into easily recalled images and arranging them against a fixed architectural background, such as the interior of a building.

To see the art in action one must imagine an orator ambling in his imagination through a particular building and stopping to gaze upon the various images he has placed in set locations, such as windows or alcoves. In recalling these images, which may be either static or dynamic, the orator enables himself to remember the salient points of his speech, and in the correct order (the images preserving the details, and the locations the sequence in which they should be recalled). Today, when structuring an argument, we might still use the phrase 'in the first place'—a long forgotten remnant of a time when the use of the art was widespread.

The effectiveness of Simonides' method was based upon the premise that sight was the strongest of all the senses, and that images were better remembered if they were exceptionally beautiful, disturbing, comic, or even erotic in nature. Opponents of the art, however, claimed the creation of such images posed a danger to the mental and moral wellbeing of the practitioner and they were confirmed in their opinions by the recent adaptations of a former Dominican, Giordano Bruno, who had taken the art into the realms of magic and the occult by introducing powerful astrological images, magical incantations, mystical religious messages and an obsession with the number thirty.

No–one could say for certain that Sir John Bathe was a practitioner of the Brunian art, but they must have had their suspicions. Indeed it was common knowledge about the court that, shortly after her meeting with Bruno, Elizabeth I had requested Sir John's elder brother, the late William Bathe, to instruct her in the finer points of the Brunian art. Bruno's subsequent demise at the hands of the Roman Inquisition notwithstanding, the practice of his art had remained extremely fashionable amongst some of the more influential of London's Catholic families. By the time William arrived in London, however, even the classical form of the Art of Memory had become irretrievably associated in Protestant minds with popery, and in particular with the activities of London's Catholic underground.

There is no way of knowing what form of the art Sir John taught William, but it was most likely the classical form. It was also most probably Bathe, himself a renowned master of the art, who was responsible for initiating William into the practices that in later life would allow him to quote, from memory, exceptionally large extracts from all manner of books, and to such an extent that he could even recall the page or paragraph numbers.

Perhaps the real significance of William's involvement with Sir John Bathe, however, is that it existed at all. That he had been sent to study with a man of Bathe's calibre suggests that William was moving in some very illustrious circles indeed, and it leaves one with a lingering suspicion that his father's protracted absence from Ireland during the negotiation of the 'Spanish Match' was something more than a coincidence.

The 'Art of Memory', however, was not learnt in a vacuum, but was intended to help William along an accelerated path of learning in the study of other subjects, such as the standard texts of classical Greek and Roman literature. As he was being tutored in these subjects by his guardian, it seems probable that the youngster's equally famous linguistic abilities were developed, at least in part, with the help of an educational tool first developed by Sir John's Bathe's elder brother, the Jesuit linguist William Bathe.

An exceptionally intelligent and multi-talented man, William Bathe had, during his time as a musician at the court of Elizabeth I, not only presented her with a 'harp of a new dimension', but also published a book on the 'Art of Music'. Sometime about 1595, however, for motives that were as much political as spiritual, he fled to Spain to join the Society of Jesus and to write what was to become his seminal work—a methodology designed to facilitate the rapid assimilation of languages by Jesuit missionaries.

Known as the *Janua Linguarum* or 'Gate of Languages', this pioneering work involved the learning by rote of some 1,330 sentences, systematically arranged under various headings, and presented in parallel columns of different languages. The method relied heavily on the student's capacity for memory but was said to enable him to make in three months 'as much progress in the study of Latin as others made in three years'. Published by the Irish Jesuits in Salamanca, the *Janua* had become famous throughout Europe and was frequently copied and imitated. An English version, *The Messe of Tongues*, was widely available during William's residence in London.

One of Charles' first acts as King had been to declare war on Spain. But foreign wars were expensive and parliament had been disinclined to provide him with the necessary funds until such time as he had rid himself of his incompetent and much reviled first minister, the Duke of Buckingham. Unwilling to stand for such an ultimatum—he was, after all, a king by *divine* right—Charles bypassed parliament and attempted to raise the money himself by way of forced loans.

Charles' fundraising met with some initial success, but the money quickly ran out and he was soon faced with having to dip again into this legally suspect honeypot. Before he could do so, however, it was revealed, early in 1628, that he had actively encouraged the Attorney General to falsify a judgement handed down in a challenge to the legality of his forced loans. So enormous were the implications of this revelation, that Protestants and Catholics alike began to debate the morality of disobeying the edicts of an 'unworthy kinge'. For the more radically minded of Charles' opponents, the scandal represented nothing less than a God-given opportunity.

A Catholic underground movement, under the direction and control of the English Jesuits, had established in London such a complex network of spies that even the Duke of Buckingham was said to be within their reach. A popular revolt, they believed, would be very much to their advantage. If the rebels were subjugated, then the King's mercenaries would end up being paid out of confiscations: if they won, the mercenaries would mutiny. Either way there would be a serious groundswell of discontent that could only be of assistance to Charles' Catholic enemies.

At roughly the same time, following a tip-off that the poor women of Clerkenwell were delivering a suspicious amount of meat to a certain Catholic household in London, a warrant was issued to search the premises. Ten men and one woman were seized; seven of whom were said to be Jesuits. The house, it turned out, had been functioning as a seminary—much like the one that William had recently attended in Dublin.

How William came to be involved in underground activities is unclear; but naïve, impulsive, and intoxicated by talk of martyrdom, revolution and regicide, he got caught up that summer in the drafting and dissemination of a short Latin pamphlet in defence of the Roman Catholic faith. He called it his '*Defensio Fidei contra Carolum Anglie Regem et suam fidem* . . . A defence of the faith against King Charles of England and his belief', and he had been posting it about the city with some friends when he was arrested and imprisoned.

Given the rather delicate negotiations in which Sir John Bathe was engaged with the King, it is unlikely, though not impossible, that William had been acting with the consent of his mentors. A more plausible explanation would be that he had acted out of a sense of fraternal solidarity with the Jesuits who had recently been seized at Clerkenwell.

William would later claim that not only did he compose this seditious pamphlet, but that it was entirely his own work. Be that as it may, the title, the company he was keeping, and his age suggest otherwise. It is more likely that he had managed to get his hands on a banned book of a similar title and adapt to his own ends the arguments of its author—a Jesuit whose dangerous arrogance held enormous appeal for an embittered youth whose keen sense of natural justice had already been forged in the fires of religious bigotry, discrimination and subjugation.

Just fifteen years had passed since the radical Jesuit theologian, Francisco de Suárez, published his infamous '*Defensio fidei Catholicae* . . . A defence of the Catholic faith', and his equally notorious '*De legibus, ac Deo legislatore* . . . On laws, and God the law giver'. In his *Defensio fidei*, a work even the Roman Curia disapproved of, Suárez argued against the oath of allegiance and refuted the claims of James I to the divine right of the Lord's anointed without being under the direct authority of the Pope—so enraging James that he ordered the public hangman to burn a copy on the steps of St. Paul's.

In his *De legibus*, Suárez declared that a state could justly exist only through a social contract to which the people had *freely* given their consent and, more controversially still, that 'the Pope has the right of deposing heretical and rebel kings' and that monarchs so deposed 'may be killed by the first who can reach them'. The Parlement of Paris held such theories responsible for the assassination, in 1610, of Henry IV.

Suárez' concept of a social contract was neither novel nor imaginative (echoing as it did the assertion of the Roman Jurists and Scottish

Calvinists that imperial power was essentially a gift of the people), but his justification of regicide and the right of the people to revolution had so scandalised the royal courts of Europe that a hot reception was all but guaranteed for any subsequent re-hashing of his ideology—an ideology, that had made so deep an impression on William that many years later, when arrested by the Spanish Inquisition, one of the first books he would request in his efforts to frame a defence would be Suárez' *Defensio fidei*.

In the light of the King's financial difficulties, one can readily see why some Catholics might have felt that Suárez' philosophy might be more enthusiastically received this time around and why, when William and his young friends were arrested for disseminating such seditious material throughout London, they should have been in fear for their lives. Under the Act of Slander they risked being charged with high treason—serious enough in its own right—but the nature of the material they had so recklessly attempted to distribute meant they also risked being tried as Jesuits (just five months later a certain Edmund Arrowsmith would be hung, drawn and quartered for such a crime).

Several days after his arrest, however, William was to be found on the wharves of St. Katherine's Docks. He would never say what became of his friends and the details of his 'escape' remain obscure, but the bribing of turnkeys was not uncommon; nor was the use of influence at court, even on behalf of suspected priests. Such influence, in fact, had already been used by a former Lord Treasurer in effecting the release on bail of the Clerkenwell Jesuits, and Sir John Bathe was equally well-connected and an intimate of the powerful Duke of Buckingham.

But no matter how it had been secured, William's escape had not amounted to a pardon and he had little choice now but to flee the country. Accompanied by his Jesuit guardian he set sail on board a Scottish merchantman heading for the French port of St. Malo and an Irish colony with a long tradition of harbouring fugitives and from where it was hoped he could make his way safely to Spain.

(5)

*W*ILLIAM NEVER MADE it to St. Malo. Before the heavily laden merchantman upon which he was travelling could get within sight of the French coast, it was overtaken by a small fleet of English pirates. Stripped of his cargo and fittings, the Scotsman had little incentive to continue with his journey and little choice but to set back to London.

Return to London, of course, was an impossibility for William and whether he left freely, or whether he was taken captive to supplement the frequent losses of crew that were part and parcel of pirate life, the upshot of it all was that he bade farewell to his Jesuit guardian and boarded a pirate vessel where, neat as a bridegroom and impeccably coiffed, he stood out like a silk scarf in a rag pile.

The descendant of an Anglo-Norman knight who had invaded Ireland with Strongbow in 1170, he spoke an antiquated dialect of old Saxon English and, in the French manner, stressed the second syllable in disyllabic words. He came from a world of wood-panelled rooms and wainscot chairs; of box beds and feather mattresses; of red meat and rich wine; of Aristotle and Horace, Euclid and Pythagoras; a world of breviaries and catechisms, pater nosters and salve reginas. Seraphic of countenance and small for his age, he was not particularly well built, nor was he suited to physical labour: his long slender hands being callused only in the quill grip between thumb and middle finger. Truth be told he could easily, if dressed appropriately, pass for female.

His new comrades, on the other hand, were hardened mercenaries: defiant of God, contemptuous of the Devil, frequently inebriated and mistrustful of those who were not. Should any one of them take a mind to harm him—and it would be only too easy for a youth of his looks and background to give unwitting offence or attract the attentions of a drunken pederast hell-bent on teaching him the 'secrets of the sea'—

then there would be precious little he could do about it. There was nowhere to hide and no-one to turn to for protection.

But he was nothing if not resilient. He had lost so much over the course of the last six years that resignation to the vicissitudes of Fate had become something of a habit. Life may not have prepared him for piracy, but he was no clueless landsman: the sea was in his blood. The son of a wealthy merchant from the port of Wexford in the southeast corner of Ireland, he had been reared with the scent of tide wrack in his nostrils and he knew his way about a ship.

Impressing his 'captors' with his willingness to please, he rapidly became something of a holy novelty—a mirror, perhaps, of their better selves; perhaps even, like the pages of the Spanish armadas, an innocent vehicle better suited to the transmission of their prayers to the almighty. Four days later he was invited to go 'on the account'.

What exactly his duties were, he never actually said, but at thirteen years of age he lacked the physical strength necessary to perform the more physical labours of a ship, and there was little other work a boy of his age could be assigned to other than the duties of a page. In this role, apart from running messages and errands for captain and crew, he would have been responsible for such tasks as cleaning, tidying, preparation and distribution of meals, keeping watch and turning the sand clocks.

Joining the crew of a pirate ship, however, was no simple matter: there were oaths to be sworn and articles to be signed. Between them they governed duties and punishments, compensation rates for injuries and the sharing out of booty. They also bound him to the ship until such time as he had 'earned' his keep, and all but guaranteed that one day he would be asked to take a human life. Even for a thirteen-year-old this was no light undertaking; but he had little time to brood over the ramifications. Just sixteen days later, during a skirmish with a Dutch flotilla, he was baptised into the bloody mayhem that passed for naval combat in the seventeenth century.

With the sighting of Dutch colours, the ship rapidly became a hive of industry. Men and boys raced to their stations, guns were run out and loaded, decks were sanded and cooking fires extinguished. And then they waited—for the vessels to close and the lottery to begin.

At the first exchange of broadsides the engaging vessels were enveloped in a billowing curtain of acrid smoke that was penetrated only by the orange flashes of ordnance and the white flicker of muskets. To the relentless thunder of the big guns, the recoil from which ensured that the ship was constantly heaving, frenetic pages stumbled in and out of the fog, dodging falling timber and swinging tackle, and roaring orders from the captain. Direct hits lit up the smoke bank, sending splinters of wood and bony flesh flying in every direction and sluicing the deck in a river of blood. There was no skill or artifice that could guarantee survival: Fate alone would select the survivors.

The clockwork efficiency of the Dutch notwithstanding, the pirates succeeded in running clear and tacked away from their crippled pursuers greatly relieved and not a little deaf. Amongst the carnage William noticed that a young Frenchman he knew only as 'de Conde' (most likely a hispanisation of *Duconte*), lay fatally wounded. It was not his first encounter with death—he had already suffered the loss of his mother and an elderly Augustinian tutor—but it *was* his first with mutilation and gore.

After the dead had sewn into their hammocks (the last stitch being made through the nose to guard against mistakes) they were weighted down with shot and heaved over the side. A meeting was then convened before the mainmast where, in accordance with the traditions of the sea, the clothes of the dead were sold and their successors, as appropriate, voted in.

Much to his surprise, and out of eleven possible candidates, William found himself elected to succeed 'de Conde' to the post of 'general'— not a term that enjoyed wide nautical currency amongst English sailors at that time, but which to Spaniards denoted the commander of a fleet. In all probability, however, the post most likely entailed little more than being an innocent figurehead or principal page who gave formal voice to the 'general' will of the crew and led such religious services as were deemed necessary on board (something for which his education would have made him eminently suitable). He was young, it was true, but his shipmates were adamant: they did not want another who was 'versed in the ways of avarice' (his predecessor had been the son of an infamous French pirate), but preferred 'that they themselves should participate in the decision making' and 'govern by way of council'. Mettlesome, resilient and as honourable as one could be amongst thieves, opportunity would teach him what he did not already know; the rest, or so they believed, was a matter of breeding.

Or at least that is how William, some fourteen years later, would piece together his fragmented memories of those events. He would never say who actually held the post of captain, being content to create the impression that he himself had been in command (though he did identify two of the three captains as being Englishmen by the names of Cox and Hull).

Of the three pirate ships that survived this latest encounter with the Dutch, none were in any fit state to defend themselves from another attack, let alone instigate one of their own. There was little for it then, but to cut away the damaged masts, jury-rig replacements, and limp 'with just the hulls' to the safety of the Norwegian boatyards. Here, if they could avoid another encounter with the Dutch en route, they could lie privately for a while, tend to their ships and their wounded, and perhaps even recruit some reinforcements. At the very least they could replenish their supplies of fresh water.

Refits completed, they set to sea once more in September 1628 and, desperate to fly at higher game than fishing boats and timber merchants, headed south for the Bay of Biscay. Here they ran straight into what appeared at first glance to be yet another Dutch flotilla, but on closer inspection proved to be a patrol of the newly formed French Navy, sailing in Dutch-built vessels and under the command of the Duke of Guise. They were endeavouring to blockade the port of La Rochelle.

The last bulwark of Calvinism in Catholic France, and for many years a hotbed of Protestant disaffection, La Rochelle offered those who held her ready access to the very heart of France. Ravaged by famine and disease, the town was currently in the hands of rebel Huguenots who had been promised military support by the English. Having already made one feebly ineffective attempt to raise the siege, the English were expected to make another any day now.

The French despatched an envoy ('El Príncipe de Rucoy' according to William's recollection) and his proposition was enticing. A cash bonanza shortened everybody's ties to the ship and what harm, in any case, could befall them that they did not risk daily on the open sea? A vote was taken, but the result was never in doubt. Following the French through a narrow gap in the mile-long dyke of wood and stones that the French commander, Cardinal Richelieu, had constructed across far reaches of the harbour, the pirates dropped anchor and settled down to await the arrival of the 'English heretics'.

Day after day, night after night, with little to occupy their imaginations other than the vocal grief of the starving Rochellais and the daily departure of corpses over the walls (there being nowhere within the fort to bury them and few men left with strength enough to dig), they kept a weather-eye on the mouth of the estuary for the first hint of a vertical shadow or flickering lantern. They knew a little of conditions within the town—it was said that not a single dog or cat was left living and there were occasional rumours of cannibalism—but that was neither their problem nor their responsibility and for young William the word 'heretic' was all the balm his Catholic conscience required.

But if they knew little of what was happening on land, they knew even less about what was happening out at sea. There was just no way of knowing how soon the English might approach the dyke, or indeed how large a fleet they might send. They could not even be certain that the English *would* arrive. The only certainty in all of this was that the stubborn and desperate Rochellais would never surrender as long as there was hope, however slim, of relief. Becalmed in a sea of misery, with their victuals in limited supply, all they could do was wait, and hope that the English would come soon.

It was not the type of combat the pirates were used to. On the open sea there would typically be a moment of sighting, a decision to attack or flee, and then a flurry of excited activity as the ship was cleared for action. There would then follow a brief period of waiting as they gave chase or attempted to flee. That type of waiting they were accustomed to: this was unnatural—more a job for engineers than fighting men. There was just far too much time to think.

On Thursday 28 September, the waiting came to an end. A fleet of over a hundred sail under the command of Lord Lindsey arrived at Chef-de-Baie, a fortified promontory to the west of La Rochelle. Two days later, the bells of the besieged city began to peal as the first of the English ships approached the dyke.

But Lindsey was not about to be rushed. If the siege was to be lifted, then the dyke, which had been fortified with cannons, had to be breached. There was also the small matter of Richelieu's 20,000 land troops—more than a match for his own 5,000.

After three days of deliberation, Lindsey finally unleashed a ferocious barrage of some 5,000 balls at the French infantry and directed incendiary barges loaded with explosives at the dyke. But the barrage did little to reduce the odds and, in difficult seas, most of his incendiaries ran aground. The following Tuesday, at least according to William's account of the battle, the pirates took five English galleons by surprise and then gleefully watched a storm roll in that raged with such unrelenting fury that by Sunday it had sent the bulk of Lindsey's fleet scurrying back to England. Lindsey made one last attempt to breach the dyke on 10 October, but lacking the wholehearted support of his captains the attack quickly petered out.

Fearful of yet another attempt to lift the siege, the French continued to hold the pirates to their contract and they were still idling at anchor on 28 October when, finding that there were no longer even enough rats left to eat, the hapless Huguenots—of whom just 5,500 out of 28,000 survived—reluctantly surrendered. Thirteen days later, the walls of the city having been demolished and the last of the English ships having headed for home, the pirates were finally paid off and allowed to return to their quondam profession.

The next two years washed over William without too many misgivings and his sense of Englishness gradually buckled under the weight of his Catholicism and his status as a fugitive. Inured to hunger, fatigue and the sight of human blood, the unusual fabric of his daily life gradually assumed an aura of normality and routine. But though it was a profitable time for pirates (they apparently took more than a hundred sail in prizes during this time), their tiny fleet still lost more crew than William would later care to remember. It was only a matter of time, he realised, before he too was captured; purely a matter of luck that he had not been maimed or killed already.

Pirate ships rarely put into port. The risk of crew absconding was far too great. Restricted to the offloading of prizes and taking on of supplies, opportunities to flee were scarce, but it was not impossible, if the will was there. Despite later protests to the contrary, it seems more likely that William had remained on board all of this time of his own volition; having found both place and purpose aboard his ship; perhaps even a much needed sense of community in the collective isolation that inevitably resulted from spending so much time together at sea.

And yet at fifteen years of age he was already older than his years—mature enough at any rate to wonder what exactly this unorthodox apprenticeship was fitting him for and how much longer it could be before no other life would be possible. With his face burnished by salt, his hair permanently raddled, his cuffs covered in the gritty black stains of gunpowder and his clothes threadbare and pungent, he more resembled a street-urchin than the young gentleman he still knew himself to be.

Perhaps, on one of those languorous summer nights when the breeze dropped away to a calm and the binnacle lamps rocked a gentle golden lullaby, he realised that he missed his books or the company of his own kind; perhaps his pride, wounded by some unexpected verbal or physical reproof, had sought shelter in the belief that he was destined for higher things; perhaps he had simply grown weary of weevil-frass on his biscuits and the emery-paper sensation of salt in his shirt and undergarments and longed for a decent meal and the chance to cleanse his louse-bitten body in fresh water; perhaps he simply realised that he was approaching that age when boys became men and were expected to take on some of the more physical and risky labours of the ship and begin their maritime apprenticeship; but, in the early summer of 1630, as they doubled the Pointe-de-Grave and sailed up into Bordeaux, he decided to jump ship. The risk he was taking was grave: the traditional punishment for desertion was death.

More in hope, perhaps, than expectation, he set out immediately for Paris, where he failed, presumably, in his efforts to harness his service at La Rochelle to the yoke of his scholarly ambitions. Perhaps thinking that family connections might succeed where service and talent had failed, he headed next for Nantes, where his older brother, John, had been sent by the Franciscans to further his religious education at the Convent of Recollects. But he was too late. Following his ordination as a deacon, John had moved on to Bilbao.

Hitching a ride with a Basque merchant ferrying oranges to Santander, William attempted to follow, only to find that his brother had already left Bilbao for the University of Salamanca. At this point he gave up on the chase. In urgent need of friends, and influential ones at that, he headed next for the largest of the Irish enclaves in Spain—Galicia.

(6)

*H*E TURNED UP later that summer in La Coruña, at the home of Don Pedro de Toledo y Leyva, the first Marquis of Mancera. He was still a pretty boy whose voice had yet to break and whose cheeks had yet to feel the attention of a razor, but he was no longer a child. With a certainty and arrogance that belied his years, he introduced himself as an Irish gentleman of rank and quality.

He used the term 'Irish' loosely. Truth to tell, he did not know what he was anymore. For almost four hundred years his family had seen themselves as English and had professed temporal loyalty to the English Crown. They might still be doing so now, had not the years either side of his birth witnessed a shift in the focus of official discrimination from anti-Gaelic to anti-Catholic. A little over a decade later he would still be incorporating within his coat of arms a harp crowned in much the same manner as on the Anglo-Irish groat of Henry VIII and Anne Boleyn, and occupying the same position as it occupied on the royal arms of Great Britain.

Born at the height of this communal crisis of identity, he had been reared amongst a community bound by race and language to one throne, and by religion to another; a community struggling to come to terms with their sudden exclusion from the arenas of power and cursed with the insecurity of exiles. Instead of a sense of place, Fate had bestowed upon him an indestructible sense of rootlessness.

At just fifteen years of age, he was probably as incapable of articulating the enormity of his uncertainty and dislocation as he was of fashioning a new identity for himself, but he carried the sense of it within him like a stone in his shoe and clung like a limpet to the only other constants in his life—his faith and his pride. His family, he explained, had long been loyal supporters of their Most Catholic Majesties, and had suffered greatly for it. But he had not come looking for alms, rather an opportunity to serve.

A gentleman of the King's chamber and a member of His Majesty's Supreme Council of War, Mancera was one of the most powerful and influential men in all Galicia. He came from a family with a proud record of piety and beneficence—his father having endowed a convent for Teresa of Ávila and both his brother Enrique and sister Isabel having taken Carmelite habits. He was generous and warm-hearted, but he was no soft touch: nor was he particularly accessible.

Exactly how William came by his introduction is unclear, but it was most probably through the offices of Mancera's sister, María Francisca, the Marchioness of Montalvo. Before taking up his post as Governor of Galicia, her late husband had twice served as Spanish ambassador in London, where the couple had become good friends of William's old mentor, Sir John Bathe, from whom William, one suspects, had received a letter of recommendation. But however the introduction had come about, what Don Pedro heard from William was a tale unusual even for those uncertain times.

At forty-five years of age, Mancera probably thought he had seen and heard everything; but William's story enthralled him. What's more, the youngster could actually back up his claims with genuine ability. He had a prodigious memory, a natural bent for mathematics and an uncanny gift for languages.

A soldier himself since the age of fifteen, Mancera understood better than most the nature of William's most recent experiences and, taking the young fugitive under his wing, he arranged for him to be provided with a scholarship to Saint Patrick's College for Irish Nobles—an establishment in Santiago de Compostela where the children of the exiled Gaelic nobility were frequently sent to complete their secondary education before entering the University of Salamanca. The timing could not have been better.

In recent years the patronage of the Irish colleges by the Spanish monarchy had become an integral part of Spanish foreign policy. In her dispensation of patronage to the more talented of the Irish exiles, Spain hoped to exert, not just her influence, but her moral and political authority over *all* of the Irish abroad so that they might become, in the words of the Count of Gondomar, 'an annoyance to the King of England, a source of fear to him and of authority to Your Majesty'. In this regard the Spanish Crown was keen to avoid favouring any particular racial group over another and, with the help of the Jesuits (whose Irish members were predominantly of Anglo–Norman stock), had opened the colleges to Old English and Gaelic Irish alike.

Saint Patrick's was now preparing students to enter, not just the priesthood, but Spanish civil and military service. Enrolment, therefore, was no simple matter. The Spanish were peculiarly touchy about the slightest *mancha* of Judaism or Islam in even the most remote branches of a man's family tree and, before he could enter the college, the purity of William's Catholic blood, or *Limpieza de Sangre,* had to be formally guaranteed. For the first time since he left London, William was obliged to write home.

The reply, when it eventually arrived, consisted of a letter from his father and a character reference from the man who had ordained him, Dr John Roche, the new Bishop of Ferns (a man William could never actually have met, Roche having only arrived in Ireland in July of 1629). Together with the certificate of citizenship that Mancera had procured for him from the Deputy Governor of Toledo, they were submitted and accepted as proof of his Catholic purity.

That November, swapping his colourful English silks for a puritanical black doublet and stiff white collar, William enrolled at Saint Patrick's to study mathematics, poetry, logic, theology, philosophy, metaphysics and scripture. Fate had handed him a second chance and he was determined not to waste it.

𝒯HE MAGNIFICENTLY TITLED Saint Patrick's College for Irish Nobles
was in reality a rather modest establishment. Housed in a two-storey
townhouse on the western side of the Rua Nova, it had a small walled
garden, its own well and a few vines. It was not entirely dissimilar to the
Back Lane seminary in Dublin, but the experience was very different.
The passage of time, and a white lie about his age, had removed the
unwanted burden of precocity (according to a document in the Salamanca archives he was now claiming to be two years older than he actually was).

Saint Patrick's was small by Spanish standards, housing no more than
a dozen or so students, and space was at a premium: but that was no
great hardship for a sailor. His fellow students, on the other hand, were
another matter entirely. Predominantly of noble Gaelic stock, they considered him an Englishman and treated him as such (just six years previously a number of 'Irish prelates and lords' had complained to the
Spanish Council of State about Jesuit colleges admitting students who
were 'totally ignorant of the Irish language').

William could always, had he so wished, have claimed distant ties to
any number of prominent Gaelic families; but there was little point in
him trying too hard to integrate. He was what he was and attempting to
pretend otherwise would have been seen as a sign of weakness. But he
was not entirely alone. Robert Plunkett, a twenty-year-old from Garris-
town in north County Dublin, was also of Old English extraction and he
shared something far more important than race and mother tongue with
the young Wexfordman: he, too, was there because he wanted to be. Dili-
gent and conscientious, their behaviour contrasted starkly with that of
their Gaelic colleagues.

Ever since 1611, when the King handed the college over to the Jesuits
in order that they might instil in their students the soldierly values of

discipline and submission, Saint Patrick's had been run with military rigour and efficiency. Students were expected to be strict in their religious observances and were forbidden from leaving the premises, keeping private funds, or sending letters without the prior approval of the rector. It was a strict regime, and it grated on the sensibilities of the more privileged.

Felix O'Neill, an arrogant and self-confident young upstart, and the social power in the dormitories of Saint Patrick's, had been behind almost every prank or disturbance encountered at the college since the day of his enrolment. His activities, like those of his devoted sidekick, Bernard O'Hagan, were well known to the college authorities, but thus far the pair had been afforded an unusual degree of latitude. In June of 1631, however, they pushed their luck too far.

The celebrations of Corpus Christi were the most important event on the Spanish religious calendar and the endless processions of priests and friars, guilds and confraternities, gilded pyxs and thuribles, traditionally went hand in glove with a secular festival of theatre, bullfights and dancing. Thousands would descend upon the towns from the surrounding countryside, churches would function as temporary inns and hostels, and sweet vendors would install themselves about the plazas. Determined to protect the reputation of his college from the exuberance of his students, the Superior, Father Alonso Bazquez, confined them to the college and locked their dormitory at night—to little avail. Somehow O'Neill managed to secure a key to the chapel, through which he led an excited parcel of students into town.

Alone in declining the invitation to accompany the revellers on their merry jaunt, stood Robert Plunkett and William Lamport. Being that little bit more mature than his fellow students, Plunkett had little time for such puerile escapades, and William's last two years at sea had purged the young Wexfordman of the need for meaningless adventure. It was not, perhaps, the normal behaviour of a sixteen-year-old, but he had far too much to lose.

The truants' absence, in any case, was eventually discovered and a hearing was set for July. Faced with imminent expulsion, O'Neill scurried about the college attempting to inveigle students and faculty alike into signing a petition that would absolve him of personal responsibility for the breakout. He even approached William, ordering him to sign lest there should be 'seditions of a provincial nature'. When the official enquiry began, however, neither of the Old English students lost any time in distancing themselves from their troublesome Gaelic peers.

On 27 July, having sworn upon the Holy Cross to tell nothing but the truth, Plunkett informed the investigators of O'Neill's night-time departure from the dormitory, his spending of private funds, and his recent death threat against a fellow student. Invited to testify on the following day, William recalled how O'Neill had left the building with several others and how he had earlier skipped classes despite being in good health.

The surviving manuscripts do not tell of O'Neill's fate but, despite having signed his petition, William escaped without censure and was still a student at the college several months later when two Franciscans arrived in La Coruña bearing news of the anchoring of two suspicious ships in a sheltered bay near Puebla del Deán (today Caramiñal)—a small town on the Galician coast. The ships were suspected of being pirates; perhaps even the same pirates who, under the command of a certain Mos Duconte, had so recently terrorised the coast of Bayona.

Because of his recent experience of piracy, and the fact that he had previously served with the son of this same Mos Duconte, William was summoned by Mancera, now Governor of Galicia, and sent with F _____ Francisco Basurto and Francisco Ximenes (the latter of whom was the guardian of the Franciscan Friary in Puebla del Deán), to see if he could identify the vessels. Boarding a Spanish warship, they sailed as fast as the wind would carry them for Puebla del Deán.

There was no mistaking the largest vessel. He knew her as intimately as his own body: every nook and cranny; every orifice and scar. He knew her fragrance and he knew her voice; her memories had been his memories, her secrets his secrets. Through fair weather and foul, deep water and shoal, he had seen little of the world that he had not shared with her; had gone nowhere that her bowsprit had not pointed the way. For a little over two years she had provided him with both a home and family of sorts, and it must have been with very mixed emotions that William confirmed her identity.

As they closed on the pirate vessels, the larger of the two engaged them in battle while the other fled for the open sea. But the battle, such as it was, was short lived and, after the prisoners had been immobilised, a small party was placed on board to stand guard over them while William's galleon set off in chase of the smaller vessel. In no time at all they had run her down and her crew were taken to join their colleagues in Santiago de Compostela and the prisons, not of the civil authorities (which were probably too small to cope with such numbers), but of the Spanish Inquisition.

Founded in 1478, following the re-conquest of Spain from the Moors, the Spanish Inquisition, or Holy Office, was essentially a tribunal of inquiry with procedures similar to the judicial bodies of most Christian countries of the time. Created initially with the sole intention of rooting out suspected Muslims and Jews, its writ had more recently been extended to include the halting of the spread of Protestantism.

Under the rules of the Inquisition, matters of faith were decided by specially appointed judges rather than juries, and prisoners were presumed guilty until proven innocent. Torture was commonplace and those convicted of being 'unrepentant' heretics were invariably sent to the stake. Unlike the Roman Inquisition, whose Inquisitors were appointed by the Pope, the Inquisitors of the Spanish Inquisition were appointed by the King and often used, as they appear to have been on this occasion, as a branch of the civil power.

During the early years of the Reformation, the Protestants of northern Europe had taken little or no interest in the plight of Muslims and Jews in Catholic Spain and saw little that was unacceptable or unusual in the Inquisition's treatment of heretics. In 1560, however, when the Duke of Alba and his *Conseil des Troubles* (or 'Council of Blood' as it was more popularly known) began the systematic execution of Protestants in Flanders, the Spanish Inquisition quickly become a byword for slaughter and sadism—an impression frequently reinforced by the gruesome tales of garrulous old sea-dogs returning from Spanish ports. Their imprisonment by the Inquisition, therefore, would have come as quite a shock to William's old shipmates (the vast majority of whom were English) and their imaginations would almost certainly have been running riot.

Perhaps because he had in-depth knowledge of the trade and traditions of piracy; perhaps simply because he spoke English and was available; but William was invited 'by a certain Inquisitor de Sea' to work as an 'interpreter'. Over the following three days—the brevity alone suggesting a commercial rather than an ecclesiastical or civil process—he helped to negotiate the enlistment of all 250 of his former colleagues into the service of the King, in effect saving their lives (at least for the time being) and the civil and ecclesiastical authorities time, money and a lot of bothersome paperwork.

Delighted by the windfall of confiscated ships and booty, the new governor, the Marquis of Mancera, recommended the young Wexfordman to the King and ordered, at least according to William's telling of the story, a night of illuminations in La Coruña and the singing of thanksgiving hymns at the Church of Santo Domingo.

Te Deum laudamus, te Domine confitemur . . .

(8)

*F*ORM AND STYLE were everything: more important even than morality or religion. If he was not to appear ill-bred, then William needed to be educated in the tribal signatures of a court so elaborately ceremonious and cryptic that, despite the proliferation of dwarves and jesters, it had come to resemble 'a school of silence, punctiliousness and reverence'. In the *Teatro de Grandeza,* even the simplest breach of etiquette could send a man toppling over a precipice of disfavour or dishonour.

In February 1632, escorted by a pair of the governor's gentlemen and two nephews of a Galician merchant in whose house he had most recently been residing, William arrived in Madrid. Mancera had procured for him an introduction to the King's first minister, the Count-Duke of Olivares. If he made a favourable impression there would be no limit to the doors that might open to him.

Not for the first time, family connections proved fruitful. Upon his arrival in the capital William was taken to the house of John O'Neill— the current Earl of Tyrone and a distant relative he regarded as an 'uncle'. A colonel of the Irish regiment in Flanders, O'Neill had come from Brussels in the hope of persuading the King to allow him renew his father's military campaign in Ireland and had been waiting the better portion of two years for an answer.

If William was to procure any sort of position at court, then the purity of his Catholic blood had to be properly guaranteed; and this time the word of his father and an Irish bishop he had never actually met were never going to suffice. His 'uncle', however, was more than supportive. With O'Neill's help he managed to harvest the signatures of such luminaries as the Spanish Ambassador to London, the Earls of Tyrconnell and Berehaven and the Apostolic Nuncio.

This was a crucial period for William: a time of circumspection and observation during which he was expected to absorb such things as the manner in which the nobility behaved, dressed and dined, while at the same time proving his scholarly worth. Asked to write a test piece in honour of his would-be benefactor, he set about composing a Latin eulogy he titled '*Laus Comitis Ducis* . . . In praise of the Count Duke'—a theme that paralleled other 'discreetly commissioned' works of the Olivares' chief propagandists. When compared to such efforts, the measure of his talent would be immediately apparent; but then no-one had said it was going to be easy. The timing, on the other hand, could hardly have been better.

Following the death, five years previously, of Duke Vincenzo II of Mantua, succession to the Italian territories of Mantua and Montferrat had been claimed by his nearest living relative, the Duke of Nevers—a Frenchman. Though fiefs of the Austrian Empire, these territories were strategically important for the defence of Spanish interests in the region as they controlled a number of important alpine passes, the road from Milan to Genoa, and the upper course of the Po. They also served as buffer states between the rival powers of France and Spain.

As the Spanish felt unable to trust the other buffer state, the duchy of Savoy, they had been more than especially concerned that Mantua and Montferrat should not fall into Never's hands, as that would amount to gifting them to Richelieu. Olivares, therefore, sent his Army of Milan to lay siege to the fortress of Casale—the capital of Montferrat. With the French tied up at the siege of La Rochelle, and likely to be there for some time, he gambled on Casale falling first; and lost. In February of 1629, Louis XIII led the French army across the Monginevro Pass, forced the raising of the siege, and garrisoned the towns of Casale and Susa.

In the pamphlet war that followed, each country endeavoured to justify their actions to a wider European public—the Spanish claiming that the French intervention had been an attempt to disturb the peace of Europe, and the French claiming that the Spanish actions had been part of a Habsburg campaign to achieve universal dominion. In the end, following a second unsuccessful attempt to besiege Casale, the matter was resolved by the two treaties of Cherasco, in April and June of 1631, and Nevers finally became Duke of Mantua.

But while the entire affair had been a source of severe embarrassment for Olivares, it had also confirmed him in his belief in the value of professional publicists and propagandists, and since then he had increased the number of writers in the personal service of the King from a more than adequate seventy-six to almost three times that figure. His appreciation of literary talent, therefore, was probably never higher.

And then there was the Royal Apartment of San Jeronimo.

At a former Dominican monastery on the eastern outskirts of Madrid, Olivares was overseeing the remodelling of the Royal Apartments in preparation for the traditional ceremony of fealty at which the Cortes of Castile would pledge their allegiance to the Crown Prince, Baltasar Carlos. The ceremony, which marked the official recognition of the prince as heir to the throne, was scheduled for 22 February and the apartments—henceforth to be known as the Palace of the Buen Retiro—were nearing completion. With so many of his recent initiatives having proved less than successful, the Count-Duke was happy, at last, to have something worth celebrating, and was in uncommonly good humour.

Born on 6 January 1587 at the Spanish embassy in Rome, Don Gaspar de Guzmán, the Count-Duke of Olivares, was the third son of Don Enrique de Guzmán, the Spanish Ambassador to the Vatican. Groomed from birth for the red biretta, an ecclesiastical career had seemed inevitable, until the deaths of his elder brothers left him heir to his father's estates. Marriage to one of the Queen's ladies-in-waiting later secured for him an appointment to the household of the Crown Prince who, upon his accession, appointed him first minister. To those he chose to favour, Olivares could be as generous as the breadth of his girth, but his combustible temperament was legendary and he did not grant audiences lightly. Supplicants knew better than to come unprepared.

Olivares was unforgettable. Short, squat, and almost hunch-backed in appearance, he gave little physical impression of power. His face was blighted by a bulbous nose and obscured for the most part by thick black moustachios and a splayed beard. Apart from a gold chain of office draped over his right shoulder, he dressed almost entirely in black taffeta—a colour that heightened his pallor and made him appear older than his years. Stricken with gout (and possibly also with syphilis) he struggled to walk without the aid of a cane and capped his burgeoning physical indignities with a rather obvious hairpiece. Up close his breath stank of stale tobacco and every now and again he would become prone to sudden head and body jerks.

Introduced by the Count-Duke's son-in-law, the Count of Medina de Las Torres, William presented his eulogy: an eclectic mixture of prose and verse. It was not a work of genius, but it wasn't bad. More promising still was the fact that the youngster was mustard-keen, lacking a secure place in society, and dependent upon patronage for advancement. There was, Olivares believed, no better recipe for loyalty and, before he knew where he was, William found himself sitting beside Cardinal Antonio de Zapata (the Patriarch of the Indies) and being ferried in his state coach on the 50 kilometre journey from Madrid to the palace of San Lorenzo el Real de el Escorial—the summer retreat of the Spanish court from the merciless heat of Madrid.

For Olivares, William's complaisance contrasted starkly with that of his current bugbear—the youth of the Spanish nobility. Believing them sluggardly, aimless and insubordinate, he had recently returned to such medieval concepts as court colleges in an effort to produce a generation of nobles more dedicated to the service of the Crown than their own self-interest. It was a grand notion, but it wasn't working. In the face of continuous attack from the religious orders (opposed to the increasing influence of the Jesuits at court) and the universities (who feared the loss of their monopoly of higher education), the new college had succeeded in attracting a meagre sixty students, not one of whom came from ranks of the nobility.

Olivares' difficulty, however, was to prove William's opportunity, and a few days later the young Wexfordman was summoned to a meeting with Don Juan de Madrid, Prior of the Royal Monastery of San Lorenzo de el Escorial. His Majesty, William was told, had granted him a scholarship to the Colegio Imperial and the use of a domestic servant and two valets. Summoned shortly afterwards to the office of Don Andrés de Rozas, the Secretary of State for the North, he was further informed that the Count-Duke had awarded him an allowance of thirty escudos a month and an annual pension of 200 ducats. It was the stuff of dreams: much more than he could ever reasonably have hoped for.

At San Lorenzo, William would have found the clement weather refreshing and a peculiar peace in the chaste austerity of the architecture. Nestled in the very heart of the Sierra de Guadarrama, at the foot of Monte Abantos, this gigantic rectangular grid of sombre grey granite commemorated the grilling of Saint Laurence the Martyr. A revel for sight and soul, it was rivalled for scale and magnificence only by the Palazzo Ducale in Venice and St. Peter's in Rome. There were even echoes of Ireland in the dry-stone walls that enclosed the groves and meadows of the surrounding farms. Granite was a familiar stone: a tactile reminder of home.

But San Lorenzo was not Wexford and he was even more of an outsider here than he had ever been at Santiago. While his knowledge of Latin was obviously up to scratch, the same could hardly be said of his Castilian, which he had been speaking for only two years, nor his knowledge and understanding of Spanish society. Here he became the stranger with the funny accent; a sailor far from the sea; perhaps also, in his outlook at least, a young man amongst children.

Having survived more than two years aboard a pirate ship, it is unlikely that he was the victim of any serious bullying. He had so little in common with his peers, nevertheless, that he tended to gravitate towards his teachers, and especially those who also knew the pangs of homesickness. They, in turn, appear to have taken an avuncular interest in him and in guiding him through an obstacle course that led to unknown horizons where the garlands of success were as unfathomable as the consequences of failure. It was just as well they did, for the curriculum he faced was daunting:

Professor *Subject/s*

Francisco Antonio Camassa *Mathematics, Military Arts, Fortification & Cavalry formations*

Jan-Karel della Faille *Nautical Geography and Hydrography*

Fray Miguel de Santa María, Fray Juan de Toledo and Padre Antonio Mauricio O.S.M. *Sacred Scripture*

Mos de la Pluma *The Secrets of State*

Francisco Isasi *Mathematics and Geometry*

Juan Palatino *Chemistry*

Juan Bautista Poza *Politics*

Claudio Clemente *Erudition and Military Arts*

Claude Ricarde *Politics, Economics, Optical Perspective, Geography, Navigation, Hydraulics and Astronomy*

Francisco de Roales *Astrology*

Juan del Espino *Architecture and Occult Philosophy*

Juan Eusebio Nieremberg y Otin *Natural Magic (1632 to 1633) Sacred Scripture, Astronomy, Occult Philosophy and Natural Magic (1633–1635)*

This, of course, was the formal curriculum, but it is unlikely to have been all that William studied. Outside of school hours he would almost certainly have received instruction in the gentlemanly arts of fencing, riding and dancing—skills equally, if not more, important to his hopes of advancement.

During the summer holidays, when the majority of his fellow students would return to their homes and families, William would head for Madrid, where he would reside at the Jesuit college of San Isidro el Real (at that time incorporated into the Colegio Imperial). Effectively an orphan, his Jesuit tutors were now the nearest thing he had to a family and, despite a tendency to draw attention upon himself and to be a trifle too anxious to please, they appear to have taken quite a liking to him. Whatever time was not spent in tutorials with Claude Ricarde, Jan Karel della Faille and Francisco Antonio Camassa, all of whom were fellow foreigners at court, he would spend ferrying *memoriales* back and forth to Madrid for his patron, the Count-Duke of Olivares. It was tiring work— a 50km trip each way—but it was an education in itself. It brought him into the homes of the rich and powerful and raised his profile at court. It also, unfortunately, had the effect of enticing him to abandon the minor heaven that lay just within his reach for a shapeless mirage, the pursuit of which had already begun to render him incapable of harmonising the burgeoning demands of his pride with the limitations of his birth.

But then it would have been nigh on impossible for it to have been otherwise. At no other time in his life had he ever had such good reason to feel positive about the future; to truly believe that anything was possible.

He may have found few friends amongst his peers, but he was still a pious, charming and eminently likeable young man who found little difficulty in cultivating the friendship of his elders, and most especially figures of authority. Having gained the friendship, in particular, of Don Manuel de Almaguer—a cousin of the Count-Duke's closest confidant, Don Francisco de Alarcón—he had even become privy to the juiciest of court gossip. Longing to be a part of it all, he became ever more eager to impress.

During that first summer in Madrid, William suddenly took to wearing the insignia of a *Familiar* (assistant/informer) of the Inquisition. It was to prove something of an embarrassment. His difficulties were occasioned primarily by the duplicity of one Denis O'Driscoll.

O'Driscoll, who had met William during his time in Santiago and recognised him as a bit of an innocent abroad, had offered to help him purchase the title of *Familiar of the Inquisition*—a much coveted patent that brought with it a certain social status and some minor juridical immunities. Theoretically awarded only to distinguished figures who had been, or could be, of service to the Inquisition, in practice the patent was often bought. It cost William, or so he claimed, the princely sum of 400 silver reals.

True to his word, O'Driscoll eventually produced an impressive looking patent on vellum parchment, the authenticity of which William never doubted for an instant. O'Driscoll, however, never expected him to wear the insignia of a *Familiar* about the royal court. But wear it he did, and the matter was quickly reported to the Inquisition of Toledo, who summoned William to an audience.

Asked to explain himself, William presented the Inquisitors with O'Driscoll's parchment only to be told, in no uncertain terms, that it was a forgery. It must have seemed odd to the Inquisitors that a young man of such undoubted intelligence could be so easily taken in: his life as a pirate, at the very least, should have purged him of such gullibility. And yet, for all that, he had an air of innocence about him. Accepting his explanations, they let him off with a warning and allowed him to keep the forgery, as a reminder to be more careful in the future.

The whole experience had been a chastening one: but it could so easily have been much, much worse. A row had recently broken out between two of William's teachers; Don Juan del Espino (his professor of occult philosophy) and Don Juan Bautista Poza (his professor of politics). Espino had recently reported Poza to the Inquisition on account of some facetious remarks he had made regarding the ease with which licences to read the Koran were currently being obtained. The whole affair had stimulated William's curiosity to the point where he had 'borrowed' a copy of the Koran from the 'Library of Forbidden Books' at the Escorial. Or at least that is what he told his friends. When questioned by the Inquisition, many years later, he would claim to have found it on the street.

But however he had come by it, the book was now a liability and William dared not be caught with it in his possession. On his return to Madrid, therefore, he sold it to a Jewish bookseller for a measly four reals. For all his good fortune, it seemed, there was still a reckless streak inside of him that he found difficult to control.

It was most likely also during these early days at court that William wrote the first of his poems in honour of Cardinal Gaspar de Borja y Velasco—a favourite cousin of the Count-Duke of Olivares and Spain's ambassador to the Vatican.

Borja had been having a rough time of it of late. In March of 1632, he had publicly accused the Pope of having betrayed the Holy Church by his refusal to support the Catholic Habsburgs in their wars against the Protestant Swedes. His outburst had scandalised Catholic Europe and his removal from Rome had since become the primary objective of the papal nuncio in Madrid. Though it was not to be published on this occasion, William was invited, nevertheless, to recite his composition before the man who had first brought him to San Lorenzo: Cardinal Antonio Zapata—Patriarch of the Indies and quondam Inquisitor General.

At a later date, on the occasion of the return of the court to San Lorenzo, William composed another work, this time in honour of the King himself. His '*Las hazañas del mayor monarca Don Felipe IV . . .* The exploits of the great monarch, Felipe IV' was so appreciated by His Majesty that it led, or so he would later claim, to a personal audience with the King and an introduction, in her private quarters no less, to the Queen.

At a time when His Majesty was invisible to the world at large and virtually depersonalized by ritual; when few men ever got to meet, let alone speak with the King; this would have represented a rare privilege.

One French nobleman, on the occasion of his visit to Felipe's court, observed that even the grandees only saw His Majesty when they accompanied him to Holy Mass and only spoke to him when business compelled them to request an audience. Even then he would stand motionless throughout, his prominent jawline endowing him with an air of perpetual sullenness and moving only to utter some brief remark as the audience came to close.

For the moment, it appeared, William could do no wrong. He was being received in the circles that mattered and was beginning to feel at home about the court. But he was just seventeen years of age and his bullish self-confidence was built upon foundations of inferiority and insecurity. For all his optimism and recent good fortune, he lacked that sense of certainty, continuity and direction that came from having roots in a community that would corroborate his identity, take pride in his successes and, when the time came, mark and mourn his passing. No matter how much he might talk up his pedigree—which in truth was hung on the outermost branches of the noble tree—it didn't make him any less of an outsider and he remained gripped by the fear of having to justify himself. Baptismal certificates, genealogies, character references; anything, in fact, that might justify his recent elevation, went into a simple wooden cigar box that he would still be carrying with him some ten years later. Thus far he had enjoyed more than his fair share of following winds; but the wind was a capricious mistress, and he had had many first-hand experiences of her changing moods.

During this, his first year at San Lorenzo, William's status as an foreigner compelled him to develop a thick skin and to rigorously apply himself to his studies. He also learnt the habit of wearing that mask of audacious assurance that for the rest of his life would be both sword and crutch to his insecurity. He even changed his name. With the permission of the Count-Duke he began to call himself *Don Guillén de Lombardo y Guzmán* (Lombardo being a rather adroit hispanisation of Lamport, and Guzmán the family name of the Count-Duke of Olivares). But the patronage of the Count-Duke was no substitute for the acceptance of his fellow students and changing his name did not make him a Spaniard. There were times, however, when a degree of isolation from one's peers could prove advantageous.

One day, during one of the young King's rare visits to the Escorial, William was sent for by the Duke of Medina de Las Torres, Ramiro Pérez de Guzmán (the young man who had previously introduced him to the Count-Duke). Led down a long, cold and dark granite passageway, he was brought to a dome-covered octagonal room deep beneath the high altar of the basilica. With no windows and just a single door, the room was about as private as it could ever get for a King.

As his eyes adjusted to the candlelight, William began to discern an altar of green Genoese marble and a series of stacked rectangular alcoves that in the years to come would hold the remains of every Spanish monarch since Charles I, Felipe included. He also discerned the unmistakably rotund figure of the Count-Duke. The King, at least according to the story William would relate to a fellow prisoner many years later, had a favour to ask. He needed someone he could trust to run an errand to Ávila. It was a serious and confidential matter concerning, or of concern to, the local bishop.

William, of course, did not need to be asked twice and he was rewarded for his co-operation and discretion with a visit to the *Pudridero*—an adjoining vault that was temporarily storing the reliquaries of Felipe's ancestors. On his arrival in Ávila, he was further rewarded by the bishop with a simple benefice (the right to receive revenue from Church property). Whatever the nature of this mysterious errand, it was important enough to ensure that Felipe would never forget the young Irishman. In the years to come, in fact, he would make some rather extraordinary interventions on William's behalf.

(9)

O N THE NIGHT of 25 February 1634, at the German fortress of
Eger, Captain William Devereux ran his halberd through the chest of
Albrecht Von Wallenstein, changing forever the course of European history and bringing a premature end to William's days as a student.

Once the most feared man in Europe, Wallenstein's dismissal from his
post as commander-in-chief of the armies of the Holy Roman Emperor,
Ferdinand II of Austria, had severely wounded his pride and by way of
revenge he had offered the use of his private army to both the French (who
were fearful of the growing power of the Vienna-Madrid alliance), and the
Swedes (with whom the Emperor was currently at war). The Vienna-
Madrid alliance had existed since the abdication, in 1555, of the Holy
Roman Emperor, Charles V of Spain. At that time his realm included all
of Spain, Austria, Hungary, Germany, the Valois duchy of Burgundy, the
Italian territories of Naples, Sardinia, Sicily and Milan, and a good deal
of the Netherlands. Deeming the Empire far too great for any one man to
hold together, he divided it between his brother Ferdinand, to whom he
gave his central European territories and the title of Holy Roman Emperor, and his son Felipe, to whom he left the rest. Since then the Habsburgs
had ruled over two empires, Spanish and Austrian, and their alliance had
made them the most powerful political and military force in Europe.

Prior to Wallenstein's assassination, a key element of Spanish strategy in their war against the Dutch had involved an invasion of the
Netherlands by Wallenstein's troops—then part of the Imperial army.
But Wallenstein, perhaps the most brilliant general of the entire Thirty
Years War, had been opposed to the offering of Austrian help to the
Spanish and his objections had driven a wedge between the Habsburg
allies. His death, however, had gone a long way towards repairing the
damage and had cleared the way for a united push by Vienna and Madrid
against their Protestant enemies in the Rhineland.

Wallenstein's assassination had been ordered by one Walter Butler, an Irish colonel in the Imperial army who, having discovered the Bohemian's plan to offer the use of his army to the Swedes, had taken matters into his own hands and laid a trap for him in the form of a banquet at the Hungarian fortress of Eger. During this banquet a company of his Irish dragoons burst into a banquet hall and set about the diners. Failing to find Wallenstein amongst them, a Captain William Devereux took six halberdiers and rushed upstairs to search for him. Kicking in a bedroom door, which had been bolted from within, he found Wallenstein standing at the window. But while it had been Devereux who had actually despatched Wallenstein, it was to be Butler who reaped the plaudits, and for a short while he became the most famous man in Europe.

The Emperor, of course, was overjoyed. Anxious to seize control of the frenzy of public interest, he paid Denis McDonnell, one of Butler's dragoons, the absurd sum of 20,000 gulden to publish an eyewitness account. Inspired, perhaps, by the generosity of the Emperor's patronage, William claimed Butler as a cousin and set about publishing an account of his own ('*Relación de la muerte del Duque de Frislan* . . . An account of the death of the Duke of Friesland').

But the expected windfall never came. The consequences of his cousin's actions were destined to be felt in other ways and in the meantime there were the far more pressing issues to be dealt with, not least of which was his application for a renewal of his scholarship to the Colegio Imperial, and an application for a scholarship to the University of Salamanca.

Reared from birth to be Cardinal-Archbishop of Toledo, the King's younger brother, the Infante Fernando, had recently escaped the constraints of his ecclesiastical leash and wrangled an appointment as Governor of the Spanish Netherlands. In the immediate aftermath of Wallenstein's assassination it was decided to delay Fernando's departure for Brussels and to send him overland from Milan, nominally in charge of a monstrous army under the leadership of the Marquis of Leganés.

This army, which would march under orders to clear the Upper Rhineland of Spain's Protestant enemies, was to be assisted, on a second front, by the armies of Fernando's cousin and brother-in-law, Ferdinand III of Hungary (the eldest son of the Emperor). With manpower shortages growing daily more acute, the threat of conscription now hung over all at the Colegio Imperial: it was, after all, a part of what they were being trained for.

That same spring, William was offered a scholarship, or so he claimed, to the prestigious Colegio Mayor de San Bartolomé. Although an integral part of the University of Salamanca, San Bartolomé differed from the majority of other colleges in that a baccalaureate was necessary for admission. Seventeen scholarships were awarded each year: five for the study of theology, ten for canon law and two for the priesthood. Selected on a competitive basis, and designed to attract the academic elite, applicants were required to be 'mature scholars' and to be 'poor'.

The pinnacle of his formal academic achievement thus far, the scholarship would have offered William the chance to network and bond with young men from noble and influential families who would leave university recognising him as something akin to a brother. Being without independent means, such contacts were vital to his chances of advancement. The Colegio Imperial may have provided a first rate education, but its students were not of the nobility.

The offer, alas, came too late. At the end of March, at the insistence of the Marquis of Leganés, a number of William's professors at the Colegio Imperial, and in particular his professor of military studies, Father Francisco Antonio Camassa, were ordered to accompany the Infante on campaign—in order that they might gain some much needed experience of the 'less theoretical' aspects of their subjects. As one of their ablest students ('well known for my excellence in mathematics and military discipline'), William was ordered to join them. Salamanca would have to wait.

On Tuesday 16 May, after a solemn ceremony in Madrid—at which he was conferred with minor orders by the Archbishop of Toledo—William left for Barcelona, from where he eventually set sail for Genoa. A little over three weeks later, as part of a small Spanish delegation, he arrived in Rome; the 'eternal city' of Hadrian and capital of the first Caesars. For a young classical scholar it must have been a dream come true. The purpose of this visit is unknown, but it was almost certainly political: perhaps another attempt by the Spanish to embarrass the pro-French pope, Urban VIII, into publicly giving his blessing to the Habsburg campaign in Germany; perhaps simply a fleeting detour to brief the Spanish ambassador, Cardinal Gaspar de Borja y Velasco.

Following the defeat of the Habsburg armies by the Swedes at Breitenfeld in September 1631, Borja had publicly accused the Pope—who had refused to open the treasure of Sant'Angelo and assist the military efforts of Vienna and Madrid—of having betrayed the Church. His continued presence in Italy, therefore, was a source of extreme annoyance to the Vatican and recent efforts to have him appointed as governor and captain-general of the State of Milan had been blocked by His Holiness, who wanted him removed from Italy altogether. But whatever the reason for their visit, the Spanish delegation was granted a papal audience, during which William found himself presented to the Pontiff.

Ever since his father took him to live at Devereux's, Fate had contrived to make William feel somewhat special. But as a devout Catholic, this topped everything. He had already met the King of Spain, and now, apparently, the Holy Father himself. If true, and we have only William's word for all this, then it would have been surprising had he *not* left for Milan with an inflated sense of his own importance.

The Spanish army finally broke camp in late June and, like a giant centipede, began to slowly wend its way through the lush valleys of Lombardy from Milan to Lake Como. At almost 20,000 strong, they were bigger than most towns of the period—and that was without counting the chaplains, surgeons, sutlers and carters of the impedimenta, without whom no army of the day could function. It also excepted the legions of female camp followers working as unpaid cooks, laundry-women, seamstresses and nurses, that struggled along behind the menfolk carrying all manner of clothing, cooking implements, poultry and children.

William had never seen such an assembly; nor had he ever felt part of anything quite so august or momentous. And yet it was perhaps the loneliest time of his life. Most of the disparate nationalities that marched with Fernando possessed some sense of purpose and knew their place in the scheme of things; but he was more a scholar than a soldier, and this was more a Habsburg cause than a Catholic one (the Pope had only grudgingly given his blessing and the French were secretly supporting the Swedes). His introduction to the Holy Father notwithstanding, there was little for him in this campaign, either personally or spiritually, and the best he could hope for, apart from survival, was that his close relationship with his professors would keep him in line for a lucrative administrative posting in Brussels when the fighting was over or, at the very least, a recall to the Colegio Imperial to complete his studies.

Keeping the blue-green waters of the lake to their right, they trudged onwards and upwards through the alpine meadows and villages of Menaggio, Gravedona and Chiavenna, finally crossing the Alps at the Passo de Maloja. They then tramped down the gentle gradients of the Engadine until they reached Zernez, at the upper end of the valley near its junction with the Val de Spöl. Following the course of the Rhinetal, they headed next for Lake Constance, from where they hoped to follow the Danube to Donauwörth.

Progress was slow, averaging no more than twelve miles a day, and stopping every third or fourth day to bake and to tend to the exhausted draught horses and to bake. Bread was delivered directly to the soldiers but meat, beer and wine had to be purchased at the camp market. Prices reflected the scarcity and the lower ranks frequently had to turn to cheap wine or cider to kill their hunger pangs. For officers like William, a square meal followed every day's march but, every once in a while, the wear and tear on clothing would have meant that even he had to endure the frustrations and humiliations of the camp market.

On 2 September they reached Donauwörth. Ahead of them, besieging the town of Nördlingen, lay the Imperial army: opposing it, the armies of Bernard of Saxe-Weimar and Horn of Sweden. Outnumbered by almost ten thousand, the Imperialists had settled down to wait for their Spanish allies.

It no longer mattered whether the war was justifiable or not. All that mattered now was survival. If his years as a pirate had taught William anything, it was that when the first shot was fired each man would fight only for himself and his comrades. He was already accustomed to the sensations of battle; had already faced the fear of fear and survived that first great conflict within himself. For many of his fellow students, however, it was only just beginning.

Weeks earlier, these raw recruits had viewed the prospect of combat with excited anticipation; as though it would be welcome relief from the tedium of endless marching and camping. Reality had since intruded in the form of the thunder and lightning of the Imperial artillery barrages and the banter had been shadowed by trepidation and reflection. All manner of crosses, *agnus dei* and images of Saint Gabriel were fingered in nervous anticipation, and new courage was sought in the company of battle-hardened veterans—the living embodiment of their hopes of survival. As they sat staring into the dying embers of their campfires, they knew only two things for certain: they were far from the comforting touch of their loved ones and this time tomorrow any number of them could be dead. Nothing tested a man's faith better than the imminent prospect of death and, for once, the *padres* were busier than the camp whores. Nobody wanted to die unshriven.

Although there could be no guarantees in battle, William found himself stationed in perhaps the only place where one might escape unscathed—the entourage of the Infante. Camped on the Schonfeld, a hilltop to the north of the strategically important Allbuch, his position commanded a panoramic view of the battlefield but was still dangerously within range of the enemy's fire. Here he occupied the position of assistant to Francisco Antonio Camassa, the Neapolitan Jesuit who had been his professor of military studies at the Colegio Imperial and who was now advising the Marquis of Léganes on tactics and deployment.

Things were moving fast. The Protestant generals, Bernard and Horn, had spotted a chink in the enemy's defences and were moving to exploit it. The Imperial forces had placed an advance guard on the ridge that joined the Heselberg and Allbuch hills and overlooked the road into the town. If captured, the Imperial position would become untenable and they would be forced to withdraw.

At 3 p.m. on 5 September, Bernard attacked the Catholic positions on the Himmelreich and by 6 p.m. he had taken the Landle. Now just a stone's throw away from the Heselberg-Allbuch ridge, he was stopped dead in his tracks by the heroic resistance of some 500 Spanish musketeers on the wooded Heselberg, and was forced to wait for Horn, who did not arrive until midnight.

The musketeers held out for another two hours, before retreating to the grassy slopes of the Allbuch. Here the Spanish had deployed no less than eight regiments, amongst them the German regiments of Salm and Würmser—the latter of which was comprised almost entirely of raw recruits, a fact that so worried the Infante that initially he had wanted to replace them with the crack Idiaquez regiment. Following the protestations of Würmser, who claimed such a move would be an insult to him personally, the Idiaquez were positioned behind him as a second line of defence.

It was now 2 a.m. and the Swedish infantry had been marching and fighting for almost twenty-one hours. Morale was poor and moans about the drizzle and damp were becoming increasingly vociferous. It was decided, therefore, to postpone the assault until morning.

Horn, meanwhile, attempted to move his troops to the right of the hill, and Bernard to take his down the valley to the left (to discourage the Spanish from reinforcing the hilltop). Horn's night advance, however, rapidly turned into a shambles. A number of wagons and canons overturned in a narrow muddy lane, blocking the advance of his infantry and giving the alerted defenders time to entrench themselves.

Divining the Swedes' intentions to charge the entrenchments, William, or so he claimed, came up with the idea of ordering the cavalry regiments of Arberg and La Tour to proceed, under cover of darkness, to positions south of the Allbuch. As the majority of the Spanish cavalry regiments were of Neapolitan origin, it seems likely that Camassa, himself a Neapolitan and professor of cavalry warfare at the Colegio Imperial, would have been, to some degree or other, in charge of their deployment. As one of Camassa's ablest students, William was ideally positioned to propose the manoeuvre.

But did he?

Surely he must have been asked for his opinion first?

William had been long enough about the fringes of the royal court to know that it was neither his duty nor his right to make suggestions to his superiors. He must also have understood by now the folly of a student making too much display of his ability. Indeed one can more readily imagine Camassa testing his favourite pupil with a problem knowing that a correct answer would flatter them both and an incorrect one present him with an opportunity to impress, than William daring to highlight an oversight on the part of his professor—an action that would almost certainly diminish them both, not just in the eyes of the Infante, but in the eyes of their Imperial colleagues. But however it had come about, the manoeuvre was to prove prudent and successful.

At about 4 a.m. the first of the campfires was re-lit and bodies began to stir. An hour later, while Horn was surveying the lie of the land, the Swedish artillery began a sustained bombardment during which one of Horn's generals ordered the Swedish cavalry to charge. Unfortunately for Horn, they advanced far too quickly and ended up, not just outstripping his infantry, but running into a hidden gully that turned south and ran away from the Allbuch. Finding themselves in difficulty, the Swedish cavalry decided to make the most of things and, deploying into line, began to charge the southernmost entrenchment of the Spanish defences. Before they could inflict too much damage, however, they were surprised in the flank by the La Tour and Arberg cavalry regiments. William's idea, if indeed it had been his, had worked, and the Swedish cavalry were forced to retire.

This small victory, alas, was soon overshadowed by the failure of the inexperienced Salm and Würmser regiments to hold their positions and they were routed by the Swedish infantry. It should have been a simple matter now for the Swedes to secure the Allbuch, but they were cursed with bad luck. In the poor visibility occasioned by the dirty-white smoke of their gunpowder, their troops on either side of the hill continued to advance and, following the unexpected detonation of a powder-wagon, contrived to open fire on each other.

Witnessing the disarray within the Swedish ranks, the Idiaquez now counter-attacked with cavalry support and, within half an hour, they had re-taken the hill. Fifteen times Horn's infantry tried to dislodge them, and fifteen times they were repelled by an inventive strategy of the Spaniards. The Swedish infantry were trained to discharge an entire unit's shot in one or two volleys in order to produce a wall of bullets. Each time they advanced, however, the Spanish hit the ground and let their shot pass over their heads. Before the Swedes could reload, the Spanish rose and fired. The Swedes fell like ninepins.

For six long hours the Swedes braved the purgatorial fire of the Spanish infantry, but by midday they were exhausted and Horn was forced to admit defeat. As he attempted to withdraw behind Bernard's lines, the Spanish on the Allbuch invoked the assistance of their patron saint and charged: *Santiago! Santiago! . . . España y Santiago!*

In a moment of panic, Bernard's army turned tail and fled, leaving

Horn and his infantry to fend for themselves. Some 8,000 of them were slain that day, and half as many again were captured. It was by far the bloodiest engagement of the war.

The turning point of the battle, of course, had been the holding of the Allbuch and, according to William, it had been his 'new stratagem and science' (occasionally he would refer to it as a 'new mathematical trick') and his 'deployment of the cavalry in a manner different to the field square to which the engineers were accustomed', that had been primarily responsible. The plaudits, however, went to his immediate superior, Francisco Antonio Camassa. But even if it were true that the night deployment of the La Tour and Arberg regiments had been his idea, William daren't complain too loudly. Patronage was a prize more easily lost than gained.

In the aftermath of victory, the ebullience of the royal encampment was quickly muted by the sight of blood-spattered women tending to the wounded, priests to the dying and peasant soldiers to the remains of the fallen (for loot and salvageable clothing). Not even the Infante could be shielded from the nightmarish immensity of the carnage or the vacant stares of the unheroic dead. Assigned a rather large house in which to billet himself, he surrendered it for use as a hospital and took up residence in a nearby farmhouse where, at the very least, he could escape the vocal agonies of the surgeons' tents.

As the stench from the incineration of amputated limbs began to waft across the valley, the Infante gave the order to move out. Abandoning the seriously wounded, and leaving the widows of the baggage train to bury the dead, they headed next for the medieval citadel of Rothenburg. It fell on 18 September. The following day they crossed the River Main and headed for the town of Aschaffenburg, about twenty miles southeast of Frankfurt. It held out for just eleven days. Less than three weeks later, having cleared their enemies from the Rhineland, they finally crossed the Flemish frontier.

On 4 November 1634, Fernando finally entered Brussels at the head of almost 11,000 troops in that flamboyant ceremonial procession so beloved of renaissance princes and Spanish viceroys—the *Blijde Inkomst* ('Joyous Entry'). Out came the flags and pennants, the extravagantly caparisoned horses, the freshly polished silver trumpets and, of course, the drums. With the usual contrived enthusiasm, the population feasted and celebrated, crowned the new governor with laurels and erected triumphal arches, stages and porticoes in his honour. Fernando, in his turn, responded by brandishing the sword of his great-grandfather, Charles V, and dressing in an elaborate costume of gold and scarlet. It was time to celebrate, and the flaxen-haired prince was intent on doing so in style.

(10)

O NE BRIGHT SUNNY morning in a district of Brussels rather opti-
mistically called *Paradijs*, a middle-aged Jesuit, trailing a nineteen-year-
old youth in his wake, came calling on an artist at his studio behind the
City Hall. The Jesuit was welcomed like a brother. He knew the artist of
old and had a favour to ask.

Shy, standoffish and perhaps a little effeminate, Antoon Van Dyck was
just two years younger than his visitor, Jan-Karel della Faille, and cut
from the same cloth. Both were the products of a Jesuit education and
the offspring of wealthy Antwerp merchants; and both were exceptionally driven individuals who had reached the pinnacle of their professions
at a relatively young age—Jan Karel having become the first man to
determine the centre of gravity of the sector of a circle, and Antoon having recently stepped out of the shadow of the great Rubens to establish
a reputation in his own right.

Antoon had worked for the della Failles before, but things were very
different now. He had just been knighted by Charles I of England and
was in great demand. Not only did the Infante and his generals want
their portraits painted, but a host of local Aldermen and diplomats also.
Nevertheless, amid the heady aroma of oils, emulsions and astringents,
a small preparatory drawing was made.

A doe-eyed and delicate youth, all ribbons and Flemish lace and
wearing a lightly brocaded student's cape, approaches his seated Jesuit
mentor anxiously seeking approval of his work (the nature of which will
forever remain a mystery as the centrepiece of the portrait: the large
poster-size document that he carries has been left blank). Directly above
his head, a hovering putto carries a coat of arms crowned in a manner
suggestive of untitled nobility and bearing his initials in monogram:
'*GLE LOA DE GUAN* . . . Guillén Lombardo de Guzmán'.

Enthroned beneath a baldachin to proclaim his authority and

pre-eminence, and wearing scholarly rather than ecclesiastical robes, Padre Falla (as the Jesuit was known to his Spanish students) appears quite a bit older than his thirty-seven years. Ardent and weary, his eyes look contemplatively into space. On a table to his right, an open watchcase or compass evokes either the virtues of temperance and prudence or his status as professor of nautical geography (the item is far from clear), while a framed *pietà* announces his devotion to Christ. Paying more than a little homage to El Greco's portrait of Cardinal Niño de Guevara, the drawing obviously flatters the Jesuit far more than his young acolyte, and there can be little doubt about who had commissioned it. Nevertheless, it is still very much a double-portrait and more or less confirms their friendship.

The portrait, however, was never painted; perhaps because royal commissions had taken precedence; perhaps because the Infante had sent William on to Venice to take care of some negotiations of a financial nature that were to detain him for almost forty days; perhaps simply because contracts had not been signed prior to Van Dyck's return to England (in the spring of 1635) or William's return to Spain (sometime between the Marquis of Leganés' departure for Paris in December 1634, and the French declaration of war in May 1635). The drawing, which hangs today in the *Szépmüvészeti Múzeum* in Budapest, remains the only known portrait of William Lamport still in existence (see also Appendix A).

(11)

*I*N THE SUMMER of 1635, William fell in love. Strictly speaking he was pushed, but his resistance was so weak it matters little how one describes it. It all started on 6 June, when the French published their *Declaration of Louis XIII*. With French charges to be answered and a wider European public to be convinced that Spain had only ever acted in her own defence, the Count-Duke decided to augment his team of propagandists. Seven years after his *Defensio Fidei* hit the streets of London, William was once again cast in the role of a pamphleteer (apparently following the recommendation of the Infante Fernando).

Assigned to a team working under the supervision of a three-man committee that met regularly in the Count-Duke's private office, William was taken to Madrid and set to work preparing pamphlets for scattering throughout France. His new duties, which liberated him from the austere confines of the Escorial and the constant supervision of his Jesuit mentors, marked something of a coming of age. It brought him into closer contact with many of the eminent gentlemen of the court and, for the first time, their daughters.

The parkland walks of the Casa del Campo, the tree-lined avenues of the Prado, and the palatial gardens of the Alcazar and Buen Retiro were frequented by an infinite multitude of young noblewomen who flittered their lives away on the fringes of the court waiting for the carefully choreographed advances of the *right* gentleman. Bred solely for marriage and motherhood, nothing was too much trouble if it helped to advance the moment of their betrothal. They smeared their lips with beeswax and cheeks with ochre, whitened their skin with *solimán*, doused themselves liberally with rosewater and passed in quiet impotence from the surveillance of their fathers to that of their husbands: resistance being a path that led only to the convent.

Ana de Cano y Leyva, however, was an exception. Little is known of

But Ana was far too intoxicated by the press of danger to be bothered with such trifles. In presenting him with that shirt she had made more than a declaration of affection; she had proclaimed her independence. In coming to his apartment she was now declaring her intention to take control. It was not the sort of behaviour one expected from a 'lady of the court' and it left William bewildered and confused.

In the well-ordered solar system of the 'Planet King' (as Olivares had styled Felipe IV), Ana was a rogue comet who frightened and fascinated William in equal measure. Over the months that followed, however, as fear gave way to anticipation and sleep to agitation, he tumbled headlong into his first romantic relationship. Emboldened by her confidence he also ceased to be quite so scrupulous about the presence of chaperones. He was far from ignorant of the consequences of discovery, but she filled such a void in his life that he felt powerless to stop. Irretrievably entangled in the brambles of a passion seductively garlanded, not just with poetry and music, but with the heady excitement of conspiracy and subterfuge, he began to explore the frontiers of catastrophe:

> What a beautiful face you possess,
> God has blessed you as a woman,
> I gaze upon you and am subdued,
> You look upon me, and I am slain.
> These mischievous eyes of yours,
> They gleam like nacre and snow;
> A poison that gives life,
> A victim who kills.

(One of three short poems in William's own hand, found at the back of a twenty-page notebook, or quinternion, dating from his days in Madrid. Its title, 'On the expeditious formation of cavalry squadrons', suggests it was written post Nördlingen).

William would remember these as his Halcyon days, but they were also days of anxiety and apprehension. Envious of the military success of his younger brother, the King was determined that he too should have the opportunity to lead his armies to victory in battle and, on 21 June 1635, he issued a proclamation ordering all *caballeros* (knights) and *hidalgos* (the lowest level of nobility) to make immediate preparations to join him on campaign. To accelerate the process he cancelled the Saint John's day festivities at the Buen Retiro.

The whole of Madrid had been looking forward to the celebrations and bonfires that traditionally marked the night of 24 June—the feast of John the Baptist. Occurring each year about the time of the summer solstice, the celebrations had their origins in Spain's pre-Christian past and had for centuries been one of the key holidays of the Spanish calendar. Their cancellation spawned a climate of urgency and vulnerability about the court and William and Ana were not alone in seeking to appease the impending trauma by 'building towers of diamonds upon straw'.

The euphoria of first love notwithstanding, William's efforts on behalf of the Propaganda Committee never flagged. One of many talented pens at the Count-Duke's disposal, his task was to produce pamphlets defending Spain's entry into the war as a purely defensive act. A small fish in a large pond that included such giants as Francisco Quevedo (one of Spain's greatest novelists) and Fajardo Diego de Saavedra (one of her greatest diplomats), there was little expectation that any of his pamphlets would hit the mark. Nevertheless, at least according to William, his '*La antipatía de los dos privados, el Conde-Duque y el Cardenal Richelieu . . .* The rivalry of the two first ministers, the Count-Duke and Cardinal Richelieu' provoked a written response from Richelieu himself.

In January of 1636, his profile rising rapidly at court, William was asked, most likely by Olivares, to re-work a poem he had once written in honour of the Count-Duke's favourite cousin, Cardinal Gaspar de Borja y Velasco, and which he had been invited to recite, just two years earlier, before the late Inquisitor General, Cardinal Zapata (d. April 1635). With the King's ambition to personally lead his armies into battle scuppered by a lack of funds, poor harvests and the non-co-operation of the Catalans, the return of Borja to Madrid was seen by Olivares as a welcome distraction and a cause for celebration—Borja's public criticisms of the Pope having made him something of a national hero in Spain. As a result, William's *Carmen Triumphale* (triumphal poem) of two columns of Latin distich were printed on posters and pasted throughout the court.

Entitled 'On the arrival of his most eminent and most excellent prince, Señor Don Gaspar de Borja, Cardinal of the Holy Roman

Church, Archbishop of Seville, and Supreme Counsellor of His Most Catholic Majesty Felipe IV etc.', William signed these posters—with a flourish of flamboyant curlicues—as a student of theology at the Colegio Imperial and a favoured protégé of the Count-Duke:

> 'Cecinit D. Guilielmus Lombardus de Guzmán, in Regio, ac ter magnifico Orbis Escurialensi Colegio Theologico imbutus focamine, Magnique Principis Comitis Ducis Alumnus etc.'

This was not the first time that the name of Guzmán had appeared in William's signature, but it is perhaps the most significant. Had it not been authorised by the Count-Duke himself it would have been seen as an outrageous and unpardonable act of effrontery. It represents a rare privilege: an honour publicly proclaimed at court. As omens for the future went, there were few better, and the expected promotion followed.

With the progress of the war now effectively stalled, William was relieved of his propaganda duties and assigned to one of the royal councils responsible for the award of titles, viceroyalties and pensions. It effectively marked the end of his life as a student and put an end to any lingering hopes he might have had of entering the University of Salamanca. This was, nevertheless, exactly the kind of entry-level position that a university degree would have fitted him for. Much as he might have liked to attend Salamanca, there was no guarantee that he would ever be offered another scholarship. It was too good an opportunity to turn down.

His new position also enabled him, or so he would later claim, to lobby on behalf of an old friend, the Marquis of Mancera, now in his fifty-first year and actively seeking a viceregal appointment to the Indies to crown his achievements. If true, it was a bold and generous gesture on William's part. Mancera enjoyed the rather dubious distinction of having shared a great-grandfather with Don Fadrique de Toledo, the Duke of Alba, titular head of the house of Toledo and, for the last two years or so, Olivares' latest bugbear.

The problems had begun back in December 1633 when Alba, having been ordered to take command of an expedition charged with ejecting the Dutch from Brazil, began to suspect he was being sent on a suicide mission and refused to leave without more ships and more men. The following July, he was summoned to a meeting with Olivares that quickly degenerated into name-calling and ended with his arrest. Three months later Olivares ordered the confiscation of his property and forced him into exile. As a public demonstration of their solidarity, the old families of Castile refused to attend the court and to provide infantry and cavalry for the war with France. They even managed, or so it was rumoured at the time, to win the support of the Queen. That William should dare to lobby a royal council on behalf of a member of the House of Toledo was indicative, not just of his highly developed sense of loyalty, but of the continuing confidence he had in his relationship with his patron.

Such was William's confidence in his future and Ana's confidence in him, that the summer of 1637 saw their relationship move onto a different plain entirely. Physical intimacy, however, was no easy matter within the confines of a court where everyone knew everyone else's business. It was further complicated by the fact that dressing and undressing was a task no noblewoman of the day could manage without the aid of her maids. Liaisons not only had to be planned; they required the complicity of others. But that is not to say they did not happen: in fact the suffocating heat of the Castilian summer all but guaranteed that they did.

The only real pastime of the nobility that was shared equally by men and women alike, was the *paseo*. But with the streets of the city perpetually carpeted with cloacal sludge and putrescent waste, this afternoon promenade was inevitably taken in a carriage—the ownership of which was seen as the sole preserve of the nobility. For young men like William, who were without the wherewithal to permanently maintain a carriage of their own, one could always be hired at the Plaza de los Herradores.

A proverb that dated back to the early days of the Renaissance did not exactly exaggerate the climate of Madrid when it described it as '*nueve meses de invierno, tres meses de infierno* . . . nine months of winter, three months of hell'. Indeed such was the heat of the city during the summer months that most carriages would abandon the traditional routes along the Alameda del Prado and the gardens of the Buen Retiro, for the cooler and greener environs of the Huerta de Juan Fernández and the river beds of the Manzanares (when the waters had receded enough). It was not uncommon, in such discreet locations, for two carriages to come upon each other 'by chance', and for the occupant of one to quickly transfer to another.

Perhaps this is how it was, perhaps not; all that is known for certain is that Ana, her heart locked in mortal combat with her honour, allowed passion to run roughshod over prudence. In her daily prayers she acknowledged one set of morals, and in William's arms another. Despite the vigilance of her chaperones, she managed to connive enough privacy to allow them consummate the relationship, thereby sacrificing both her reputation and her future for love.

It was, on the face of it, a reckless act; one no well-bred young woman of her day would ever have considered without at least the promise of marriage—a promise that in itself would be next to worthless from a man of William's station. But then perhaps that was exactly the point; perhaps the only way to secure a remedy for her passion was to leave her parents with no other choice!

(12)

*I*N THE EARLY autumn of 1637, William bade farewell to Ana and rode north to La Coruña, home of his very first benefactor in Spain, Don Pedro de Toledo y Leyva, the Marquis of Mancera. He had been offered a place in the armada of Don Lope de Hoces y Córdoba—most likely as a result of some string-pulling by his one-time professor of nautical geography, Jan-Karel della Faille, who at that time was assisting Olivares with a variety of nautical projects, one of which had William's name written all over it.

Olivares had suddenly taken a mind to recall the battle-hardened Irish regiments of the Army of Flanders to Spain, ostensibly to shore up the inexperienced infantry battalions that were currently defending the Catalan border with France. Their recall, however, was more likely a precautionary measure aimed at thwarting the persistent attempts of Richelieu to lure them into French service.

With the overland supply routes between Italy and the Netherlands now either broken or under threat from the French, it was no longer feasible to transport troops to and from Flanders by land, and Olivares was considering sending their replacements by the perilous northerly route around the British Isles. But it was not William's experience of Irish and English waters that made him particularly suited to this expedition, rather his links to two colonels of the Irish regiments: his 'uncles' John O'Neill and Hugh O'Donnell. For the first time in their history, the Irish regiments were being called upon to fight as integral units in Spain, and William was to assist with their assembly and transport.

On his arrival in La Coruña, William found Hoces and Admiral Don Antonio de Oquendo waiting anxiously in a port that was packed to overcrowding with more than 5,000 fighting men for whom accommodation was in short supply and boredom was becoming a real problem. For many there was little to do but drink and brawl; for William, at least, there was the opportunity to renew his acquaintance with Don Pedro and his wife, Doña María Louisa.

Don Pedro was not a happy man. A riot by sailors from the fleet of Miguel de Horna had left several locals dead, and the atmosphere within the port was extremely tense. He wanted the soldiers shipped out, and shipped out fast. Olivares, on the other hand, was still considering his options. The Spanish were understrength and ill-prepared to meet the superior Dutch fleet that was currently blockading Dunkirk. But pressure was mounting on him to act, and so he decided to gamble.

On Christmas Day 1637, new orders arrived for Hoces to sail immediately for Flanders with reinforcements for the Infante Fernando. Two days later, his armada of forty ships left La Coruña heading for the English Channel—Olivares having abandoned by now the idea of sailing by a northerly route. Spreading all the canvas they could safely bear they sailed with strong prevailing winds and made record time for a winter sailing. It had been three years since William had last set to sea—more than enough time to have lost his sea legs—and it would have been with a happy heart, if not a healthy stomach, that he disembarked at Mardyck that New Year's Eve.

Like many a young girl before her, it was probably not until she began to swell that Ana really believed that she was pregnant. Short of arrest by the Inquisition, it is hard to imagine a more frightening predicament, and all manner of fears would have raced through her head, from the dread of childbirth itself to the humiliation and shame that would accompany the scandal—the type of scandal that could distress a girl's parents far more than news of her death.

Time was not on her side. William's progress had been slow and there was only so much that could be concealed beneath the hoops of her farthingale in his absence. Her maid, in any case, would probably notice her secret long before it chose to declare itself to the world. She had only two choices; the altar or the convent, and as her parents would not agree to the former her fate, it appeared, had been sealed.

Very soon she would find herself leaving the opulent delights of the court and its manicured surrounds for a cavernous retreat of devotional austerity; trading her silks and satins for a habit of plain serge; forsaking the delights of poetry for prayer, dance for stillness, flirtations for genuflection; and kept forever out of reach of everything her young heart held dear. She faced sharing the rest of her days with a community seduced by the romantic hope of achieving perfection in the impersonal and active service of God; a community for whom she would become the living embodiment of the Magdalen, or at least the popular perception of her; a community whose sacrifice had been voluntary rather than imposed and whose vows of chastity and unquestioning obedience would lead many of their number to look down upon her with an unspoken admixture of self-righteousness, pity, envy and disdain. The submission she would have offered freely to her husband would now be demanded by the rule, and she would become even more of an outsider within those walls than her Irish lover had ever been in Castilian society: tolerated, but never truly accepted. For such an independent mind, the prospect must have been truly terrifying, and all for a moment of girlish recklessness.

On 7 March, along with his 'uncles' and some 1,400 Irish soldiers, William set sail on the return journey to La Coruña in a fleet of thirty warships, once again under the command of Don Lope de Hoces y Córdoba. But they'd hardly set to sea when he was roused from his sea-chest by the shout of *zafarrancho de combate . . .* clear the decks for combat'.

They had stumbled upon a Dutch convoy and the temptation of easy pickings had proved much too great. Fifteen Dutch vessels were captured that day, forcing Hoces to set back to port to offload his prizes. They weighed from Mardyck for a second time on 24 March only to run into yet another convoy. On this occasion, despite taking twelve sail in prizes, Hoces decided to press for home.

On his return to Madrid, William expected to be rewarded for his part in a job well done, but by this time Ana's pregnancy had become known and with the scandal fresh in the minds of his detractors he received nothing more than his salary. He had slighted Fortune with his arrogance and now she was exacting her revenge. There was no way on earth he was going to be able to charm his way out of this situation and, with marriage out of the question, his only other option meant abandoning everything he had worked so hard to achieve at court.

But while there is enough evidence in her one surviving letter to confirm Ana's deeply felt love for William, we will probably never know for certain how William truly felt about Ana (he appears to have never discussed matters of the heart with anyone, or at least anyone who recorded what he said). But perhaps his poetry holds some clues:

> Enchantress, Mother,
> You are my dark one,
> With your eyes you bewitch me,
> As herbs cannot.
> In your eyes, Mother,
> Love displays all its powers
> And makes of me a mark
> For its persistent arrows.
> Your eyes are its quiver,
> Your eyebrows its bow,
> With your eyes you bewitch me,
> As herbs cannot.

(Another of the three short poems in William's own hand, found at the back of the quinternion entitled 'On the expeditious formation of cavalry squadrons').

Whatever his motivation, in the early spring of 1638 William smuggled Ana out of the royal palace and carried her off to Madrid, where the pair initially 'took refuge in a church'—most probably that of San Isidro, in whose adjoining college William had once taken his tutorials in mathematics and where many of his old friends still resided. A short while later they rented a ground-floor apartment on the Calle de la Magdalena, a fashionable street just ten minutes walk from the college.

The traditional rosary of invocations to Saint Ramón Nonnato notwithstanding, it was far from a certainty that all would go well for Ana. This was, after all, an era when childbirth was a potentially life-threatening condition. Three to four day labours were not uncommon, Caesarean sections were rare on live mothers, midwives varied wildly in levels of expertise, and postpartum infections were almost to be expected for mother and child alike. Mortality rates were so high, in fact, that women of her station were frequently encouraged to make wills before giving birth. She had more than enough to be getting on with, even under normal circumstances. But these were not normal circumstances, nor were these her only worries.

Sensing that the scandal had presented them with an opportunity to embarrass the Count-Duke by association (William was still calling himself *Lombardo y Guzmán*), a number of her family began to allege that she had been abducted. By the time news of their disappearance had reached Olivares, the pair had become a latter day Hades and Persephone. Perhaps she wanted to protect herself from scandal amongst her new neighbours; perhaps she was fearful that her uncles might attempt to find her and 'rescue' her for the convent or, even worse, take her back to court and use her shame as a stick with which to beat Olivares and his detested 'creatures'; but she began her lying-in under the alias of Godoy y Rodriguez.

To the well-heeled Spaniard, children were everything. The birth of a child was more than just a family event; it was a source of joy to the whole community and something to be heralded. Whatever rancour might lie between adults, it would be put aside for the sake of the child. Children came first. From the King himself (who would sire some thirty children outside of wedlock before he died) to the humblest *hidalgo*, the *bastardo* had become something of a Spanish institution.

Amongst the less well off, however, the joy was not always unconfined. The high rate of illegitimate births had led to equally high rates of abandoned children (in some places as high one in five). But despite their much reduced circumstances, there was never any question of William and Ana abandoning Teresa. For the first time in almost ten years, William felt part of a family. Whatever difficulties they were experiencing were temporary. He'd see to that.

It was probably about this time that he wrote his '*Discurso de las lágrimas de la Magdalena . . .* A discourse on the tears of the Magdalen'; a religious treatise of a type very much in vogue amongst those orthodox Christian women for whom the Magdalen represented the ultimate model of redemption. In an attempt to curry her favour and influence, he dedicated it to Doña Inés de Zuñiga, the austere and pious wife of the Count-Duke of Olivares, to little or no avail. His pique was aggravated even further by the unexpected visit, sometime between May and July, of his older brother. Amongst a population of 150,000, John had somehow managed to track him down.

With his tonsured head and habit of dark brown serge, John was almost unrecognisable. He had not seen William for over thirteen years—the last four of which had been spent at the nearby University of Salamanca. What brought him to Madrid now, of all times, was anybody's guess; but it was probably word of the birth of his niece. His father and mother were dead, Gerald had joined the Irish Regiment in Flanders, and Catherine was still in Ireland (where she had abandoned the life of a third order Franciscan to marry). William was effectively the only family John had left.

But if he had come looking for consolation, he had come much too late. William and he were strangers to one another, and the meeting was difficult. Time had softened neither John's resentment nor William's conceit, and the reunion was strained and competitive—William at one point having to dig out a bound copy of his *Laus Comitis Ducis* in order to convince his brother that he really *had* been a student at the Colegio Imperial where 'there were none the equal of me in any subject'. His brother, on the other hand, could always point to having completed his degree; something William, for all his talent, had never managed to do.

John, however, was more interested in his brother's marital status than his academic qualifications, and Ana was particularly unnerved by the manner in which he stared at her. Finding William persisting in a union unsanctified by Holy Mother Church, and with a woman who was 'without dowry', the Franciscan was curious to know something of the circumstances. But William was evasive: he would not even confirm her identity. 'She had,' he said, 'many names'.

Stories of patronage and scholarships notwithstanding, John was more than a little sceptical. Everything he saw about him led him to believe that his brother was living in poverty. William, however, insisted that they were fine. Ana's sister was helping them out financially and they hoped to be married soon—a claim that suggests, perhaps, a legal impediment, such as Ana's age, or continuing negotiations with her family through Doña María's intercession, rather than any great disregard for social or canonical conventions, or the fact that William claimed not to have had the time to approach the sacrament of confession.

In July of 1638, a force of 18,000 French soldiers unexpectedly crossed the Spanish frontier at Irún and laid siege to the strategic coastal fortress of Fuenterrabía (now called Hondarribia). The blockade was completed by over seventy warships under the command of the

Archbishop of Bordeaux, including the famous *La Couronne:* a 1,200 ton giant boasting over 70 cannons and a crew in excess of 600.

The invasion took the Spanish completely by surprise and posed such a threat to national prestige that many of the kingdoms that had been less than supportive of Olivares' plans for a general 'Union of Arms' suddenly volunteered reinforcements. The only exception were the Catalans, who invoked their constitutional prohibition on the recruitment of troops to fight outside of Catalonia.

As two companies of infantry were being recruited in Madrid in the Count-Duke's own name rather than that of the King, it was perhaps inevitable that William would end up polishing his *coraza* and heading off, at his own expense, to join his old Jesuit colleagues and teachers. Sieges, after all, were meat and drink to military engineers and for a man anxious to mend his fences with the Count-Duke it was an opportunity not to be missed. The army, which was placed under the command of the Marquis of Mortara, was to be augmented by the 1,200 Irishmen that William had recently helped to transport from Flanders.

As the siege dragged on into the month of August, an increasingly desperate Olivares sent new orders to La Coruña. Hoces could hardly believe his ears. His ships were not yet seaworthy. The last thing he needed was to be told to put to sea again; but that's exactly what was expected of him. There was little point, however, in seeking to engage the French navy with such puny resources, so he resolved instead to land his troops on the Basque coast from where they could march to Fuenterrabía. On 12 August 1638, his armada of twelve ships sailed into the tiny harbour of Guetaría only to be surprised, soon afterwards, by thirty-three of the French fleet. With no time to improvise a screen of grappling boats against the French incendiary barges, he lost 3,000 of the 4,000 men under his command and all but one of his ships. Those who were left made their weary and sodden way on foot to Fuenterrabía. News of the catastrophe caused consternation in Madrid.

How William travelled to Fuenterrabía is unclear. He may have marched with Mortara or O'Neill; he may even have been amongst those who swam ashore at Guetaría. All that is known for certain is that at on Tuesday 7 September he was amongst 200 Irish soldiers who succeeded in breaching the French lines and entering the beleaguered fort, where he then proceeded to assist the Jesuit engineer, Francisco Isasi (formerly his tutor in mathematics and geometry at the Colegio Imperial) in organising the fortification and defence of the city until the final victory was secured. For the majority of the town's defenders, the Irish breakthrough came much too late: for Olivares it was only just in time.

Three days later, a messenger arrived in the capital bringing news of the Spanish victory. His name was Bernardino de Ayala and as he made his way through the warrens of the Barrio de San Luis people began, more or less spontaneously, to pour into the streets and follow him to the royal palace. As the news spread the capital went mad with relief. Bells pealed throughout the night and excited crowds thronged the streets to beat on their drums and give tumultuous vent to their joy. So many bonfires and torches were lit during that night of riotous rejoicing that the English ambassador wrote 'it was as if night had been turned into day'. Nine days later the same thing happened in Seville.

On 23 September the victorious Spanish army marched in triumphant cavalcade through the *Puerta de Alcalá* to receive the adulation of Madrid. Attempting to take advantage of the unprecedented orgy of triumphalism and in particular the public acclaim that was being showered upon the Count-Duke (in whose name the victorious army had been raised), William sought to procure for himself some little reward in light of his most recent services to the Crown. He was offered two *hábitos* worth 1,400 copper reals per annum; substantial sums, to be sure, but there was a catch. The awards were dependent upon his recruiting 200 infantry at his own expense and transporting them to Barcelona. He declined the offer, and began to search for alternative employment. He had had his fill of war.

Nothing had prepared Ana for motherhood. Its secrets were like those of the marital bed—shared only by wives and widows. And yet somehow she had coped. With a quiet serenity she had accepted her fate and learned to cope with being left alone in a strange house while William went to war or in search of work, not to mention the unpleasant tasks she had grown up assuming were the sole preserve of servants. But the pair were still dependent upon her sister's charity and, much as they were grateful for her help, it was not a state of affairs their pride could suffer for long.

Details of William's movements at this time are virtually non-existent. All that is known for certain is that he found employment for a short time in the service of Don Francisco Lasso de la Vega (a member of one of the most prominent Toledan merchant families) at his house on the Calle de la Victoria, and later still with engineer and military architect Luis Carducho—a nephew of the famous Florentines, Vincente and Bartolomé Carducci (court painters to Felipe IV). One of the leading lights of the Royal Academy of Sciences in Madrid, Carducho was currently employed on a project close to the heart of every Toledan merchant—the canalisation of the Tagus from Toledo to Lisbon. The post of his assistant came with the use of an apartment in a large two-storey house on the narrow and undulating Calle del Olmo, where he lived with his wife, Geronima.

Toledo had never recovered from the removal of the court to Madrid. Since 1561 its population had been halved, its textile industry had withered, and the canalisation of the Tagus was seen as the only way to arrest the decline. The project had, in fact, been mooted before. Work had even begun during the 1580s, only to be abandoned following the death of the Italian engineer who had made the plans and the venomous opposition of the merchant families of Seville (who saw the project as a major threat to their trade with Toledo and Lisbon). It was still opposed, not just by the Sevillians, but also by the Count-Duke of Olivares (who considered himself a Sevillian). For a man whose future was more or less dependent upon a reconciliation with the increasingly irascible Count-Duke, it was far from ideal employment.

Shortly after William and Ana moved in to their new apartment, in the summer of 1639, John returned to Madrid from Salamanca; perhaps to make one last attempt at reconciliation; perhaps simply to say his goodbyes. He had just completed his degree and a missionary life was beckoning. Very soon he would be exploring for himself the utopian possibilities of the New World and evangelising the natives of some distant oriental backwater. Once there he might never again hold a conversation in his native tongue and all sense of home and family would soon be bleached from his memory by merciless rays of a tropical sun. It was unlikely he would ever return.

Arriving at Carducho's house, he found William embowered in books and papers and working in a room that was packed to the rafters with charts, globes, astrolabes and other sundry mathematical instruments. Perhaps it was simply the crusader zeal of the new missionary; perhaps a sense of loss or emptiness took him unawares as he watched the unconscious intimacies that William shared with Ana oblivious to the desolating effect that such things can have on a cleric; but something within him snapped, and his tone turned admonitory. In Ana's presence he asked why, as they were still living as man and wife, they had not yet sought the blessing of the Church.

William was incensed. To dare to ask such a question in front of Ana was an unforgivable impertinence, even for a brother. Realising he had outstayed his welcome John took his cape and left immediately. His remarks, nevertheless, had cut to the marrow.

Their exile from court had not diminished the social chasm that lay between Ana and William, rather it had increased it. A fallen noblewoman was still a noblewoman; that was a matter of birth, ineradicable and immutable. *She* did not require a wealthy patron to affirm *her* identity.

Without the patronage of the Count-Duke, however, William was a nobody: one in a long line of apocryphal foreign nobility that were scrambling for a foothold on the ladder of respectability. He himself had long since become accustomed to privation, and the Calle del Olmo was far from the worst place he could be, but Ana was a child of the court. If they were ever again to live in comfort, enjoy the respect of their peers and liberate themselves from their dependence on Doña María's charity, he would have to mend his fences with the Count-Duke.

But the timing could not have been worse, especially given the nature of the scandal that had led to his fall from grace. A recent crusade at court against falling standards of public morality had forced the King to publish an edict prohibiting the wearing of fashionable low-necked bodices by all women bar prostitutes: not exactly an auspicious omen for an alleged fornicator and abductor. And then there was the ever increasing popular discontent with the policies of the Count-Duke. This was currently so vehement that he had become something of a recluse, living, it was said by at least one foreign ambassador, in constant fear of assassination. It was not the best time to be seeking a handout.

*G*ILBERT NUGENT NEEDED a place to hide. He had come to Madrid with an offer to provide Irish soldiers for the Army of Flanders and did not want his presence to become known to the British Ambassador. Unfamiliar with the Spanish court and unable to speak a word of Spanish, he sought the help of his 'cousin', William Lamport.

A brother of Richard Nugent, the Earl of Westmeath, and a relative of Henry Plunkett (one of William's tutors in Dublin), Gilbert's arrival, in September of 1639, could not have been more opportune as it presented William with an opportunity to renew some old acquaintances. Offering Gilbert lodgings in his apartment, he took his papers to Don Pedro López de Celo, Secretary to the King and Fiscal of the *Junta de Ejecución* (a small war cabinet created by Olivares in January of 1637 to ensure that important policy decisions could be made and put into effect without undue delay).

This was the first time that Ana had met any of William's 'noble' relatives and she was happy to oblige at first. Given the acute manpower shortages in the Spanish military, there was every reason to believe that Gilbert's proposal would be dealt with quickly. The first they heard from the *Junta*, however, was a request for William to retrieve his cousin's papers and summarise them in Castilian.

A blind eye was often turned in Ireland to the activities of men like Gilbert Nugent, as they were effectively clearing Ireland of unemployed professional soldiers who might otherwise be causing mischief. Under normal circumstances, therefore, he would have had little need for secrecy. But the circumstances were far from normal: Gilbert was intending to use the profits to finance a rebellion in Ireland.

The days passed slowly in the cramped confines of an apartment filled with three adults and a baby. Topics of conversation began to run dry and small talk ebbed and flowed between pools of difficult silences. After ninety days Gilbert had had enough of playing gooseberry to the adults and peek-a-boo with the baby. Returning to Ireland to report on his negotiations, he left William with the task of speeding up matters. It was a measure of just how far his star at court had waned, however, that his efforts consisted solely of written reminders to the Count-Duke's secretaries rather than personal audiences with the man himself.

Gilbert returned to Madrid early in the New Year, this time offering to ferry as many as 10,000 Irishmen to Dunkirk. At a cost of four ducats per head, he hinted, the Spanish would have to act fast. Whole regions of France were being combed by press gangs. The price was likely to rise.

The matter finally came before the Council of State on 13 February. 'Even though the proposition seems ridiculous,' Olivares finally conceded, 'we can advance the man a little money to test whether he has any influence in Ireland or the power to deliver what he promises.' Summoned to the office of Don Fernando Ruiz de Contreras, Secretary of the Council of War, William and Gilbert were given a number of blank patents: two for the appointment of sergeants major and fifty for captains and other officers. They were also awarded the sum of 44,000 ducats in silver to finance the recruitment of some 2,400 men. The money, they were told, was awaiting them in London.

For themselves personally, they were offered a number of gifts, including grants of land—also dependent upon their return to London—and two patents of fieldmaster or *maese de campo* (an honorary title that of itself did not confer military rank). William declined everything, with the singular exception of the patent of fieldmaster. It was, he protested, still much too dangerous for him to return to England.

The offer, however, seems surprisingly generous in the light of Olivares' scepticism. What exactly he was up to is impossible to tell. Perhaps he felt some sympathy for William's current difficulties; perhaps the 'scandal' had made William an embarrassment best swept under a foreign carpet. Either way, if the Irishman wouldn't go to London, then there were other places he could be sent.

Over the days that followed, a series of appointments were made that began to weave the threads of William's life into a Gordian knot of intrigue with the Marquis of Villena and Don Juan de Palafox y Mendoza. Before two months had passed, all three would be heading for a new life on the opposite side of the Atlantic. The catalyst was the current crisis in New Spain (as Spain's North American territories were then called).

(14)

$\mathcal{T}$HE EVENTS THAT triggered William's passage to the Indies had actually begun some five years earlier with the appointment of Don Lope Diez de Armendaríz, the Marquis of Cadereyta, to the post of Viceroy of New Spain. His promotion, just short of his sixtieth birthday, coincided with intensified Dutch raids on the Spanish territories, a royal prohibition on trade between New Spain and Peru, and a calamitous slump in silver production. It also coincided with a threatened revolt by the lower castes.

Almost without exception, all positions of authority in New Spain were filled by native-born Spaniards or *gachupínes* (literally 'spurred ones'). The shortage of pure-blooded European women in the western empire, however, inevitably made Creoles of their children and rendered them ineligible to follow in the footsteps of their parents. As Creoles, their children were viewed by other *gachupínes* as inferior, intellectually lazy and tainted with Indian blood. When one *gachupín* retired, another came to take his place; setting the children of his predecessor on the road to genteel poverty. Not even commerce offered a way out: all the great entrepreneurial opportunities in New Spain having already been granted to a small number of favoured families.

Beneath the Creoles in the social pecking order, came an intricate hierarchy of racial classifications based on one immutable principle: Indian blood was capable of redemption, Negro blood was not. Nouns such as *Mestizo, Indio, Cuarterón, Mulatto, Zambo* and *Morisco* came into common usage, not as pejorative terms, though they certainly had such uses, but as something much worse—the cold, aseptic classifications of a bureaucracy for whom each caste was capable only of occupying their own specific socio-economic niche. They even gave rise to a new art form, the *casta* painting—a visual means of illustrating and reinforcing the prejudice.

Barred from voting, holding public office, attending a university or religious seminary, and even from joining professional guilds, the mixed races were trapped from birth in a web of social immobility and institutionalised poverty. Race even determined how close to the altar they could sit at Mass and where each could march in religious and civic processions. Such humiliation made the Creoles, in particular, resentful and antagonistic towards the Viceroy—the ultimate symbol of *gachupín* authority. They had more or less come to accept the tradition that no high officer of the Crown could be appointed to a province in which he had ties of a personal or commercial nature, and they did not aspire to the very top posts. Below the Viceroy and Archbishops, however, there was an entire administrative and ecclesiastical bureaucracy to which they wanted access—beginning with half of the places on the *Audiencia* (a colonial government of legally trained judges or *oidors* under the presidency of the Viceroy). If another crisis was to be avoided, Cadereyta would have to act, and act quickly.

By tradition, and by law, it was required that an independent end-of-term evaluation, or *residencia,* take place into the reign of the outgoing Viceroy, in this case the Marquis of Cerralvo. This was meant to encourage the incumbent to perform to the best of his abilities and to allow his successor to get the best possible briefing for his new role. It was traditionally a courteous and consultative affair, but Cadereyta refused to meet with Cerralvo and publicly aligned himself with the Visitor General, Don Pedro de Quiroga y Moya: a move that made him immensely popular with the Creoles.

Cerralvo was furious and isolated. Unused to criticism, let alone denunciation, he was desperately afraid he would be indicted. But Fate conspired to protect him. The Visitor General died suddenly during a visit to Acapulco, forcing the King to suspend the *residencia.* Cerralvo, meanwhile, was allowed to return to Europe—a move that exasperated the Creoles.

To help bankroll Spanish military campaigns in such diverse arenas as the Caribbean, Flanders, France, Germany, Italy and the Pyrenees, Cadereyta was now expected to enforce such extreme measures as increased taxes, forced loans and confiscation of bullion. The Creoles agreed to co-operate, but demanded concessions. Apart from greater autonomy, they wanted restrictions placed on the Jesuits (who were developing a voracious appetite for haciendas) and an end to the ban on trade with Peru—the lifting of which was seen as a panacea for all of the colony's ills.

Cadereyta made vague promises but ceded little. The Creole demands, however, *were* passed on to Madrid, where they were viewed with some considerable concern. The ban on trade with Peru had been imposed to protect Spanish exports to the New World: lifting it would cause an economic catastrophe at home.

Under the leadership of Andrés Gómez de Mora and Fernando Carrillo, two allies of Cerralvo with whom William was soon to become intimately familiar, the Creoles began to openly oppose the new Viceroy. His difficulties increased tenfold when Antonio Urrutia de Vergara, a dissident army general and friend of Cerralvo, broke out of gaol and sought sanctuary with the Dominicans. The escape heralded an alliance between the Creoles and the disaffected within the military similar to that which had led to the downfall of the Marquis of Gelves (Viceroy of New Spain from 1621 to 1624). The Crown now began to receive conflicting reports regarding Vergara. Cadereyta believed him to be an evil genius and a threat to the colony, while Cerralvo, by this time in Madrid, claimed him to be the innocent victim of an over-zealous Viceroy. Unable to determine the truth of the matter, the Crown decided to put a stop to the public feuding and ordered Cadereyta to leave Vergara be. With his hands now effectively tied, Cadereyta was subjected by Vergara and his circle of friends to a relentless campaign of harassment. They were supported by the City Council, the Creole leadership and three judges of the *Audiencia*. In a blind panic, Cadereyta wrote to Madrid denouncing the behaviour of the *Audiencia* and claiming that 'a popular commotion' was imminent. That letter, the primary reason for William's impending exile, was the last straw for Olivares and Cadereyta was recalled to Spain.

On 27 December 1639, at the Monastery of San Bernardo in Madrid, Don Juan de Palafox y Mendoza was consecrated Bishop of Puebla de los Angeles, the second most important city in New Spain. Just thirty-nine years of age at the time, he initially refused the appointment on the grounds that he considered himself unworthy and only relented following pressure from the King.

The bastard son of the illustrious Don Jaime de Palafox by a young widowed noblewoman from Zaragoza, Juan was born at Fitero, in Navarre, during the Saint John's day fiesta of 1600. Abandoned by his mother at birth, and adopted by two millers, he was named after the saint on whose feast day he was born. A graduate of the Universities of Salamanca and Alcála, by the time he eventually took holy orders, at the age of twenty-nine, he had already served as Fiscal to the Council of War and was currently serving as Fiscal to the Council of the Indies. Considered one of the most brilliant men of his generation, his selection as Visitor General was an indication of just how seriously the crisis in New Spain was being viewed in Madrid—as indeed was their choice of Viceroy.

Also educated at the University of Salamanca, and a colonel of the Spanish Infantry, Don Diego Lopez Pacheco Cabrera y Bobadilla had almost as many titles as he had living relatives. The 7th Marquis of Villena, 6th Marquis of Moya, 7th Duke of Escalona and 8th Count of Santisteban de Gormaz and Xiquena, he would be the first grandee of Spain ever to rule in New Spain. He was a pious and cultured man of refined tastes, as capable of extremes of religious devotion as opulence and ostentation. So fond was he of the delights of the table, it was said, that it could only have been his equally prolific attendance at the altar that had spared him the agonies of the gout.

A direct descendant of King Manuel of Portugal and distant relative of the Count-Duke of Olivares through his marriage into the more senior branch of the Guzmán family, Villena's elder brother, Felipe, had actually sought this appointment as early as 1632. Following Felipe's death, Villena had not only inherited his titles, but also the appointment as Viceroy which, rumour had it, his brother had purchased.

But however the appointment came about Villena's brief, although potentially lucrative, was always going to be a difficult one. The Mexican mining industry was an irregulated mess, agriculture was in decline, the religious orders were in conflict and the secular clergy were seriously discontented and leaderless. Simply stated, Villena was expected to oversee the revival of viceregal authority within the colony and impose administrative reform. He was ordered, as indeed was the new Bishop of Puebla, to sail for the Indies the following March.

But while Villena and Palafox could travel openly in their official roles, Olivares had something altogether different in mind for William. Confusion still reigned in Madrid over the Urrutia de Vergara question, and Olivares needed someone willing to go undercover and weed out the truth of the matter. William was a pleasant young man, capable of great charm and, at least up to now, of keeping a secret. Even the King appeared to trust him. His talents could not have been better suited to the task and there were any number of other, more personal, reasons for sending him as far as possible from Madrid, not least of which was the fact that by William's own admission, there had already been a number of attempts to lure him into acting as a spy for the French. Well better a Spanish spy than a French one!

Late in February of 1640, William was summoned to the Palace of the Buen Retiro. He found the Count-Duke in his office and in foul humour. On the morning of the 20th a fire had broken out that had destroyed the royal quarters and forced their Royal Majesties to move to the Alcazar. Since then Olivares had been present from dawn to dusk overseeing the restoration.

Tired, impatient, and in no mood to negotiate, he apparently offered William the one thing he would be unable to refuse—a title. If he proved successful in his mission, Olivares would see what he could do about making him the next Marquis of Crópani—an impoverished marquisate in the far south of Italy. The title, which had been created as recently as July of 1622, had become vacant following the death of the current marquis, a Sicilian by the name of Ettore Ravaschiera. As there were no legal heirs, succession lay entirely within the gift of the King.

Or at least that is what William would later claim had happened. Meetings such as this, however, were rarely minuted and such was the Crown's need for cash that vacant titles were frequently sold. As loyalty no longer ennobled quite as effectively as silver it seems more likely that Olivares, believing the funding he was about to offer William would, if properly invested, easily yield the kind of return necessary for him to purchase the title, had agreed to hold off making a decision on the succession for a couple of years.

But whatever agreement had been reached, the nature of the mission remained the same, and William was told of a letter recently received from the Marquis of Cadereyta, which spoke of a threatened mutiny in Mexico. From the left-hand drawer of his desk Olivares retrieved his *pugilar* (Hebrew Manual of the Scriptures), inside of which was a cipher. William was given the cipher and ordered to use it to encrypt such private letters as he might send to Madrid. With the promise of a draft for 7,000 pesos from Olivares, and a further 3,000 from the King, William resigned himself to leaving. Excited at the possibility of travelling to the Indies, not to mention the possibility of a title, he returned to his apartment to tell his family (and redesign his coat of arms).

But there was a fly in the ointment. Whatever deal had been struck between William and the Count-Duke, or perhaps even between Ana's relatives and the Count-Duke, it did not include Ana and Teresa. William was to travel to the Indies with all due 'secrecy, caution and artful dissimulation', and he was to travel alone.

(15)

*T*HE ATLANTIC WAS an ocean of tears; so vast it could dissolve the most heartfelt of promises; so wide it could stretch the strongest of bonds to breaking. On the other side, it was said, lay an enchanted land, straight out of the book of Amadis; another Eden where dark-skinned Eves loitered like sirens. For every argonaut who returned carrying his weight in gold, there was another whose bones lay sun-bleached and scattered on some nameless beach, and yet another for whom the possibility of a clean slate or the supposedly limitless opportunities for *amancebamiento* (concubinage) had turned his conscience inside out.

There was little point in Ana seeking assurances: far too many men had disappeared with covenants of fidelity burned in their hearts. '*Júrame*', the wives had pleaded and their husbands had sworn as they were asked, only to be never seen again. The most that Ana could do was pray to the Holy Virgin to keep William safe and hope that his absence would not loosen the ties that bound them. It had, after all, been she who had initiated the relationship; she who had made it happen. Left to his own devices William might never have moved.

How long had it been since she first followed him home to his apartment? Five years? Hardly long enough, at any rate, for her to have forgotten his response to her unexpected appearance. 'Are you trying to ruin me,' he'd said, or words to that effect.

She had learnt a lot about life in the intervening years, and about herself. She had come to accept that she had been in large measure the author of her own misfortune and that the object of her desire was less than perfect; though no less worthy of her affection. She could never really be certain, however, that her singular devotion would be enough to deflect him from the sort of temptation that she herself had so easily led him into. Oaths, in general, guaranteed nothing more than a few grains of hope and comfort. There was one, however, that offered a morsel of self-respect.

Prior to the Council of Trent, in 1563, the Church had always taught that the constitutive factor of marriage lay in the mutual consent of the partners, rather than the blessing of a priest. Put another way, the priest did not marry a couple, they married themselves. Secret or clandestine marriages, however, were seriously frowned upon by the Church, as their existence could not be proved before the law should either party ever deny it. Such unions, nevertheless, were extremely common, especially amongst young men and women anxious to pursue their own destinies and marry partners of their own choosing.

At the Council of Trent, however, the *Decree Tametsi* declared a marriage to be null and void unless it had been presided over by a parish priest in the presence of at least two witnesses. This decree was contentious, to say the least. Many prominent theologians doubted whether the Church had the right to alter conditions for validity that had been fixed by Christ himself, and no fewer than sixty bishops defied the Pope and voted against it. Just seventy-five years later, there remained a large body of opinion that still believed such marriages to be valid in the sight of God.

But whatever the nature or validity of the oath that passed between them, the upshot of it all was that Ana believed herself to be married, and for the time being that was good enough for William, who still hoped for the day when they might legitimise their union, thereby restoring themselves to favour, and Ana to her inheritance or dowry. If things worked out, William promised, he would send for her and they would be legally married. It would take some time, however, to set himself up (spying was not a full time occupation, hence the large monetary advances), but when next they met he hoped to be a Marquis.

The last fourteen years had been an endless rosary of goodbyes. Each had marked the death of one life and the birth of another: but this time William was leaving in the expectation of reunion; as an immigrant looking to the future rather than an exile looking to the past. It was with a lighter than usual heart then, that he suffered the separation and made his way south to Escalona—home of the Marquis of Villena.

He could not resist the temptation, however, to bring something of his history with him and, along with his clothes, he packed an old wooden cigar box containing his birth certificate, character references, a printed poster containing the poem he had written in honour of Cardinal Borja (proof he had once been a protégé of the Count-Duke) and every letter he had ever received from the King, the Count and Countess of Olivares and various royal secretaries. Whether they were intended to serve as the tools of self-aggrandisement, or as some form of insurance in the event of discovery, is difficult to tell; but it was most likely the former. An outsider for as long as he could remember, and bound for yet another land where he would be without roots, it was perhaps only to be expected that he would cloak his vulnerability with pride, and exalt in his imagination what little status he could salvage.

Located on the banks of the Río Alberche, halfway between Ávila and Toledo, Escalona was a sleepy hamlet that had not witnessed a commotion of this magnitude since the departure of the Moors. The majority of travellers had worked all their lives for their appointments and had every reason to celebrate. But a long sea voyage lay ahead of them and each was wary of making an unfavourable impression on the others. Despite the feasts and celebrations, a cautious reserve was the order of the day. Nobody, least of all William, wanted to find himself on the outside of a clique.

On 10 March 1640, the great caravan set off for Cádiz, Villena himself leading a procession of eight coaches, two litters and a train of two hundred mules (half of which carried his larder). Travelling initially by way of Fuensalida to the city of Toledo, they continued south through the windmill flecked plains of La Mancha and the towns of Moya, Consuegra, Villahorta, La Membrilla, and El Torre de Juan Abad. At every stop along the way, Villena refused the use of sheltering canopies, offered his seat to members of the clergy, and declared his preference for the Franciscans by lodging, where possible, in their monasteries. He would persist with these seductive displays of generosity and piety (he heard at least two Masses every day) all the way to Mexico City. Those of his entourage who did not lodge with him were found alternative accommodation in monasteries, inns and the houses of prominent local families.

From El Torre de Juan Abad they more or less followed the course of the Guadalquivir through the heart of Moorish Andalucia to Córdoba, where the bishop and local nobility rode out to meet them and accompany them back to the *Mezquita*—an eight-century mosque that now functioned as the city's cathedral. One of the most magnificent Islamic buildings in Andalucia, the *Mezquita* had retained much of its original structure—including a forest of brightly coloured pillars and arches that suggested an oasis of date palms. It was unlike any church or cathedral that William had ever seen before.

From Córdoba they travelled by way of Ecija and Fuentes to the tiny fortified town of Carmona, at which point William made a brief detour to the city known far and wide as the '*puerto y puerta de Indias . . .* port and gateway of the Indies'. It was probably only now that any real sense of the scale of the adventure that lay before him began to hit home. Seville was not just any old port: it was where the treasure fleets unloaded and the *only* Spanish port allowed to trade with the Indies. The rows of magnificent buildings that gazed out upon the busy wharves of the Guadalquivir had for decades attracted all manner of ship-builders, tradesmen, merchants and adventurers. They had seen fortunes made and lost, and the corruption of Spanish society reach its zenith.

The city's landmark towers, *La Giralda* and *El Torre del Oro*, were testimony to a Muslim past that could no more be disguised than the wealth of the city's merchants, and its taverns reverberated each night to the clamour of gravel-voiced ululations, ricocheting heels, and a peculiar activity so abhorrent to the Spanish nobility that it was all but considered the sole preserve of Jews—commerce. Nobody, be they Christian, Moor or Jew, left this decadent labyrinth of minarets and *mudéjar* arches without designs on becoming the latest gilded plebeian to purchase a title of nobility. Indeed, if sailing on to the Indies, it became something of an expectation—with even the humblest mariners indulging in the odd bit of clandestine trade or smuggling.

Why William made for Seville remains a mystery. Perhaps it was to collect some of the money he had been promised; perhaps there was not sufficient accommodation for all of Villena's entourage in Carmona; perhaps it was simply that, realising that he might never return to Spain, he wanted to see this fabled city just once. More likely, however, is that he was running an errand for Villena to the *Casa de Contracción* (House of Trade), which handled the regulation of all maritime matters from the licensing of seamen to the registration of all ships and passengers. What he most certainly did not go there for was to visit his brother, John, who was staying at the local Franciscan monastery, for when their paths eventually crossed on the streets of the city, William more or less ignored him.

William rejoined the viceregal caravan as it left Utrera for Lebrija and the port of Santa María: the mouth of the Guadalquivir and the principle port for the galleys of the King's navy—giant vessels propelled as much by the lash as by the wind, but upon whose protection they would soon be almost entirely dependent. Here, beyond the masts and yards of the local shrimpers and sardine boats, they found the *flota* of Don Roque Centeno y Ordoñez, busily completing for sea: yards square; sails stowed neatly in the gaskets; and flags, streamers and pennants bedizening the masts as they awaited their pre-departure *visitas* from the inspectors of the House of Trade.

The atmosphere in the ports that dotted the bay approached that of a public holiday. The wharves were bustling with sailors and burghers, and the air reeked with the smell of caulking and rocked to the hammering of coopers. Bakers, butchers and salters worked late into the night and every bed was taken and every stable full. Amid the crunch of cartwheels, the creak of pulleys, the squealing of pigs and the incessant bleating of lambs, goats, merchants and mountebanks, one could almost touch the optimism. Where profits were not already being made, they were being dreamed of.

In the midst of this mad mêlée, William once more ran afoul of his elder brother, and this time there was no avoiding each other. His worst fear was confirmed: John was travelling in the same fleet. It was a complication he could have done without. Such was the public perception of married passengers travelling to the Indies without their wives that, since 1549, it had been made illegal for them to do so. Enforcement may have been unusually lax of late, but prosecutions were not unknown. If William was claiming to be married, he would not have wanted it known: if not, he risked being labelled a rogue.

Hardly anything is known of what passed between William and John that day in Santa María, but from what little there is, the meeting appears to have been strained. William said nothing about his clandestine mission for Olivares and when questioned by John about his reasons for travelling, he reply was somewhat enigmatic. He was, he said, sailing to the Indies to collect some *libranzas* (orders directing the payment of money) from 'those who wished to remember the relatives of Doña Ana'. They saw nothing of each other after that, at least until they arrived in Veracruz—William returning to the entourage of the new Viceroy, whom he accompanied on his round of visits to such local nobility as the Duke of Medina Sidonia and the Duke of Maqueda.

It was also in Santa María that the saga of William's fabulously embroidered shirt finally came to an end. So friendly did he become with Don Martín, the Chief Constable of the Royal Palace (with whom he was probably lodging), that not only did he advance him an undisclosed sum of money, but entrusted him with the care of his famous shirt (most recently admired by the Duke of Medina Sidonia). William never saw it again. The last tangible memento of his halcyon days was gone. He had nothing left but stories and a few old letters.

On Easter Sunday, attended by scenes of tearful goodbyes and heartfelt wishes of good luck, the fleet finally made preparations to leave. To a fanfare of trumpets, the Viceroy, his family, and his own personal navigator (a famous sea captain by the name of Juan Romero), were rowed to the *capitana*—a giant Biscayan *nao* that was to serve as flagship of the fleet. Accompanied by the Duke of Maqueda and various other gentlemen of the nobility, they were welcomed aboard with a salute of whistles and a salvo of artillery.

At three o'clock the following afternoon, the wind rose up from the south in what Villena's chaplain described in his diary as 'a very great hurricane'. It came as a particular shock to those embarking on their first sea voyage to suffer their first bout of seasickness or *almadiamiento* (literally, 'fainting spell') before they had even left Spanish waters. But with the wind howling like an agonised soprano, scrolls of spumy white caps filling the bay, and even experienced sailors recommending their souls to Saints Christopher and Barbara, only a complete idiot would venture topside without good reason, let alone attempt to reach the shore.

There was nothing to be done but sit tight, keep one hand constantly free to steady oneself against the gusts that were violently jerking the ship against her cable, and pray that a falling mast would not capsize them. The storm raged for ten days, and could hardly have failed to put

Roque Centeño in mind of the disaster of 1606, when his entire fleet was wrecked on a sandbar at nearby Sanlucár. Three days of repairs and restocking followed the calm and allowed those who had been continuously working the bilge pumps to recover from the physical and psychological exhaustion of their labours.

On the morning of 21 April, the order was finally given to weigh anchor and 'ease the ropes of the foresail in the name of the Holy Trinity'. As it would for the remainder of the voyage, the *capitana* led the way. Slowly doubling the mouth of the estuary in a light north-easterly breeze, they watched the star-shaped walls of the Castillo de Santa Catalina, the gleaming towers and whitewashed houses of Cádiz, and the vineyards above the Playa de la Caleta disappear behind them to larboard, knowing that this might be the last they would ever see of Spain.

As they reached the open sea, a scurry of pages roused William from his sea-chest. Villena wanted the entire ship's company, men and boys alike, mustered on deck. Addressing the assembly from the rail of the poop deck, the Viceroy invoked the figure of Jonah and urged all present to confess their sins and take communion. Five hours later, as if God had duly taken note of their piety, a freshening wind began to comb the rigging and the wooden hull began to creak to the movement of the larger waves under her bows.

At this point the thirty-odd ships that made up the heart of the fleet were joined to windward by the heavily armed galleons of the *Armada de la Guardia:* a formation they would maintain all the way to Veracruz. The *capitana* always led the way, even at night—when a giant lantern would be hung from her poop. A pilot or captain who dared to lose sight of her risked losing his cargo, a crippling fine, and a ban from sailing to the Indies for up to two years. In severe cases, where an unauthorised change of course was deliberate, a captain might even face the death penalty.

Herded like milch cows along the west coast of Africa, the fleet clawed its way slowly towards those latitudes where it expected to pick up the trade winds for the Indies. After the Easter storms, the rhythm of the ship now seemed almost musical in its constancy—pitch, and roll, and heave, and roll—and for those accustomed to the sea it was a song to be savoured. But as they entered the hotter latitudes the inside of the ship became like an oven, and the heat hot enough to melt the tar that sealed the seams.

It was just about then, when the illusion that they could complete such a voyage without major incident was beginning to take hold, that a caravel bound for Cartagena took a blow one night from a large wave and began to ship water. Dismasted and in immediate danger of sinking, she came alongside the *Covalonga*, which broke its bowsprit, beakhead and ram in attempting to rescue her crew and passengers. By daybreak the entire ship's company had gathered on the deck of the *capitana* to watch the continuing attempts to save her (Villena having ordered the entire fleet to wait).

A small skiff of divers, carpenters and caulkers was despatched from the *capitana* to the stricken vessel and before the day was out the caravel was once again seaworthy and taking up her allotted place in the fleet. William had seen such scenes many times before and for him they were just part and parcel of life at sea: but for many others, the drama, like their unquenchable thirst, was an untimely reminder of their vulnerability.

Before they knew it a week had passed and, at 10 p.m. on 27 April, they could just about discern the silhouette of a group of islands known to Plato as 'Atlantis' and to Homer and Saint Brendan as the 'Islands of the Blest'. To modern geographers they were known simply as 'the Canaries' and they would be the last land they would see before reaching the Indies. Early next morning they caught clear sight of the Island of Gran Canaria and a little while later passed the island that had marked the prime meridian for Spanish navigators since the time of Ptolemy.

As the steep cliffs and lush green valleys of Hierro sloped away to the west, they revealed a harsh and arid landscape of blood-red boulder fields and small volcanoes; a subtle reminder, to those who would hitch their fate to the trades, that the Atlantic, too, was a desert of sorts; and demanding of the utmost respect.

SHIPBOARD CONDITIONS WERE damp and tightly confined. If one man caught a cold, the entire ship's company had it in days. Fresh water spoiled easily and raw sewage was often dumped directly into the bilge. Wet clothes, sunburn, dysentery and seasickness proved a constant scourge, and they lived in the continuous fear of calenture, flux and fever.

The commander of the fleet, Don Roque Centeno y Ordóñez; the ship's captain, Don Tomás Manetto; and of course the Viceroy and his family, were each provided with private cabins on the quarter and poop decks of the sterncastle. They also enjoyed the Viceroy's immense private stock of food: a stock that included 12 calves, 200 rams, 2000 hens and six trunks of sweets and viands. Various beasts would be slaughtered every other day and transferred from the victualling ships, that is, if the rats didn't get them first. And where there were rats, of course, there was the risk of plague (though the link would not be discovered until 1894).

Villena's larder was excessive, but he could well afford the expense. As he had already shown by his decision to bring along his own private navigator, he was extremely nervous of the journey. In good conditions the voyage could take six weeks, in bad it could take at least twice that. Such were the risks of tropical storms, attacks by pirates or Dutch galleons, and shipboard fires, brawls and disease, that there could be no guarantees that they would arrive safely at all. Villena, therefore, was determined to ensure that if he had to die upon the *Carrera de Indias*, it would not be from starvation.

William's civilian status on this voyage warranted nothing more in the way of privilege than the sharing of a claustrophobic, malodorous and lice-ridden recess of what, on an armed galleon, would have been called the gun-deck. He shared this tiny lodging or *rancho*, with a *camarada* of

Villena's servants and the Viceroy's personal chef—a man who struggled daily to satisfy the demanding palate of a grandee of Spain.

And yet if a man had to share his living space with anyone, then the Viceroy's chef would probably be his first choice of companion. It meant an occasional share in the sumptuous provender of the Viceroy and a welcome break from the cheap wine, weevil-infested hardtack and endless stews of legumes and salted meat that was daily slopped up for the crew. And unlike the majority of the crew, who simply slept where they fell, he had at least been allocated a space.

Given his privileged past, it would also have been surprising had William not by now acquired a copper urinal, the possession of which would have marked him out as different from the majority of his fellow travellers and excused him from the necessity to line up, pants in hand, and relieve himself in front of the rest of the queue that formed each morning in front a wooden grating that jutted out over the sea at the prow (officers and rich passengers having sole access to the more comfortable latrines of the poop deck). He may even have brought along his own fishing line to pass the time and supplement his rations—there was hardly a mariner alive who did not—but other than that, there was little to distinguish him from his peers. On a voyage of this duration, where a man measured his free space in centimetres, every tiny advantage represented a potential source of resentment.

The greatest challenges, of course, lay in keeping busy. Some brought prayer manuals to help pass the slow procession of days, others books of chivalric and romantic adventure. Occasionally a literate passenger would read to his illiterate colleagues, or a guitar would make an appearance for a sing-a-long, but in general there were more hours of daylight than activities to fill them and the Devil frequently found work for idle tongues.

Everyone had their own way of coping with the boredom, but none surpassed the enthusiasm with which Villena's chaplain and confessor, Father Cristóbal Gutiérrez de Medina, attended to his diary. Every day, following the taking of the noonday altitudes to establish the ship's latitude, the 42-year-old sycophant drove master and pilot to distraction with queries on position, course and daily progress. Such was the pitch of his zeal that his obsequious scribblings came to more closely resemble a log-book than a journal, but then he was nurturing the dream of publishing a book.

Day after day, night after night, the winds continued to hold fair and they sailed into one blood-red sunset after another. By the end of their second week the landsmen amongst them had finally grown accustomed to the pitching and rolling of the ship. They no longer heaved their rations over the lee nor scanned the immense cerulean womb that enveloped them with a respectful terror. Their noses, too, had become numb to the stench that wafted from the foetid lower decks (except when the bilge pumps were employed), and their ears deaf to the rush of water along the sides, the interminable creaking of the rigging, and the chorus of psalms and prayers which announced the turning of the sandglass and which had so frequently disturbed their sleep during the first nights of the voyage.

The ladies, who up to now had been reluctant to leave the comfort of their cabins—lest the sun dry their skin or salt stiffen their hair—now began to lift their noses from their breviaries and take a turn on deck. During the *guardia de cuartillo,* when the heat of the day had passed, they would seek relief from the boredom in polite conversation and the sighting of saddleback dolphins playing on the bow wave or the occasional school of trigger fish or dorados. Great delight was taken too, in the shoals of flying fish that leapt from the water having mistaken the shadow of the hull for a giant predator. During the hours of darkness it was not unusual to hear these wonders of nature crashing into the side of the ship or even to see one beach itself upon the deck.

Questions about the workings of the ship (still amongst the most complex machines of the age) now gave way to questions about the Indies and, inevitably, about each other. To anyone who asked after his background or what his role was to be in New Spain, William was almost always evasive. Once, however, when pressed on the matter by an Irish Carmelite to whom he did not wish to appear rude, he claimed that he was to be made 'Fiscal of the Inspectorate of Apothecaries'.

As the days wore into weeks and the ship settled into its Atlantic routine, the first signs of boredom began to manifest themselves. Clothes were washed and mended, firearms were cleaned, swords and daggers were whetted, and games of cards, dice and backgammon were played.

But tempers still frayed easily, even amongst the old salts: solitude being an unobtainable luxury aboard a vessel cradling four hundred souls.

Having successfully made the crossing on two previous occasions, Don Roque Centeno was acutely aware of the risks that ennui and inattention posed to a ship, and from time to time he would request that a feast be prepared. The first was held on 3 May, the day of the Holy Cross, and it began, to the accompaniment of an orchestra of whistles, flageolets, bassoons and cornets, with Mass beneath the mainmast. To add some much needed lustre to the occasion, Villena, whose cabin was said to have more resembled a monastery than a palace, loaned all manner of carpets and hangings for the decoration of the deck, and fabulous 'jewels and riches' for the adornment of the altar.

Later that day, the merciless monotony of the voyage was further assuaged by the spontaneous gaiety of poetry competitions, the staging of mock bullfights and the dancing of saraos—the memory of which would still be a balm for frustration and homesickness many days later. The festivities would be repeated with equal success on the Feast of Corpus Christi and other apposite opportunities throughout the voyage.

The occasional human drama also generated much animated discussion: none more so, perhaps, than miracles being effected in the poop cabin of the *San Esteban*. On the morning of 2 May, just five days out from the Canaries, Doña Esperanza María, wife of Villena's butler, Don Francisco Pérez, gave birth to a baby girl. A difficult labour left her unable to breastfeed, and for the next eight days the child survived on a twice-daily dose of lemon conserve, until she developed a high fever and stopped feeding altogether. After three days of taking nothing at all, the ship's surgeon abandoned her to her fate.

Don Francisco, however, refused to give up on his daughter, and when he discovered that one of the Viceroy's game dogs had recently given birth to a litter of pups, he had the bitch brought to the baby to see if she would permit the child to suckle. Amazingly she did, and the child was thriving on her milk. The bitch's acquiescence was hailed as a miracle throughout the fleet; evoking the inevitable comparisons with the she-wolf who had given suck to Romulus and Remus. The voyage, it seemed, had been truly blessed.

At about the same time the merchant ship, *La Serena*, began to take on water. In immediate danger of sinking, she launched a small two-masted lifeboat and sent it to the *capitana* with eighteen Franciscan friars and some of the Viceroy's servants to plead for help. They were granted temporary refuge aboard the *capitana*, which lay alongside while carpenters and caulkers carried out repairs, and for a couple of days the emergency engaged everyone in a fresh novelty.

Four and a half weeks after they left Cádiz, a ribbon of seaweed on the bow-wave sent a rush of sailors aloft. Within hours, they had sighted the verdant peaks and gleaming white sands of the Leeward Islands. With sails stiff with salt and bleached by the sun, they by-passed most of the islands until, at 5 p.m. on 21 May, they sailed into the Great Bay of San Martín—a tiny island north-west of Antigua that the Spanish had more or less ignored until the Dutch began extracting salt from the Islands ponds. Just eight years had passed since the Spanish ran the Dutch off the island and a garrison fort had been erected on the eastern rim of the bay to discourage them from returning. For the first time in weeks they were able to enjoy fresh fruit.

They left their anchorage at San Martín at 6 a.m. on the morning of the 29th and moved quickly on to Puerto Rico, a considerably larger and more populous island roughly the size of Corsica. At 9 a.m. on 1 June they approached the bay of San Juan—one of the biggest natural harbours in the Caribbean. As she glided slowly to her anchorage, the *capitana* received the customary salutes from the fortress of San Felipe del Morro, whose Batería de Santa Barbara covered the bay from a rocky bluff over-looking the entrance. Beyond the bowsprit to the west, they could see the verdant hills and rainforests that gave the island its nickname of *La Isla Verde,* and to the south the walled town that for more than a century now had been Spain's most important military outpost in the Indies.

The following day there was a rush of passengers for the shore (crew were generally forbidden from doing so for fear of desertions). Friends and families that had not seen each other for weeks jumped for joy, embraced each other on the wharves and traded stories of the events that had occurred on their individual ships. At last they could wash the ingrained salt from their persons with fresh water, gorge themselves on fresh food, and replenish their supplies of tobacco. A wet nurse was even found for the miracle baby of the *San Esteban.*

Having settled into their rooms in the inns, monasteries and palaces of San Juan, those who could afford to began to purge themselves of their cabin fever with a frenzy of sightseeing and musical feasts. On one particularly memorable morning, Villena and his entourage wandered into a village in which a native woman was giving birth. Scarcely had the cord been cut than they descended upon the poor woman to dote upon the child. Bishop Palafox offered to baptise the infant there and then and Villena, entering into the spirit of the moment, agreed to stand as god-father.

After a couple of days recuperation, the fleet set sail on the final leg of their voyage—a three-week sail westward along the northern coast of Hispaniola, through the Windward Passage and the Yucatán Channel, to the Bay of Campeche. They left San Juan in good heart and high spirits, but by the time they had passed Cuba's Cape San Antonio, on 17 June, Villena was notified of an outbreak of sickness that was spreading rapidly throughout the fleet and causing much alarm.

In his diary the Viceroy's chaplain attributed the sickness to the affects of the heat and strange food, but it was more likely due to a fever picked up in San Juan, or the ravages of body lice. On the majority of vessels sailing to the Indies such infestation would normally manifest itself in bouts of intense itching and excoriated skin rashes, but the lice could also spread disease. Whatever the cause, the captain of the *almiranta*, upon which Palafox was a passenger, had already counted thirty-six ill and two dead.

The following day, they doubled the tip of the Yucatán peninsula and the translucent turquoise of the Caribbean finally gave way to the darker waters of the Gulf. As they rode to their anchorage off the shark-infested cays and *islotes* of Cape Catoche, a sheltered anchorage on the northernmost tip of the Yucatán peninsula, most remained oblivious to the fact that just 123 years earlier this same featureless landscape of semitropical palm groves and hardwood forests had provided the very first sight of Mexico to the Conquistadors. Of more pressing concern was the lack of fresh water and the ever-increasing numbers that were falling prey to disease.

Anxious to control the outbreak, Villena detailed his personal physician to attend to the afflicted and ordered his private supply of victuals and fresh water put at their disposal. His actions were seen as generous at the time, but they were also astute. Aboard the *almiranta* was Bishop Palafox, the new Visitor General—a man with whom Villena would have to work very closely in the months ahead: assuming, that is, the good bishop survived to see his new diocese. There was also the fact that they were now no more than three days from Vera Cruz and Villena had little use for the vast private stock of food that remained. His gesture, in truth, cost him very little.

An uncertain impatience now filled the air. The outbreak had not only infected the travellers with an anxiety for dry land, but had focused their attention on the calendar. It was now well into the month of June—the start of the hurricane season—and while there could be no guarantees, if it pleased God to permit it and the winds continued benign, there was every chance they would arrive in time for the Saint John's day festivities.

(17)

$\mathcal{A}$T EIGHT IN the morning of 24 June, the feast of John the Baptist, a shout of '*Tierra, Tierra*' started the customary rush into the rigging. For those below, many of whom were shedding tears of relief and thanking God for their survival, another hour would pass before the same white flash could be discerned with any degree of clarity. It was the summit of *Orizaba* and snow was the last thing the newcomers had expected to see in such sweltering heat.

'Oh Lord', Villena's chaplain noted in his diary, 'if only mankind could crave heaven as these people crave the sight of land.'

As the exuberant vegetation of the Veracruz coast came more plainly into view, the ship became a hive of frenzied activity. Doublets were brushed, cuirasses burnished, and gowns and jewels unpacked for wearing. Sea chests were locked for transport and the ships' barbers were run off their feet. By three in the afternoon the order was finally given to shorten sail and, in what seemed no time at all, they were listening for the last time to the rumble of the anchor cable racing through the hawsehole. With topsails furled and the *capitana* swinging gently to her anchor, the worst of the journey was now behind them. It was time to celebrate their deliverance and sing Te Deums to the Almighty.

To a blast of trumpets and a volley of ordnance, Villena and his colour party were ferried by barge to San Juan de Ulúa—a small island off the mainland where a native shrine to *Tezatlipoca* had been usurped by a Franciscan chapel and a Spanish fortress (whose dungeons would replenish the natural wastage of the galleys). William, in contrast, was rowed in the stern sheets of a shore boat to the port of Veracruz—a pestilential shantytown called home by only the hardiest of customs men, innkeepers and traders. A feast of venery was promised by the knots of *Mulatta* whores that had gathered along the shore, sweat beads glistening like pearls on their smooth chocolate skin. The sun was glaring bright. It was very hot.

Leaving the shore to the Creole foremen with their shimmering West-African slaves, and the Indian fishermen to their crates of red snapper and enormous looking shrimp, William headed uptown past the *Mestizo* merchants and their exotic and unfamiliar produce—vanilla, acuyo, chiles, tomatoes, avocados, papaya, mamey and zapote. Despite the town's importance there were few stone buildings, most being constructed of wooden planks. Taking a room at a local inn while he waited for the departure of the caravan (the road to the capital being so infested with bandits that it was considered dangerous to travel alone), he arranged for his laundry to be done and set about hiring some mules and horses.

For the first time since he jumped ship at Bordeaux, he was completely in charge of his own life, and under different circumstances he might have felt excited. But Veracruz was a nightmare. Every evening after dusk, endless squadrons of mosquitoes would descend upon the town to gorge themselves on its inhabitants, making it impossible, initially, to sleep in their presence. No matter how many a man killed each evening, there would always be more the following night. Hiding under the bed sheets made the heat, which seemed more intense after dark, even more unbearable and like every other virgin traveller to the Indies he quickly learnt the folly of scratching the bites.

Early the following day, the local nobility and principal Indians came calling on the fort to kiss Villena's hand and present him with bouquets of flowers. Villena, in his turn, ordered his steward to pay the cost of the welcoming celebrations and everything his family might consume during their stay. He also ordered a festival of illuminations (the public lighting of streets with lanterns and torches) and a three-day festival of bullfights. It was to the start of what would prove to be a four-month binge of feasting and celebrating.

The town being small and the festival bringing so many onto the streets, it was perhaps inevitable that John and William would cross paths again. But once again William merely acknowledged his brother's presence with a brief salutation and continued quickly about his business. They would continue to ignore each other all the way to the capital and, according to John, they 'never again enjoyed any fraternal emotion in either the humours or manner of living'.

On the morning of 2 July, a salvo was fired from the fort cannons that sent hundreds of yellow-eyed starlings whistling from the ramparts. To the accompaniment of two trumpeters, and in a brightly painted barge positively gushing with awnings of diaphanous crimson, the viceregal party departed for the mainland. Awaiting them on the beach stood two companies of cavalry, another two of infantry, and the better part of the local nobility. They presented Villena with a thoroughbred mare, upon which to make his ceremonial entrance into the town.

The solemnities of the official welcome completed, William attached himself to the great mule-train as it took its leave of the oppressive heat and prolific greenery of the *tierra caliente* and set out on the long sluggish haul into the highlands. They headed westward at first, through the savannah and deciduous forests of the coast, and then upwards, and in a more northerly direction, through the towns of Rinconada, Venta del Río and Lencero, towards the more temperate semi-tropical climes of Xalapa.

A town of steep narrow streets and prodigal vegetation, Xalapa lay on the southern slopes of the *Cerro Macuitépetl* and more or less marked the spot where the mountains of the Sierra Madre Oriental began their descent to the Gulf of Mexico. Approaching the town under an opalescent sky, they found themselves enveloped in the warm and welcoming embrace of the *chipi-chipi*—a misty afternoon rain that drew a grey veil over the gleaming white peak of a rapidly retreating *Orizaba* (in the clear light of morning it had seemed so much closer). Unlike Veracruz, the nights were cool.

Leaving Xalapa eight days later, they rose by energy-sapping oxblood tracks to a panorama of rolling hills of oaks and conifers, and thereafter past a succession of misty green gorges and spectacular waterfalls. Here, at last, daytime temperatures became more merciful and their aching limbs were refreshed by the sweet perfume of dew-soaked pines, the sour tang of freshly rutted earth, and the lyrical whispers of running water that echoed unseen from the penumbra. Wirh breeches caked with mud and doublets stained by rain and sweat, they descended next on the town of Xico.

From Xico they headed for Perote, the town which more or less marked their arrival upon the vast volcanic highlands that, prior to the arrival of the Spanish, had housed the great cities of the Aztec Empire. The indigenous inhabitants—short and squat as their adobe dwellings, with soft round faces and an insatiable appetite for flowers, chocolate and maguey juice—gave Villena a welcome worthy of an emperor. Outside his bedroom, he counted four fountains of milk, honey, scented water and fine wine, each flowing into great flower-covered vats. The rest of the mule train camped in the open or lodged at local inns and convents.

Despite the temptation to stay longer, the caravan was soon descending through the mists, skirting the pine-covered slopes of *Matlalcueyetl* and making toilsome progress towards a plateau of rocky escarpments and Lion's Claw grasslands not unlike the heathery hills of William's Irish childhood. Even the rain, which occasionally fell in torrents, seemed eerily comfortable and familiar. The illusion, however, was soon broken. On the outskirts of Tlaxcala, beating rhythmically on their *teponaxtlis* and dancing their hypnotic *mitotes* and *tocotines,* hundreds of natives came rushing out to meet them in a wondrous concert of coloured cotton smocks and iridescent feathered head-dresses. The hospitality equalled that of Perote.

Days later they descended onto a broad fertile plain attended by the Romeo and Juliet of the Aztec Pantheon. Dominating the horizon to the northwest, the snowy volcanic cone of *Popocatépetl* stood watch over the shrouded ridge of a somnolent and couchant *Iztaccíhuatl*—the daughter of an Aztec emperor who expired of grief while her warrior prince, Popo, was away at war. On his return, Popo had built two mountains, laid his sleeping princess on one and stood holding her funeral torch on the other. It was from the pass that separated these giants that Cortés had first laid eyes on the great Aztec capital of *Tenochtitlán.* For the moment they provided a spectacular snowy backdrop to the caravan's next stop, the second most important city in New Spain—Puebla de Los Angeles.

This time it was the turn of the local clergy to come out in their hundreds and, on seeing them approach, Villena dismounted and strolled into town on foot—a humble gesture, much appreciated by his clerical public. At the Convent of the Sisters of the Trinity, he found his passage blocked by a triumphal arch that spanned the width of the street. On a

115

stage to the right, in a painted wooden cloud, a young boy dressed as an angel recited verses on behalf of the 'City of Angels'. Following the presentation of keys and the opening of the doors to the city, so many citizens poured onto the streets that Villena's chaplain thought their displays of public dancing akin to 'an army on the march'.

At this juncture, Palafox announced his intention to withdraw. He had decided to spend the first months of his tenure getting acquainted with his new flock and the diocese he would come to refer to as his 'Rachel'. 'The constant rule,' he would often say, 'is that a bishop should live and die in his first diocese just as a husband must with his lawful wife'. There was no persuading him otherwise. The new bishop was not a man of opinions, but of convictions; the type of unbending certainty that builds cathedrals; the kind of adamantine rectitude that would lead him, in the not too distant future, to simultaneously hold the four most important posts in New Spain.

Unburdened of the inhibitions of travelling with a man who, despite the circumstances of his birth (or perhaps because of them), had extremely high moral standards, the travellers suddenly felt free to return the smiles and the greetings of the scantily clad *Mulattas*. With his cavalier good looks and his cupid's bow moustachios, Villena attracted most of their attention. 'With such a fine face,' they teased, 'you will certainly accomplish fine things'.

Skirting around the edges of the pine-tufted highland volcanoes, the caravan crawled onwards through Cholula, Huejotzingo, Otumbo and a procession of lesser hovels and hamlets that had sprouted along the trail, until finally, bone weary and saddle sore, they reached the outskirts of the capital and the beautiful weeping *ahuehuete* woods of *Chapultepec*. Here, at a hilltop castle built upon the ruins of the royal retreat of the Aztec emperors, Villena and his entourage took temporary lodgings while preparations were made for his 'joyous entry' into the city below.

From the castle ramparts William could survey the woods, lakes, causeways and canals, the 900 arches of the great aqueduct that brought drinking water to the city from the mountains 27km away, and the imperious myriad of bell-towers and cupolas which endowed the city with a splendour the equal of any European capital of the day. Leaving the new Viceroy to settle into his quarters, and taking his leave of his travelling companions, William continued into the city that was to become his new home.

Over the days that followed he saw the small flat-bottomed canoes that carried people and provisions along the myriad of narrow canals that criss-crossed the city; he saw the fine European buildings and the ubiquitous churches and monasteries; and he saw the market squares full of mules and Indian traders whose hands, unlike those of the Spaniards, were always full. What he did not see was any evidence of Cadereyta's threatened 'popular commotion'.

At 3 p.m. on 28 August, the feast of that other pious *bon vivant*, Saint Augustine of Hippo, Villena finally emerged from the castle and began his official entry into the city. All along the route of ceremonial arches that led him towards the Plaza Mayor, the welcome he received was sincerely joyous. The news of his decision to pay for everything he had consumed had travelled before him, as had his decision at *Chapultepec* to use up the remainder of his provisions rather than burden the citizenry of the capital with unnecessary expense. For the time being he had won the hearts of the populace and it was beginning to look as if William had been sent on a fool's errand.

(18)

*H*AVING COLLECTED A draft for 7,000 pesos from one of Olivares' agents, William set about his mission of insinuating himself into the heart of colonial society. Three men had been named by Cadereyta as the likely instigators of any rebellion: Andrés Gómez de Mora, Antonio Urrutia de Vergara and Fernando Carrillo. His first call was to Carrillo—Chief Notary of the *Cabildo* (City Council).

An authoritative figure with shrewd eyes and a nose for a killing, Carrillo lived with his wife and family in his official residence—an expensive apartment in the *Casa de Cabildo* (City Hall). Though he had recently sided with the Creole conspiracy to oust Cadereyta, naked self-interest had also led him in the past to vehemently oppose Creole demands for the abolition of forced Indian labour, face down their opposition to the 'Union of Arms', and use his friendship with Cerralvo to line his own pockets at the expense of essential drainage schemes that might have saved hundreds, if not thousands, of those who had died in the floods of 1629. Archbishop Manso once described him as the 'curse of this republic'. His wife, in contrast, was considered something of a saint.

William approached Carrillo with a view to getting his draft cashed and, unable to contemplate such an enormous sum slipping through his fingers, Carrillo persuaded the Irishman to form a company in partnership with his wife: a company that would lease farmland around Tacuba, where Carrillo already had several haciendas, to grow wheat. The land was rich and had the potential to yield enormous profit. His wife would match William's investment peso for peso.

For William this was a tantalising prospect, and temptation overwhelmed him. He had inherited nothing of his father's entrepreneurial instincts, nor had he been overly blessed with the gift of prudence. Having worked for the Junta responsible for the awards of titles and pensions he would have known exactly how little Crópani was worth—it may even have been him who suggested it as a possible reward in the first place. Cursed by the shadow of unfulfilled promise, he invested the entire 7,000 pesos.

For the same amount of money he could have purchased any number of fee-paying public offices, perhaps even the post of Fiscal of the Inspectorate of Apothecaries that he had claimed during the voyage from Cádiz was his for the asking. But such investments took many years to turn a profit and, like so many ambitious new arrivals in the Indies, he wanted a quick return (Viceroys were replaced every three to five years and posts were generally auctioned afresh by the new arrivals). He may have known little about agriculture, but it didn't take a genius to work out the implications of two harvests per year. He saw a city that was built upon land reclaimed from the waters of Lake Texcoco. He saw nearby mountains that were permanently snow-capped and a bower of plenitude that had been peaceably farmed for generations. What he did not see, or chose to ignore, were the risks.

By 1640 the ranching practices of the haciendas had all but destroyed the natural habitat of the Valley of Mexico. Indeed a meagre forty years after the first Spaniards set foot in New Spain, the *Conquistador* Bernal Diaz del Castillo found himself shocked at the level of deforestation:

> I never tired of looking at the diversity of the trees, and noting the scent of each, and the paths full of roses and flowers, and the many fruit groves. All these wonders I then beheld, today are overthrown and lost; nothing is left standing.

But not only were trees being cut down, Aztec irrigation channels were being diverted to power Spanish mills; and Aztec dykes had been allowed to fall into such a state of disrepair that floods had by now become a common occurrence in the valley. The last one, in 1629, had submerged the city for almost five years and occasioned the loss of more than 30,000 lives.

Nor were floods the only problem. Cattle and sheep were grazing the land bare, and in many places water was running off it before it could be properly absorbed. There had been a minor drought the previous year, but nothing really serious had occurred since 1624. The decade prior to that, however, had seen no less than five. It was only a matter of time before the next one struck.

There was now just one loose end to be attended to. John was still living at the Monastery of Saint Francis and, though he knew nothing of William's mission in New Spain, he knew enough of his personal circumstances to embarrass him. At the first opportunity—the funeral Mass of a priest who was to be buried at the cathedral—William went to speak with him.

This time their meeting was more cordial. William was deftly conciliatory and John careful to avoid the subject of Ana. He had been posted, he told William, to Zacatecas—a frontier town in the far north and one of the main centres of silver production. But William, somehow, knew this already, and he asked his brother to deliver some letters for him to Don Sancho Guevera Dávila, the local *Corregidor* (municipal administrator). Dávila and his wife were currently involved in an unholy row with the Bishop of Guadalajara, who had excommunicated them both following an incident in which they had publicly branded him a 'vile clerical blackguard'. The dispute had scandalised the entire colony, and William's attempts to contact Dávila must have signalled to his brother that he was up to his neck in activities of a political rather than a commercial nature.

But that was far from the end of the matter. William had yet another favour to ask. From this point onwards he wanted John to behave as if they were strangers. Not even in private letters were they to refer to each other as brothers!

John was somewhat discomfited by the request; perhaps even a little wounded. But whatever story he was spun he agreed to comply and left for Zacatecas soon afterwards. They never met again.

Over the course of the months that followed, William began to cultivate the friendship of young Creole militia officers (this being where the greatest threat to the colony was thought to lie). It was not a difficult task. Poorly trained and lacking first-hand knowledge of so many facets of military life, his military education, battlefield experience and title of *maese de campo* acted like a magnet. He became particularly close to two: a young Mexican captain by the name of Don Manuel de Pedrosa y Tapia, and a 26-year-old Spanish ensign by the name of Don Francisco Solís y Corral, a native of Salamanca.

He also contrived an introduction to the infamous Don Antonio Urrutia de Vergara, the dissident army general whose gaol-break had precipitated the crisis that had brought him here in the first place. Having married the daughter of one of the richest men in New Spain, however, Urrutia seemed more intent on increasing his fortune than fomenting rebellion. Everything was progressing smoothly for William, except for one little thing: he had never been so idle in his life.

To relieve the boredom, he struck up a friendship with his tailor—an Italian who went by the name of Saboyano and from whom he had recently ordered a new doublet embroidered with a cross of blue-green velvet that he claimed was the insignia of the Order of Saint Patrick (an unknown order that should not be confused with the current Order of Saint Patrick, which was only established in 1783). The congeniality of their exchanges would probably have been impossible in Madrid, but social constraints were much more relaxed in New Spain and the pair shared a keen interest in astrology. Despite the fact that William had studied the subject under Francisco de Roales at the Colegio Imperial, it was actually the tailor who was the more experienced practitioner and in no time at all Saboyano had more or less assumed the role of tutor.

His renewed interest in astrology provided William with an enjoyable means of passing the time and a disciplined, if largely solitary, process into which he could channel his intellect. But even that was not enough to fill the empty hours. Alongside his sidereal observations he also began to develop an interest in the magical arts of herbalism and healing, and to actively seek out Indian sorcerers and shamans in order to learn from them. He was not the first, and would not be the last, to find in sorcery the intoxicating illusion of self-empowerment.

And learn he did—as much about the power of suggestion as the medicinal properties of plants. Working not by means of salves and unguents, but rather simple herbs and magical incantations, he quickly acquired a reputation as a *curandero*. To one client he gave some words to chant with 'a medicine that had to be taken each morning in uncorked wine'; to another, who came looking for a cure for impotency, a piece of paper containing a spell which would 'invoke in his mind a personality of darkness' that would take the form of a cat or a dog. Should this vision appear, William warned, he should take care not to become agitated or to bless himself, less the apparition 'explode some wall or cause the house to fall down'. It was also important, he advised, to have present a lighted brazier and a red hot iron, and to continue to chant the words he had written down so that the 'force of the person he had bound himself to would confess him and present him with the remedy to free himself'.

(19)

*I*T WAS AN act guaranteed to raise his predecessor's hackles, but Villena could scarcely have cared less. As part of his campaign to repair vicere-gal relations with the Creoles, he released almost all of the political pris-oners gaoled by Cadereyta and invited those who had earlier fled the city to return.

Even after he had learnt of Villena's arrival, Cadereyta had continued to appoint his friends to positions of influence. Villena, needless to say, replaced them with appointees of his own. He sold the post of High Sheriff for the enormous sum of 120,000 pesos, gave the post of Com-missioner of Pulque to his stableman (from whom he later collected 50,000 pesos in kickbacks) and rewarded his personal physician with the post of Inspector of Apothecaries. He also placed his cronies in charge of the public granary and the public water supply, and plagued Palafox with so many gifts that His Excellency felt compelled to protest to the King.

Having invested so much in the purchase of their posts, the new appointees had to make them pay quickly and the corruption of the pre-vious regime was rapidly supplanted by that of the new. Just as it had been in Castile, official corruption was endemic—even judges were known to purchase their robes and split imposed fines with the accus-ers. For all its golden promise, New Spain was not so very different from the old.

Just two months later, Palafox arrived in the capital and threw him-self into his work like a man possessed. Already in Puebla he had gained the reputation of a zealous reformer and a paragon of precision and piety. He had ordered the cathedrals scrubbed and cleansed, had encouraged the secular clergy to dress more modestly, had reformed the nunneries and cleared the prostitutes from the plazas. But Puebla was essentially an Indian and Mestizo city; the capital was a Creole one. The task that lay before him here was a different proposition entirely. Taking immediate possession of the four carriages of papers left behind by the previous Visitor General, he began his examination of the regimes of Cerralvo and Cadereyta, and initiated the trials of all officials thus far accused of corruption. The first to be tried were Andrés Gómez De Mora (whom he acquitted) and Antonio Urrutia de Vergara (whom he fined the paltry sum of 2,000 ducats). In little more than a year he despatched over a hundred such cases and in the process further enhanced his reputation as a reformer. He also began the task of informing the King on the true state of the colony and the extent to which Cadereyta's allegations of sedition had any basis in fact.

Having begun his secular campaign, Palafox now turned his reforming zeal on the Church. In the city of Puebla alone there were over 600 diocesan or 'secular' clergy, the vast majority of whom considered themselves poorly provided for. It vexed Palafox to see mendicant orders like the Franciscans becoming as rich and powerful as the Jesuits, and monasteries that served no genuine purpose staffed by priests and friars who had become lazy, corrupt and dependant upon native sweat for their existence. It was especially galling to find the greater part of his own diocese under their control.

In December 1640, he decided to do something about it. He ordered the mendicant priors—who controlled about thirty-seven Indian parishes in Puebla—to submit their curates for examination in morals and languages, in accordance with the royal *cédula* of 1624. All but one refused. On 29 December, beginning with the town of Tlaxcala, he set about seizing all parishes under mendicant control and placing them under diocesan supervision. The majority of confiscations were suffered by the Franciscans, who, by way of retaliation, entered into something of a guerrilla war against the bishop and his allies.

The day after the taking of Tlaxcala, a friar carrying a sack of flour to a local Franciscan friary was set upon and badly beaten by a mob of Indians loyal to the local curate. The following July, a dozen Franciscans armed with knives and sticks broke into a chapel in Cholula and made off with a jewel-encrusted Virgin much adored by the local Cholultecs. But this was fundamentally a diocesan issue: it did not directly affect the Creoles and was not really any of William's business. Or at least it wasn't, until the Viceroy decided to intervene. The civil unrest forced Villena's hand. Not only did he prohibit further confiscations; he publicly voiced his support for the Franciscans of Puebla. The result was a power struggle between the Viceroy and the Visitor General that posed a far greater threat to the stability of the colony than the political aspirations of the Creoles. It could only be a matter of time before William would be asked to take sides.

(20)

$\mathcal{J}$UST AS THE Spanish Empire had been built upon the ruins of the Aztec one, Mexico City had been built upon the ruins of the Aztec capital of *Tenochtitlán*. Aztec buildings had been replaced by Spanish, old rulers by new, but the spiritual, commercial and political heart of the city remained the same.

Bordered to the east by the red *tezontle* stone walls of the Viceroy's palace, to the south by the *Casa de Cabildo* (City Hall), to the west by the balconied townhouses of the aristocracy, and to the north by the imperishable grey façade of the Metropolitan Cathedral, the Plaza Mayor was no longer as spacious as during its Aztec days but it remained one of the world's largest city plazas. One hundred and twenty years earlier, this same square had housed the palace of the Aztec Emperor, Moctezuma II Xocoyotzin, and the infamous *teocalli*, upon whose racks Cortés had discovered the skulls of some 136,000 sacrificial victims.

Despite the demolition and reconstruction little had changed. Raised by the Spanish from the rubble of the demolished Aztec palaces and temples, the Metropolitan Cathedral more or less straddled the foundations of the giant pyramid that was once the political and religious epicentre of the great Aztec metropolis, and the plaza it overlooked still played host to temporal entertainments, religious and civil processions, whippings, hangings, mutilations and burnings. Just as in its Aztec days, it functioned as marketplace, theatre and school for the populace.

It was here each morning that the city stirred from its slumber. Even before cockcrow the place would be buzzing with the activity of Indian traders as they arrived from the hills around Guadalupe, driving their pigs before them and carrying the fruits of their labours to the maze of wooden stalls that constituted the city's main market. Here one could buy coal, cigars, rope, fish, fruit, nuts, vegetables, livestock and, on occasion, African slaves.

But if the political and commercial heart of Mexico City was the Plaza Mayor, the social heart of the city was the Alameda—an oasis of greenery in a city whose exceptionally broad thoroughfares offered precious little protection from the sun. Every day, at about 4 p.m., the elaborately attended élite of Creole society came here to take their afternoon *paseo;* the men resplendent in silver buttons and spurs, and the ladies in sumptuous high-necked gowns, glinting with constellations of gilded buttons, diamonds and pearls.

It was here that the women of Creole society really came into their own: powerful and influential women attended by trains of servants and slaves; sumptuously attired women with velvet beauty spots glued to their cheeks; and cherubic young debutantes who spoke in pious platitudes and surveyed their rivals with a heady mixture of envy, suspicion and disdain. They came here not just to walk, but to see and be seen: the women being especially observant, as it was here that the most important business of their lives was conducted—the arrangement of alliances.

Foremost amongst them all strode the crypto-Jewish matriarch, Blanca Enríquez. Her daughters, Beatriz and Juana, had landed the biggest catches in town—the merchant Simón Váez Sevilla (one of the richest men in all of New Spain), and his agent, Tomás Núñez de Peralta—two men with whom William would soon become intimately familiar. The Enríquez and Váez families belonged to a tightly-knit community with a clandestine Jewish past that dated back to 1492, when the King of Spain ordered all non-Catholics to convert to the true faith or resign themselves to perpetual exile. Derisively called *Marranos* (literally 'swine' or 'filth') and often the target of suspicion and abuse, they had fled to the Americas to begin a new life with a clean slate and, in many cases, new identities.

In the absence of rabbinical instruction, the *Marranos* had struggled in New Spain to maintain contact with their religious roots, and their orthodoxy had, with the passage of time, been diluted almost to the point of oblivion. They still observed the *Shabbat*, celebrated the *Pesach* and *Sukkoth*, kept to a kosher diet and fasted for *Yom Kippur* and *Purim*, but their observance of Jewish ritual had become haphazard and they had become dependent for instruction upon such scraps of information as could be harvested from the Old Testament, aged relatives, and the edicts of the Inquisition (which named, described and banned the practice of various Jewish rites).

In such a vacuum, the emergence of a certain degree of syncretism—which could vary wildly within any given family—became inevitable; as did divided loyalties. Indeed, rumours that they might be in league with the Dutch were causing such alarm in Madrid that, on 7 January 1641, a royal decree was issued authorising the interception of mail from all suspected Portuguese sympathisers and prohibiting the immigration to New Spain of any Portuguese not normally resident there (the terms 'Portuguese', 'Jew', and 'crypto-Jew' having by now become synonymous to the average Spaniard).

Believing the threat to be grossly exaggerated, Villena decided to ignore it. It was a decision he quickly lived to regret. Just three months later word arrived from Madrid that, in the wake of a Catalan revolt, the Duke of Braganza had thrown off his allegiance to Castile and declared himself King João IV of Portugal.

But if news of the Portuguese revolt had disturbed William, whose future was almost entirely dependent upon the whims and favours of the Count-Duke, it was nothing to what it did to the colony. The enemy without rapidly found its reflection in an enemy within, and Villena's apparent indifference to the 'problem' began to feed the rumour mill. Within weeks there were wild mutterings of the Viceroy's plans to send two ships to Flanders with 80,000 pesos to purchase the arms and munitions necessary to continue Braganza's revolt in New Spain.

Rumours of a Portuguese massacre of Spaniards in Brazil also began to surface, and allegations that the local Portuguese were stockpiling weapons received a more sympathetic hearing than prudence should have allowed. In the heat of the moment, Palafox wrote to the Council of the Indies to 'remind' them that, not only was Villena a relative of Braganza, but descended from a family of Castilian Jews.

Amongst the mixed races, in contrast, the news of the Catalan and Portuguese rebellions planted the noxious weed of nationalism. They saw Spain as a house divided against itself and believed they were witnessing nothing less than the collapse of the Spanish Empire. But though some Creoles began to speak openly about autonomy, years of conditioning had made them cautious; and while they dithered events inevitably overtook them.

(21)

$\mathcal{T}$HE VALLEY OF MEXICO had really only two seasons—a dry season, between November and March, and a rainy season, between April and October. A dry April (the planting season) was always a cause for concern, but a dry June heralded catastrophe. The canals slowed to a trickle, exposed the sewage on their bottoms, and began to stink. As the price of maize began to rocket, the capital's shrines disappeared under a mountain of votive offerings from an impotent population desperate for a miracle. From within the clouds of incense and candle smoke there arose a general clamour for the return of the Virgin of Los Remedios.

The Virgin of Los Remedios was to the white population of Mexico what the Virgin of Guadalupe was to the Indians, and the Mexican clergy were not given to appealing to her except during the most dire of emergencies. But this *was* an emergency: a similar drought had precipitated the collapse of the Mayan civilisation. On 13 June 1641, therefore, following a period of consultation between the ecclesiastical and secular authorities, a decision was made to bring the Virgin from her shrine on the summit of the *Tototepec* to the Metropolitan Cathedral, where candles could be lit, promises made, and all manner of bargains struck for her intercession. But despite numerous *pro pluvia* rogation ceremonies at the cathedral, the rains refused to come. Neither the Virgin, nor the rain god *Tlaloc* for that matter, saw fit to intervene and William's problems began to multiply like flies upon a carcass.

Although he never openly admitted as much, the weight of circumstantial evidence suggests that William, like so many others whose fortune was tied up in agriculture, lost everything to the drought. By summer's end he was petitioning the King for more money and working as a humble Latin tutor. Having spent the greater part of his life struggling to blend in, this was his greatest fear made manifest, and the blow to his self-esteem was enormous. Without money he would cut a ridiculous figure and his aristocratic hauteur would become something of a local joke. As for Ana and Teresa, even if he wanted to he could not send for them now. Rather they should hear nothing, than hear of this.

But just when his predicament seemed hopeless, Doña Inés offered him a lifeline. Perhaps she felt partly responsible for his loss; perhaps his patrician features and courtly airs reminded her of her family's noble past; whatever the reason, she approached him with a proposal. Her sons, Sebastián and Juan, were in need of a tutor.

Like most elite households of the time, the Carrillo apartments were home, not just to the nuclear family that ran them, but to all manner of relatives and visitors, not to mention the small army of domestic servants and slaves who waited on them. It was not unusual for such families to share the family home with their business partners, and the offer gave William the opportunity to save some face. But it was not entirely an act of charity. William had an excellent mind, a prodigious memory, and spoke Castilian like an aristocrat. As learned in the fathers and councils of the Holy Church as he was in the heavenly bodies, he had studied mathematics, philosophy, and theology with some of the greatest minds of his generation and could debate metaphysics as though he had been an intimate of Aristotle or a favoured protégé of Francisco de Suárez. Marinated for almost two decades in the classical literature of ancient Greece and Rome, he could also recite from memory large extracts from the works of Virgil, Horace, Plato, Menander, Euripides, Cicero, Ulpian, Justinian, Juvenal, Quintilian, Prudentius, Pliny and Seneca, and with only minor flaws. Eloquent, cultivated and refined; he possessed all of the gentlemanly accomplishments that a lady like Doña Inés could have wished for her sons and, as a natural raconteur and exceptional table companion, was something of a social acquisition.

Confined for the most part to her home, the life of the Creole wife was insipidly pious and unchallenging. Her rooms were filled with caged parrots and images of the Holy Child of Atocha or serpent-trampling Virgins. The only social luxuries she could afford herself were conversation, fantasy and harmless flirting. Holding court in what was commonly called the *salón de estrado*—an essentially feminine space with its own strictly observed traditions of layout, furnishing and etiquette, she emphasised her authority by sitting on a raised platform (*estrado*) covered with expensive rugs and exquisite cushions, while her male guests, seated around her on chairs or settees, engaged her in vapid persiflage through a fog of cigar smoke and a carillon of tinkling chocolate cups.

William swept into this austere and secluded world like a gust of mountain air, regaling Doña Inés with the latest advances in the arts and sciences, the scandals and novelties of the royal court, and the latest news of home (even third generation Creoles were inclined to think of Spain as home). Within months they had become so familiar that she would take him riding with her at the family hacienda in Los Remedios.

But he was still essentially an employee and the comedown offended his pride. So poor had he become of late that he was grateful to accept the odd gift of second-hand clothing from one of Doña Inés' occasional guests, Don Jacinto de Soria Naharro—a native of Puebla with whom he had struck up a close friendship. The solution, as obvious as it was time-honoured, may have been more than a touch unpalatable; but he was desperate.

For Creole women, marriage to even the poorest European constituted a form of racial purification. For similar reasons, a Catholic with a history of pure blood made a desirable match for ambitious Jewish debutantes. As an unmarried *letrado* with first-hand experience of the royal court, William would have been socially in demand, would have sat in the foremost pews in church and, with enough money in his pocket, would have had little difficulty insinuating himself into the higher echelons of colonial society. Being Irish, in this regard at least, was even better than being Spanish: the Irish having never been corrupted by Moorish or Jewish blood. With his brother by now safely ensconced in Zacatecas, William resumed his visits to the Monastery of Saint Francis; this time motivated less by the desire to renew his faith or socialise with other Irish ex-patriates than the expectation of a chance encounter with a young heiress who lived nearby. Her name was Antonia de Villarías y Turcios, and her mother, Doña Beatriz de Turcios, was the wealthy widow of both Don Alfonso Ulloa de Castro and Don Francisco de Villarías. They had occasionally met socially.

Antonia's family was no longer exceptionally esteemed nor influential. During the late sixteenth century, it is true, one of their number had held the office of Chief Notary of the *Audiencia*—the colony's parliamentary court/governing body. Another had recently served as *Corregidor* of Puebla. These days, however, they were probably better known as the owners of a sugar refinery.

Perhaps it was simply a matter of honour and expediency; perhaps he really did have feelings for Antonia; but William soon became such an established fixture at the Villarías house that he felt free to come and go as he pleased. Before the year was out, he was calling Antonia his *Antandra* (after one of Penthesilia's Amazons) and making overtures to marriage. As for Ana and Teresa, their existence was something he endeavoured to keep very much to himself.

But inconstancy exacts its own price. For all of his adult life William had taken pride in being an honourable man: a model of Castilian *pundonor* whose commitment, bravery and trustworthiness had never been questioned. Such a man could hardly renounce his fiancée, let alone his daughter, without some discernible crisis of conscience, and while it was not yet certain that he would be able to go through with a marriage that set pride at odds with honour and duty, his situation demanded that *something* be done. For Spanish gentlemen of his generation pride and dignity were the stuff of life itself, and without money, and the independence it brought, both were compromised.

$\mathcal{P}$RIOR TO DROUGHT, Villena's standing with the Creoles could scarcely have been higher. But things were very different now. His appointees had quickly proved themselves more rapacious and venal than their predecessors and contrived such a stranglehold over the commercial life of the city that its citizens were effectively held to ransom. They controlled the supply of meat; they controlled the supply of cocoa; they even controlled the supply of drinking water.

Prices began to rocket. One-*real* portion of meat would once have fed an entire family, now it barely fed one person. Reduced to drinking water from saltpetrous ponds, the poorest began to starve and little by little disease took hold of the city. Complaints were useless; few, if any, would ever reach the Viceroy's desk. Kept constantly rapt in new delights and lavish entertainments, he had been neutered by his staff. Discontent was ripe and waiting to be harvested. All that was lacking was a catalyst.

On 28 August 1641, a certain Luis de Mezquita received a letter from his brother Fernando concerning a rumour, currently circulating in Veracruz, that a ship carrying 150 Portuguese infantry had recently docked at the Canary Islands en route to New Spain. When the same, or similar, rumour reached Puebla, it sent Palafox scuttering off to the capital accusing the Viceroy of complicity with the Portuguese and complaining about the appointment of two Portuguese merchants to key posts in the administration.

Sebastián Váez de Acevedo was Provider General of the *Armada de Barlovento* and his brother a captain of an infantry battalion in the capital. Their appointments, Palafox asseverated, had prejudiced the defence of New Spain. Together the brothers controlled enough arms and munitions to bring the colony to its knees.

But Villena was having none of it, and rallied to their defence. The brothers Váez, he retorted, were loyal subjects of His Majesty. There was no need to panic. He had everything under control.

Enraged by the Viceroy's refusal to act, and exhausted by a recent illness, Palafox turned instead to the Holy Office. But the sympathies of the Inquisition lay very much with the Viceroy. Like Villena, they did not believe that the Portuguese community, many of whom they knew personally, posed any real threat. They were much more afraid of Palafox's scaremongering and the rumours he was spreading concerning the intention of Portuguese malcontents to massacre the Inquisitors of the Holy Office. Such prophesies had a tendency to become self-fulfilling.

Given the explosive history of Church-State quarrels in New Spain, and the reasons for his appointment in the first place, Palafox had to consider his next move with care. If he was to inform the King of his opinions, he had to do so without appearing to interfere in matters that were not his direct responsibility. And so he asked William to provide independent corroboration of his concerns.

William, of course, was only too willing to help and on his return to the capital he began drafting a report, which he completed during a brief holiday at Doña Inés' hacienda in Los Remedios. Despite all that had happened since his arrival in New Spain, the dream of Crópani still danced in his head and the twenty-page report he fired off to Madrid detailed the corruption that was rife in Villena's administration, the manner in which high offices were being auctioned, and Villena's apparent sympathy with Braganza. Also despatched was a personal letter in which he petitioned the King for a further grant of funds.

Lest his report be intercepted by Villena's spies, he had one of Doña Inés' servants, a certain Sebastián de Almeida, carry it to Puebla with instructions to hand it to Gregorio de Segovia (one of Palafox's secretaries), who was supposed to despatch it by a circuitous route to Madrid. But unknown to William, Segovia was working as a spy for the Inquisition and, before the letter could be sent, a copy was made and sent to the Inquisitor, Don Bartolomé González Soltero. It would seem that the Inquisition was already aware of William's activities in New Spain and were anxious to ensure that there was nothing in his reports which reflected badly on them.

Despite the obvious need for secrecy, William also took the time to send a letter to Don Jacinto de Soria Naharro, at that time also resident in Puebla, informing him of what was happening and prophesying the fall of Villena. Information such as this would have been grist to the mill of any merchant in New Spain, and William probably felt under an obligation of especial gratitude (Soria having recently gifted him an expensive suit of clothing). He also revealed the contents of his report to Doña Inés.

Although sent to New Spain to spy on such families, William had by now grown so close to Doña Inés that he had come to look upon her as much more than an employer. Perhaps it grieved him to have to keep secrets from her; perhaps conceit had loosened his tongue; perhaps he thought that the Carrillos too might be able to turn such information to their advantage; but one day, during one of their early morning rides at Los Remedios, he confessed the true reason for his presence in New Spain and the nature of the confidential reports he had been sending to Madrid through the secret intercession of a Jesuit priest by the name of Juan de San Miguel: a man so close to Villena that it beggars belief that the Viceroy could have been unaware of the Irishman's activities.

Three months later two letters arrived for William: one from Don Pedro López de Celo (Secretary to the King), and the other from Don Manuel de Almaguer (a cousin of Olivares' closest confidant, Don Francisco de Alarcón and an old friend of William's from his days in Madrid). The letters confirmed the safe arrival of the report which William, in the meantime, had published anonymously as a pamphlet.

Allowing any spy, however insignificant he might appear in the grand scheme of things, to become too involved with his target was a serious matter. Even the *possibility* that William was becoming attached to the Carrillos should have been worthy of some concern. But the Portuguese rebellion had turned everything on its head and it was no longer the activities of the Creoles that were uppermost in Villena's mind: it was not even those of the local 'Portuguese'. What was of most concern to Villena, at this juncture, was the increasingly emotive ranting of the Bishop of Puebla.

William had always had a raconteur's propensity to mythologise his life. Since his arrival in the Indies, in fact, he had reworked and recycled so much of his life that, even now, it is difficult to divine the truth. But his colourful exaggerations were losing, of late, an essential thread of credibility and assuming the sad swagger of desperation. Lost in a forest of guilt, hurt, embarrassment and anxiety, the last thing his humiliated spirit needed was for someone to unrealistically raise his expectations: but that is exactly what happened.

In one of the aforementioned letters, someone, it would appear, had the bad sense to suggest that not only would Olivares honour his promise to make William the next Marquis of Crópani, but that the title would pave the way for the King to appoint him Viceroy! However it had been worded, the effect on William's mental health was corrosive and he fell prey to the cruellest of delusions.

His friends did not know how to react. Up until now they could dismiss his occasional conceits and pretensions to omniscience as the eccentricities of an intellectual. A leap of faith on this scale, however, required the suspension of all his critical faculties—and it was well known that they were considerable. Given his ties to the Count-Duke and his apparent closeness to Palafox (who had to have financed his most recent propaganda work), his claims were not impossible and they were reluctant to gainsay him to his face. In their heart of hearts, however, they must have suspected that he had finally abandoned himself to his demons.

The dispute between the bishop and the Viceroy, meanwhile, was rapidly degenerating into a public slanging match. At every opportunity Palafox sought to heighten the tension and his repeated claims that the Portuguese were stockpiling weapons eventually forced Villena into ordering the surrender of arms by all Portuguese residents. From the 419 families who registered, however, just sixteen firearms were collected.

Failing to learn from his earlier mistakes, and overestimating his influence at court, Villena wrote to Madrid complaining about Palafox's scaremongering and demanding that the troublesome bishop be stripped of his commissions and recalled immediately to Spain. His difficulty, had he but known it, was that he was attacking the reputation of a man considered irreproachable in Madrid: perhaps the only man that Olivares still trusted fully. It didn't help either, that other members of Villena's family had recently been caught conspiring against the Crown.

Villena, in the end, found himself reprimanded by the King for obstructing Palafox's reforms—'so desired by both Spaniards and Indians'. Sooner rather than later, the animosity between the bishop and the Viceroy was bound to come to a head, and when it did, William dare not be on the losing side.

(23)

*I*F WILLIAM HAD discovered anything since his arrival in New Spain it was that it was not the Utopia he had once been led to believe. If paradise *was* to be found here, then it lay behind the shuttered balconies of the palaces, the high walls of the monasteries and the crested doorways of the old families, and not amongst the Indians in their coarsely spun mantas and rough leather sandals, who shambled about the plaza like foreigners in what was by now a very Spanish city.

Shortly after the Spanish conquest of the Aztec Empire, the level of public debate in Spain regarding the juridical status of these natives became so intense that the King invited the most eloquent advocates of either side to argue the matter before him. Before setting foot in the Indies, the details and ramifications of that debate would have coloured almost everything William had known about this strange land or its inhabitants.

Following in the footsteps of Aristotle, Juan Ginés de Sepúlveda had proposed that not all men were equal and that the natives of the New World were natural slaves who had been justly conquered. Bartolomé de las Casas, on the other hand, had argued that all nations and races shared a common humanity and were capable of civilisation. The conquest of the New World by force, therefore, was immoral. Only by peaceful conversion could it be justified.

Slaves or free men? Human or subhuman? The debate raged for almost fifty years. At its conclusion a compromise was arrived at. The Indians, the King instructed, were not to be treated as slaves but given a type of second–class citizenship under which they would be subjected to the supervision of their Christian betters, whose responsibility it would be to protect them from exploitation and instruct them in the faith. In return for this protection, the Indians would be required to perform certain services for the Crown.

It all sounded very well in theory, but in practice, as William was slowly discovering, the promised protection from exploitation had been superseded by the Crown's desperation for silver. A legal loophole, intended to be used only for 'necessary public works', had been exploited to provide forced Indian labour for the mines. Able-bodied Indians were being rounded up by corrupt public officials and supplied to the mine owners at a price. The same was true of many of the larger haciendas. William's eyes were being opened and he didn't like what he was seeing.

It was about this time that the renewed efforts of the Viceroy to collect settlement fees for land and water rights saw William taking temporary employment as a royal surveyor. The project was one of numerous land and water surveys that were being used to pressurise reluctant landowners and townships into paying the fees assessed against them. Disputes over the level of fees assessed would see the royal surveyors descend upon the affected town or hacienda, where they would billet themselves and carry out their work at the expense of the town council or landowner. So quickly, in fact, did costs escalate, that a settlement was invariably reached before the survey was ever completed. Indeed such was the Crown's need for cash that in many cases dubious or fraudulent titles to land were confirmed in exchange for prompt payment, in effect legalising the theft of land by rich landowners (who realised that the best way to obtain cheap labour for their haciendas was to deprive impotent peasants of their plots).

The land grabbing was not unlike that inflicted upon the Old English by New English settlers in Ireland and, despite the nature of his employment, it made William more than a little sympathetic to the plight of the dispossessed. In Michoacán he noted how it broke the hearts of the 'less powerful farmers' to see the rich man 'take over their fields without a right'.

It was shortly after this, in March of 1642 in fact, that William was first introduced to Ignacio Pérez—a thirty-year-old Indian from the village of San Martín Acamixtla, near Taxco. Shrewd, well respected amongst his people and, courtesy of a bout of smallpox, blind since the age of two, Ignacio had come to the capital in the hope of finding a legal remedy for the maltreatment of Indian labourers by 'Spanish miners'.

He wished, in particular, to complain about the activities of Don Alonso de Cerecedo, the *Alcalde Mayor* (district governor) of Taxco. His only companion was a young boy, whom he employed as a guide.

Complaints against the activities of the *Alcaldes Mayores*, however, were as frequent as they were futile. It was common knowledge that many were illegally using royal funds to engage in trade or usury with the mine owners, who responded to their pressure by demanding impossible productivity from their workforce, but there was no official will to stop them. The abuse of Indian labourers could often be redressed before the General Indian Court when the Indians were the plaintiffs, but putting a stop to the illegal activities of the *Alcaldes Mayores* was going to be a far harder nut to crack. The only person who could realistically do so was the Viceroy, and no Viceroy yet had been willing to allow such a valued source of patronage to be diminished in the eyes of potential recipients.

Don Ignacio Fernando Pérez, however, was no ordinary Indian. He was what the Spanish called an *Indio Principal*—the lesser of the two upper ranks of native nobility recognised by the Spanish after the *Conquista*. Despite the general ban on such things, *Indios Principales* were often permitted to use Spanish honorifics such as *Don* and *Doña,* to dress like Spanish nobles, to carry arms and to ride horses. They represented Spanish authority before their Indian subjects and their Indian subjects before the Crown: many, in fact, held positions as town governors or mayors. Fluent in both his native Nahuatl and Castilian, Ignacio was intelligent and articulate. Despite the picture he would later attempt to paint of himself, he was nobody's fool.

By the time Ignacio arrived at the *Casa de Cabildo* (presumably to speak with Fernando Carrillo), he had spent most of his money on scribes and was facing a quick return to San Martín. Knowing that her husband's views on such matters were unlikely to be of much help, Doña Inés offered him temporary accommodation in her home. In no time at all William—who had an encyclopaedic knowledge of the law and experience of dealing with grandees—was helping him to draft his memos to the Viceroy.

There were just three years between William and Ignacio in terms of age and despite the Irishman's affectations they got on famously from the start. Ignacio's noble status appealed to William's vanity and afforded him an opportunity to show off the breadth of his education. Whether it had been Doña Inés' intention or not, the challenge was just the tonic William needed, and he took to the task with zest.

His conversations with Ignacio also forced William to confront his apathy toward the vast sea of misery and resentment that existed beyond the cities—misery that up to now had passed unfelt and unseen by the majority of Spaniards and Creoles. With the drought now in its second year, many Indian families had abandoned agriculture to seek alternative employment in the towns, and the roads were strewn with the corpses of those who had left it too late. Parents buried children, children their parents. Drained of all grief and compassion, the survivors dragged themselves to the capital in a desperate attempt to cheat Death of his due.

But there was only so much work, or indeed alms, to go around, and William, struggling to square his full belly and Christian conscience with such overwhelming evidence of unnecessary suffering as seemed to make a mockery of the faith, slowly began to identify with the oppressed. Not only did he discuss such matters with Ignacio, he even hinted—with a strange and enigmatic conceit that perplexed and intrigued the blind Indian in equal measure—that he would soon be in a position to offer him 'a remedy' for his troubles. It was a peculiar boast. The only man who could effectively 'remedy' the current state of affairs was the Viceroy!

On one of his darker mornings, in May of 1642, William asked Ignacio to go to the Plaza Mayor and fetch him a half-real's worth of *peyote*. But Ignacio had no money on him and neither, for that matter, did William and so he told Ignacio to ask Don Jacinto Soria Naharro, who had recently returned from Puebla, for the loan of two reals in his name. Having collected the money without any great difficulty, Ignacio headed for the Plaza Mayor.

Directly opposite the viceregal palace, outside the arcade of silk shops, a handful of cross-legged Indian women held court, wrapped in colourful mantas, nursing their babies, and selling medicinal plants in much the same place and with much the same aura of invulnerability as they had for centuries prior to the *Conquista*. Used to cure common illnesses and ailments by Spaniards, Creoles and Indians alike, the close relationship between the medicinal use of these plants and their role in native religious rituals had led the early Spanish clergy to associate them with acts of idolatry, witchcraft and heresy. To confuse the clergy and frustrate the Inquisition, they had learnt the habit of re-classifying the local flora with a suitable Christian nomenclature. *Matlalcuahuitl*, had become 'Holy Staff', *Yoyotli* had become 'Friar's Elbow', and *Tlachichinoa* had assumed the rather poetic appellation of 'Saint James' Tears'.

Under the very noses of the Spanish administration, they also sold (to those who knew how to ask) a plant so notorious amongst the Spanish clergy that it had only ever been known by its Aztec name: *peyote*. Because of its strong hallucinogenic properties, and its role in shamanistic ritual, its sale and consumption had been outlawed by the Inquisition. William, however, was not unfamiliar with its properties and this was probably not his first purchase—he would later describe its action as being similar to an Irish plant called 'tams' (presumably *Tamus Communis* or Black Bryony), which 'if put on the head in a certain manner, at times of carnival or Christmas, would attract heat to it'.

Ignacio returned later that same morning with two buttons of peyote wrapped in a small rag. He gave them to William along with the one and a half reals change, and set off about his business. Three days later, he was sent for again. William, who had ground the peyote into a fine powder in anticipation of his arrival, asked Ignacio to consult the spirits regarding the timing of the arrival of the new Viceroy and, in what seemed like an instant of remorse, whether a certain woman to whom he had once been engaged was still alive.

'No-one,' warned William, 'not even Doña Inés, is to know of what passes between us.'

The use of peyote in prophecy and divination would have been well known to William, especially since the publication, in 1629, of Hernando Ruiz de Alarcón's famous *Treatise on the heathen superstitions and customs that today live among the Indians native to this New Spain*:

> If the consultation concerns something lost or stolen, or a woman who has fled her husband, or something similar . . . the divination is made in one of two ways: either by fortune-

telling or by drinking peyote, or ololiuqui, or tobacco . . . or
by ordering that another person drink it . . .

Although not entirely an unwilling participant, Ignacio was nervous.
He was afraid they might be overheard. The walls of the apartment
were, after all, made only of timber and he knew that what he was being
asked to do was illegal. To allay his fears, William led him to the *salón de
estrado*, brought him the peyote, an empty gourd and a jug of water.

Placing the peyote into the gourd, Ignacio dissolved it in water. Its
consumption, however, was not a particularly pleasurable experience
and required time, commitment and solitude—the local custom being
that the 'consultor' should be allowed to retire to his 'oratory' and be left
in solitude for as long as the 'consultation' might last. Despite this,
William insisted on waiting until the gourd was empty, before retiring
to his room to get some sleep.

Next morning, at about 8 a.m., the entire household gathered, as was
their custom, for morning Mass in Doña Inés' private oratorio. After the
Ite missa est, William called Ignacio to one side and, dismissing his guide,
led Ignacio to his room. The approaching fleet, Ignacio reported, was
indeed bringing a new Viceroy, but as for the woman, he had been unable
to ascertain if she was alive.

William was flushed with anger.

'If you do not know these things,' he raged, 'then you could not have
consumed the peyote.'

Ignacio was taken aback.

'Did not you yourself give it to me? Were you not there when I drank
it?'

William calmed himself, but offered nothing remotely approaching
an apology. Unable to shake the suspicion that he had been duped by his
friend, he continued nevertheless, over the weeks that followed, to write
letters on behalf of those Indians from Taxco who continued to seek his
assistance—the majority of whom were being sent to him by Ignacio
(though this may not have entirely have been an act of charity, it being
customary in New Spain for suitably educated *letrados* to be paid from
fines or levies on the Indian community for acting on behalf of those
Indians who came before the *Audiencia* as plaintiffs). William also

resumed his reports to Olivares, sending them now to Puebla with an old hunchback servant of Doña Inés—his previous courier, the Jesuit Juan de San Miguel, being too close to Villena to be trusted.

(24)

ON 23 MAY 1642, a courier arrived in Puebla bearing news of the arrival of the ship *San Francisco* in Veracruz. Amongst the sealed orders she carried, were the nomination of Bishop Palafox as Archbishop of Mexico and authorisation for him to oust Villena, if and when he saw fit.

The inordinate delay in relaying the papers to Puebla—the *San Francisco* had actually docked on 4 May—was most probably deliberate. By the time Palafox received his new orders, the Inquisition had already adjusted its position. Abandoning Villena and their usual diet of false priests, bigamists and readers of forbidden books, they turned on the Portuguese community with a sudden and surprising ferocity.

First to be arrested, on 17 May, were Doña Blanca Rivera and three of her five daughters: Margarita, Isabel, and Clara—a simple-minded girl who enjoyed the reputation of a *parlanchina*. The eldest daughters, María and Catalina, avoided capture. Realising the threat posed by the arrest of the loose-tongued Clara, María made immediate efforts to contact Simón Váez Sevilla. They met at his home the following midnight.

A crisis meeting was in progress when María arrived, and amongst those present she counted sixteen of the most influential Jews in the city. Flanked by her teenage sons, Rafael and Gabriel, she offered to allow herself be arrested in order to coach her younger sister. To ensure she was placed in the correct cell, she wanted a thousand pesos with which to bribe the guards.

There was a general acceptance amongst the *Marranos* that should any one of them be arrested by the Inquisition they would, if necessary, confess to being practising Jews and limit their implication of others to immediate family members. Clara, it was agreed, would be a loose cannon. María was given everything she asked for.

The following morning, María asked a Negro slave who worked at the prison to take a message to Clara. The letter, as anticipated, was intercepted. But though arrested as planned, María and Clara were kept apart. Ironically enough Clara would testify against relatively few; María, on the other hand, would end up implicating no less than 175, including her own sons. Neither would survive their imprisonment.

On hearing of the arrests of the Riveras, Juana Enríquez, the highly strung wife of Simón Váez Sevilla, made her way to her kitchen. Seated on a trunk of crockery, she cried at her slaves in desperation.

'Look here,' she wailed, 'do we not eat stew and chicken like every-body else. And if we do not eat lard or pork, is it not because I have a weak stomach?'

Similar scenes were taking place throughout the capital.

(25)

THOUGH HIS INITIAL reaction had been to refuse his appointment, Palafox arrived in the capital on 6 June to formally take charge of his new see. At 10 p.m. on the 8th, before any other clique or conspiracy could act in a similar manner, he sent messengers to over eighty civil and religious officials requesting that they attend an emergency meeting in the Archbishop's Palace at dawn.

Having secured their permission to act, he sent Don Antonio Urrutia de Vergara and a squad of thirty men to the Viceroy's palace. Anyone who wished to, he insisted, should to be allowed to leave, but on no account was anyone to be allowed to enter.

Shortly after 6 a.m., Palafox marched into the palace at the head of a column of soldiers and officials. They roused Villena from his sleep, handed him the royal decree, and ordered him to read it. Dishevelled, half-dressed and not a little dazed, he was given a two-mule carriage, a solitary valet and ordered to leave immediately. He was not permitted to pack.

Ousted unceremoniously from his home, Villena headed straight for Churubusco—a tiny settlement on the southern shore of Lake Texoco. Here, at the friary fortress of Santa María de los Angeles, he was given sanctuary by the local Franciscans. He had supported them in good times; they would support him now in bad.

In a sense the Creole revolt had finally taken place, albeit under the control of Palafox, whose actions had succeeded in wresting control from those factions he considered potentially disloyal to the Crown. Believing that it had been *his* letter to Olivares that had prompted this sudden turn of events, William expected to be rewarded (a post on the tribunal controlling the colony's tobacco industry had apparently been mentioned at some point), but apart from a summons to brief Palafox on the state of the colony's defences nothing in the way of reward was forthcoming. Or was it?

At a much later date an acquaintance of William's would recall him mentioning 'that Don Juan de Palafox had promised him that he could take care of the administration of the kingdom's tobacco industry on behalf of His Majesty, but that he had refused, as he wanted that it should be for him alone, and to give a certain amount each year to the King'. If this offer was indeed genuine, why on earth should William have refused it, unless he had even higher ambitions? At this point in time Palafox had total control of both the religious and political reins of the colony—a situation William knew the Crown would not allow to persist for very long. The next fleet would surely bring better news.

In the meantime, William attempted to get another letter to Olivares, this time criticising the Holy Office of the Inquisition and the disastrous effects the arrests of so many prominent merchants on the 'pretext of Judaism' were having on the local economy. As before, he asked Doña Inés' servant, Sebastián de Almeida, to carry it to Puebla and hand it to Gregorio de Segovia to despatch. This time, however, William must have discussed the contents with Almeida, for the servant took it straight to the Inquisition. Luckily for William there was little in the letter that could be construed as heresy or suspect in the faith, but he was now a marked man.

Palafox's coup was not the outcome that William had expected his report to Olivares to provoke, and though he still remained one of the bishop's most fervent admirers, Palafox's exceptionally harsh treatment of Villena left him racked with guilt. Perhaps he had exaggerated Villena's faults; perhaps, in his efforts to impress Palafox and Olivares, he had even been untruthful. Be this as it may, his conscience, or, as he put it himself, 'the Holy Spirit' began to nag at him, and he felt compelled to make amends.

Three days after Villena left for Churubusco, William went to the Monastery of Saint Francis and called on Fray Juan de Prada, the Commissioner General of the Franciscans. There may yet, he suggested, be a way out of this mess. Having assisted the Count-Duke in refuting the charges of Richelieu, he had a great deal of experience in such matters and was therefore offering his assistance to the Marquis, should he intend to draft a refutation.

The following night the Commissioner General collected William in Villena's carriage and drove him to the monastery at Churubusco. They found the distraught grandee not yet recovered from his ordeal and struggling to grasp how comprehensively his actions and intentions had been misinterpreted. Even his selection of a Portuguese mare over a Spanish one was being touted as evidence of his support for Braganza! He could not believe that the King had given credence to such rubbish.

For the next four days and nights William was given bed and board at the monastery, where he slowly came to the conclusion that Villena was not quite the villainous voluptuary he had been painted and more a victim of circumstance and incompetence than a traitor. In an effort to raise his spirits, he asked a servant to request the date and hour of the Marquis' birth in order that he could compile an astrological chart. It was a neat touch: one of Villena's less notorious ancestors was the famous Henry the Astrologer (Enrique el Astrologo, Marquis of Villena 1378–1434). How seriously the chart was taken is impossible to judge but, like every other grandee of Spain, Don Diego was exceptionally susceptible to flattery.

Over the course of the following week, William shuttled back and forth from Churubusco and Mexico City where, with the help of Juan de San Miguel, he started to compile a defence of the ex-Viceroy. Just a few weeks earlier he had been unwilling to trust this Jesuit—a man Palafox had once described as being 'kind to neither his enemies nor his friends'—with the posting of his letters to Madrid: now he sat so comfortable in his company that he could recount hazy recollections of a dream in which he himself had become Viceroy, and of another in which he had cut Villena's throat. As the revelation of these guilt-ridden visions were not covered by the seal of the confessional, it would have been surprising had the Jesuit not reported them to Villena, and yet neither appeared to have any qualms about trusting him.

To his closest friends, William's sudden *volte-face* reeked more of hypocrisy than madness and they were not beyond giving him some grief over the apparent contradiction posed by his previous denunciation and current defence of Villena. William, however, brushed their criticisms aside. The former, he claimed, had been inspired by the Devil, the latter by the Holy Spirit.

With the crozier in one hand and the sword in the other, Palafox now held the four most important positions in the colony: Viceroy; Visitor

General; Archbishop of Mexico; and Bishop of Puebla. Still protesting that he was taking charge only until such time as replacements could be sent from Spain, he began to purge his enemies from the government, to take action against the Portuguese, and to initiate a moral crusade against corruption, prostitution, and the immodest dress and erotic dancing of the *Mulattas*.

A week later the first hint of why he had acted so hastily emerged. On 14 June, a close friend of the Rivera family was arrested. In his pocket was found a copy of the mutual assistance treaty agreed between the Dutch and the Portuguese. Two days later Tomás Núñez de Peralta was arrested and four days after that the warrant for Simón Váez Sevilla was signed (though it would take another twenty-three days before it could be executed).

Up until now, nobody believed that this latest purge was anything more than a temporary squall that would soon blow over. The arrests of Váez and Núñez, however, changed everything. A river of fear, thus far contained within the banks of precedence, suddenly burst its banks. Panic spread like floodwater and the colony was submerged in a collective paranoiac anxiety and seized with a fear of fifth columnists.

Palafox now had the Creoles exactly where he wanted them—turning to the Crown for protection and temporarily forgetting about increased autonomy or independence. But it was no longer the Jews or Creoles who were thinking of seizing power, but an unusual Irishman said to possess the gift of tongues and, as he put it himself, a 'mastery of all the sciences'.

*W*ITH FAMINE AND disease rampant throughout the drought-stricken highlands, morale in the capital plummeted. Even the news that a new Viceroy, the Count of Salvatierra, had been nominated, did little to raise the spirits of its beleaguered citizens. Having boasted to his closest friends that Olivares would make him Marquis of Crópani and the next Viceroy of New Spain, the news was particularly humiliating for William. The fleet may even have brought word from his friends in Madrid of the King's decision to recognise the claims of Geronimo Ravaschiera, a Sicilian relative of the previous Marquis, to the Marquisate of Crópani. To humiliation, in that case, could then be added a sense of betrayal.

The disappointment sent William plunging into an Avernus of despair. He slept little, spoke infrequently, and more or less confined himself to his room. Like a bird with a broken wing he dragged himself from the shadows only occasionally, and then like a breath of cold air that was there one moment and gone the next. His friends were concerned and anxious to console him, but he refused to receive visitors. Don Francisco Solís y Corral, nevertheless, drafted a note of condolences, had it signed by many of his closest friends, and delivered it personally to the *Casa de Cabildo*. William accepted the letter, which expressed the hope that he might yet receive his promised title, but it served only to intensify his embarrassment.

For perhaps the first time in his life, William found himself unable to abide the capricious cruelties of fate that he had once accepted as easily as a change in the weather. Like a good sailor he had always picked himself up, brushed himself down, and got on with his life: but this time it was different—humiliation being a wound that never closes and next to impossible to conceal. The more he dwelled upon it, the more irate he became. Such intense anger was far from consonant with his character and lent no great logic to his compensatory impulses, nor reason to his avenging stratagems. It did, however, at least succeed in lifting him out of his lethargy.

He would not, he resolved, allow himself to become a figure of ridicule. He would not be mocked. One way or another he would regain his dignity (this was, after all, a time when a Spaniard's behaviour and self-esteem was shaped as much by the plays of Calderón de la Barca, with their recurring themes of honour and revenge, as by Holy Scripture). The colony, he thought to himself, was being destroyed by incompetent government. But it could so easily be different. It could so easily be a meritocracy where everyone, regardless of the circumstances of their birth, could have the opportunity to share in its munificent bounty. What was needed was not the perpetuation of *gachupín* corruption, but the type of imaginative and intelligent leadership that a man like himself could easily provide.

The enormous distance from Spain and the poor state of the colony's defences were such that a relatively small army could, with little difficulty, seize control. Having recently advised Palafox on the danger to the colony of an attack from within, he knew exactly how it needed to be timed, the number of men he would need to accomplish it, and how much would be required to finance it. If the Spanish would not make him Viceroy, then he would approach the Dutch (who had supported the Portuguese) and the French (who were supporting the Catalans). On 30 July, drunk on a deadly cocktail of bitterness, pride, resentment and frustration, he set out to write to them both. He had nothing left to lose.

Two days later, his spirits restored by a renewed sense of purpose, he finally left the confines of his room and headed for the Monastery of Saint Francis to confess his sins, renew his faith and receive the Portiuncula Indulgence. Inspired, perhaps, by the ease with which Palafox had ousted Villena, he hired an Indian forger to counterfeit various official documents and the royal seal of Felipe IV. To cover himself, in case of discovery, he also sent a letter to the Jesuit, Juan de San Miguel. He was, he wrote, about to smoke out any remaining Portuguese sympathisers by dint of some forged letters and the illusion of another coup, and he required, therefore, an expert opinion regarding the circumstances in which certain secrets 'concerning matters of crime, lese-majesty, Judaism and heresy' might be morally kept or disclosed.

The Jesuit, who scribbled his reply in the margins, could think of no legal or moral obligation that might force a man to respect a *secreto natural*. But though he refused to be drawn into giving specific advice, the Jesuit's reply was enough to convince William that 'matters of state did not have to be prejudicial to the soul'.

As they were perhaps the only group to have benefited from Palafox's coup, there was little point in William chasing Creole support. His ideas on racial equality and land reform, in any case, were unlikely to appeal to a class whose primary objective was to replace *gachupín* monopolies with monopolies of their own. The Indians, on the other hand, were a different proposition entirely. Although the arrival of Old World diseases such as smallpox had decimated their race, they still greatly outnumbered the colonists and Palafox had recently contrived to alienate himself by ordering the destruction of all Aztec antiquities collected by his predecessors and the removal of the Aztec symbols of cactus, eagle and serpent from the city's coat of arms.

Not content with having attacked their symbols, Palafox had also promised the hacienda owners that he would help them to increase their permanent Indian workforce by extending the system of debt-peonage—an institution that prohibited Indians from acquiring debts in excess of forty *reales*, prevented them from leaving their masters while in debt to him, and made such liabilities hereditary. Kept perpetually in debt by small advances of wages, the Indian who worked the land became chained to his master as surely as the labour force that worked the mines were chained to the mine owners and *corrigedores*.

This was quite an about-face for Palafox, but the reforms of the *repartimiento* instituted by Cerralvo and Cadereyta had not only led to the Indians enjoying a greater degree of self-determination with regard to employment, but to acute labour shortages. Palafox was anxious, furthermore, not to provoke the hacienda owners at such a delicate moment in the negotiations over settlement fees. The collection of these fees was intended to finance the building of the *Armada de Barlovento*—the creation of which was due in no small part to his having convinced the Count-Duke of the need for a special Caribbean defence squadron. Having been so closely associated with the decision to go ahead and build such a fleet, Palafox could hardly abandon it now.

But by authorising a number of farmers to detain their Indian labourers for debts, the amount or nature of which was never specified, Palafox was not just bequeathing enormous problems to his eventual successor; he was single-handedly destroying the reforms of his predecessors and putting a permanent halt to the official campaign for Indian liberties at the very moment when the goal of complete freedom for Indian workers seemed in sight—quite an achievement for a man who, paradoxically, was the author of a famous work in defence of the Indians. Hardest hit by the corruption, drought and famine of recent years, the Indians now had more than ample cause to rebel. All they were lacking, to William's mind, was leadership and training.

Despite niggling doubts about the incident with the *peyote*, William again sought out Ignacio, who was on the point of returning to Taxco. He had decided, he told Ignacio, to take the matter of corruption and injustice into his own hands and he needed someone to spread some propaganda in his favour. He also needed someone to suborn a native army of 300 expert archers from amongst the disaffected miners, to support the 400 men he himself would recruit 'with the utmost alacrity'. Together, he said, they would liberate the Africans and restore the land to the Indians.

The steep and cobbled backstreets of Taxco should have been a hotbed of discontent, but Ignacio was either unable or unwilling to mould the obvious ill feeling into any form of organised resistance. The brutal truth of the matter was that the Spanish had inflicted nothing upon the Indians that the Indians had not, for many centuries prior to the arrival of the Spanish, inflicted upon themselves. Having lived for so long under one yoke or another, they were extremely cautious of quick-fix solutions.

Long before the arrival of the Conquistadors, the abandoned ruins of the Mexican highlands had stood as monuments to the fact that colonisation was a virus that eventually destroyed its host. Empires had risen and fallen, old masters had been replaced by new, and the pantheon of the gods had been filled to overcrowding. For the placid and fatalistic Indians time was not just a cyclical entity, but a living one. As one cycle died, another would be reborn. The Spanish were merely another in a long line of invaders and in time they too would go. The Spanish, in consequence, were always much more afraid of a rebellion by their Negro slaves (as had happened in 1537).

Just eight days after he left for Taxco, Ignacio returned to the capital to take care of some outstanding legal business and decided to pay a courtesy visit on Doña Inés. Finding her not at home, he sat down to pass some time in conversation with one of her slaves. Hearing his voice, William called him aside.

'Did you tell them everything?' he enquired as he led the Indian to his room.

Ignacio told William exactly what he wanted to hear. He had, he said, spoken to the men in his village and to the disaffected miners. All were happy with the Irishman's plans and were awaiting the day they would be freed from their troubles. They would even, he claimed, be able to raise the required 500 pesos.

It all seemed too good to be true.

'And how, pray tell, do they intend to raise such a sum?'

'With nuggets they will steal from the mines.'

Three days later Ignacio returned to his wife in San Martín, leaving William so secure in the belief that he had managed to recruit his 300 archers that he made no attempt to verify their existence. He trusted Ignacio as he had trusted Olivares. A nobleman's word of honour had always been enough.

(27)

$\mathcal{F}$OLLOWING IGNACIO'S DEPARTURE, a conspiracy of whispers in the capital began to speak of a wife and child that William had left behind him in a Spanish convent. The gossip spread quickly and soon reached the ears of Antonia's mother, Doña Beatriz de Turcios.

Forced to defend himself, William avowed that he had never married Ana de Cano y Leyva. The most he had done, he said, was to promise marriage; and even that was only after he had been 'drugged' by her scheming relatives. Though not entirely convinced, Doña Beatriz permitted the courtship to continue, but the wedding was postponed until the truth of the matter could be determined. The rumours, however, had already done their damage and William and Antonia quickly drifted apart.

The demise of this relationship, the losses he had incurred during the drought, the discomfiture and humiliation that had followed Salvatierra's appointment as Viceroy, and his continuing sense of rootlessness and disconnection were trouble enough for any man; but what followed next eclipsed all other sorrows.

The last year or so had brought to the Valley of Mexico yet another outbreak of a swift and highly lethal haemorrhagic disease known to Indians and Spaniards alike as *cocoliztli*. Its virulence had been increased significantly by the drought, and fatalities (which usually occurred within three to four days of the first symptoms) were reaching epidemic proportions—especially amongst the Indians.

With so many on the move a pestilential noose began to tighten around the capital and those who could afford to more or less confined themselves to their homes, constantly examining themselves for the first signs of the disease and driving themselves mad with anxiety at the first sign of a headache, nose-bleed or raised temperature. But the plague was democratically indiscriminate in its choice of victims and for many of the city's most prominent citizens the recall of the Virgin of Los Remedios to the Metropolitan Cathedral came too late.

The deaths, that summer, of Don Fernando Carrillo and his wife, Doña Inés Maldonado, hit William hard. As the will of the Almighty it had to be borne with humility and fortitude, and faced with a stoical composure: on the inside, however, there remained an awful sense of loss. Doña Inés had been perhaps his closest friend in New Spain and her passing, in so many respects, left a hole in his life that could never be filled. Almost entirely dependent now on the goodwill of her children, her passing left him disconsolate and powerless: bowed, but not yet broken.

Shortly after the funeral of their mother (their father had died first), the Carrillo brothers were forced to extirpate themselves from their father's official residence to make room for Palafox, who in turn had vacated the viceregal palace to make room for the new Viceroy. They moved into a much less expensive mezzanined apartment at the *Casa de los Condes de Carrion*—a little under a kilometre away in the market neighbourhood of *La Merced*—and 'spent almost 30,000 pesos' in furnishing it. In accordance with his mother's dying wish, Sebastián brought William with him and continued to treat him as one of the family.

The move, however, did little to lift the gloom and there was little that William could do to alleviate it. He had lost a dear friend and confidante, but the boys had lost a mother. Their respective losses bore no comparison and there was no point, as he knew well from bitter experience, in trying to offer false comfort. There would be no easy release from their silent and tearless suffering: their grief was a private matter that time alone would heal.

For the time being, the new apartment remained soaked in mourning and entertained few visitors. The rooms no longer echoed to the fluttering of fans or the tippling of hot chocolate, and what little conversation took place was empty, joyless and served only to renew the sorrow. Deprived of an appreciative audience, the stimulation of intelligent conversation and finding himself face to face once more with the mortal and the transitory, the nights became interminably long and William began once more to turn in on himself.

Antoon van Dyck: double portrait of William Lamport and
Jan Karel della Faille

The entrance to the college: Royal
Monastery of San Lorenzo de el
Escorial.

The Independence Monument in
Mexico City. A statue in memory of
William stands in the vestibule
(beneath the lion in the picture).

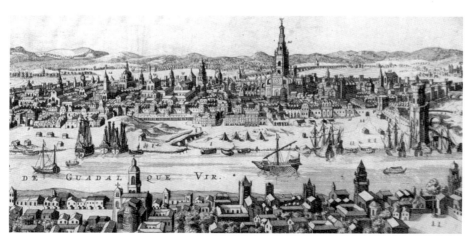

Seventeenth century Seville: port and gateway to the Indies.

The Casa de Cabildo, where William lived with the Carillos. Modified in the eighteenth century, these days it serves as the Departamento del Distrito Federal.

The Metropolitan Cathedral, Mexico City, in 1899. The two bell towers were not completed until 1813. In the last century the cathedral has sunk considerably into the lake bed.

Statue of William Lamport

(28)

*H*IS SELF-ESTEEM AT an all-time low and his future more precarious than ever, William redoubled his efforts to instigate a rebellion. In his quest for a legal and moral justification, he began to seek refuge in the old argument that the conquest of the Indies had not just been immoral, but illegal. The actions of the Conquistadors, he proclaimed to any and all who would listen to him, had run contrary to every divine precept and Christian ideal of justice. The Indians, therefore, had every right to defend themselves.

It was all very well, of course, espousing the right of the Indians to self-defence and self-determination, but there was just one small problem. The obsidian-tipped arrows and lances of Ignacio's promised recruits would never be sufficient to hold the colony: they would, in fact, be next to useless in the face of organised firepower. What William desperately needed was military discipline and access to firearms; and so he turned once again to the underpaid and undervalued officers of the colony's military.

First to be approached was the young ensign, Don Francisco Solís y Corral—a likeable rogue for whom he had previously done some favours. If he could recruit the 26-year-old Castilian, there was every chance that the popular ensign's militia colleagues would follow suit. In early September, he told Solís of his plans and promised him a lucrative position in his new administration. But Solís refused to bite.

A week later William invited the reluctant ensign up to his apartment and showed him various forged documents he claimed to have recently received from the King. Though not entirely convinced, Solís, or so it appears, at least agreed to set up a meeting.

Some days later, at a newly opened boarding house facing the Balbanera Convent, William sat down to dinner with Solís and a couple of his more senior militia colleagues—Captains Don Sebastián de Isasi and

Don Manuel de Pedrosa y Tapia. The meeting did not go well. While discussing the state of the colony William became exceptionally animated and fiercely critical of the King—describing Felipe as a weakling who only ever rewarded the toadies and lickspittles of the royal court and holding His Majesty personally responsible for his failure to receive the title he had been promised before sailing for the Indies.

Criticising the government of the colony, however, was one thing, indeed it was something of a national pastime, but attacking the honour of the King was quite another and Solís was having none of it. He demanded that William retract his remarks.

William refused.

'Let him be, Don Sebastián,' Isasi cried as he stepped between them, 'can't you see that he's mad!'

Solís did not believe William to be mad, and neither, apparently, did the Marquis of Villena (for whom William was still preparing a refutation of the charges laid by Palafox), nor indeed Palafox himself (who had recently sought his opinion regarding the defence of the colony and, allegedly, had also offered him a high-ranking position in the public service). Joining his friends, Solís got up from the table and left William to cool off alone.

(29)

$\mathcal{T}$HE COUNT OF SALVATIERRA was long overdue. Having sailed from Cádiz in mid-July, in the fleet of Don Pedro de Ursúa, he should have arrived in Veracruz by early September at the latest. Almost a month overdue, he had by now been given up for lost. His apparent demise was a source of such encouragement to William that during a social visit to the home of the Carrillo brothers, Doña Francisca de Soto y Salinas, a young married woman in her early twenties, was left somewhat bewildered on finding the Irishman in ebullient mood, 'drinking his chocolate with such majestic grandeur as though he were some great lord', and boasting, 'amongst much other humbug', that 'should the Count of Salvatierra fail to arrive, he himself was to become viceroy'.

Some days later, on Wednesday 1 October, William asked Sebastián to accompany him on a day trip to Ixtapalapa—an Indian village adjacent to Coyoacán. Site of an Aztec temple and the centre of the native *Fuego Nuevo* rituals, Ixtapalapa had for centuries been associated with Aztec astrologers. But it was not an astrologer that William was seeking, at least not on this occasion, rather a hermit believed to possess the gift of clairvoyance. Still cradling the hope that Olivares would honour his 'promise', he wanted to quiz the old man about his future.

Sebastián had no problems with astrology—just six months earlier he had asked William to compile charts for both himself and his younger brother—but the notion of visiting a clairvoyant for some reason filled him with dread. Perhaps a little afraid he might be seen and reported to the Inquisition, he told William to ride out alone. Like Ignacio before him, the old hermit told William exactly what he wanted to hear: bad news never turned a profit.

Just three days later, after an epic thirteen weeks at sea, the battered and half-starved *flota* of General Pedro de Ursúa finally limped into Veracruz. Salvatierra had survived. It took almost two weeks for the news to reach the capital but when it did it prompted yet another visit from William to his tailor.

Saboyano handed William a hand-written prophecy. The last three Viceroys of New Spain, it read, would wear in their turn a biretta, a hat and a crown. If the biretta was Palafox, William surmised, then the hat must be Salvatierra. That just left the crown! All of a sudden the post of Viceroy ceased to be the limit of his ambition.

His tutor's recent erratic behaviour was making Sebastián—long accustomed to William's minor eccentricities—more than a little anxious. The youngster, nevertheless, remained no less in awe of his tutor's intellect than his mother, and no less of a friend to him than Solís. Consequently, he kept his mouth shut and his concerns to himself. The genie, however, had already left the bottle.

William's plan to raise himself by popular vote to the throne of Mexico was soon being whispered on the streets of Puebla and Taxco, though with a new and surprising twist. Knowing that the Indians would not elect just anyone as their King, no matter what manner of land reforms he was offering, William had plundered the nooks and crannies of his fertile imagination for a cover story. Embroidering the tapestry of his picaresque life with a thread of royal silk, he adopted the persona of a bastard half-brother of Felipe IV—the result of his widowed mother's affair with Felipe III. When he came of age, his story now went, he travelled to Madrid to meet his royal half-brother, who set him on the path to an ecclesiastical career and granted him a scholarship to the Colegio Imperial. The rest of the story more or less adhered to the truth.

Having done all that he could to encourage Indian support for his revolution, William now returned to the not inconsiderable matter of firearms. He had not yet succeeded in obtaining modern weapons for his recruits, but he knew a man who could. It was time to pay him a visit.

(30)

On the eve of the feast of Saint Teresa, William called on his next-door neighbour, Felipe Méndez y Ortiz.

Unlike the poorly trained and grossly inexperienced Creole militia, 48-year-old Méndez was a battle-hardened veteran of the Army of Flanders. More importantly, as a captain of the Viceroy's guard, he had access to arms. Chatting about nothing in particular they wandered the streets of the capital for a few hours (being a Sunday the taverns were closed) until they found themselves back at the *Casa de los Condes de Carrion*. William invited him up to his room.

'Are you capable, Don Felipe, of keeping a secret,' he asked as they entered, 'even if it be contrary to the faith to do so?'

'I would die first,' replied Méndez.

It was not the reply William had been expecting but, given the manner in which the question had been framed, it could hardly have been otherwise. At a time when the Inquisition had eyes and ears everywhere, a man's best strategy when matters of faith were raised in conversation was always orthodoxy or silence.

It left William in something of a quandary, and for a moment he lost his bearings. As the son of a ship's pilot, he knew better than most the consequences of laying on sail in uncharted waters. He should have been dropping his lead line and proceeding with the utmost caution: but time was running out. He decided, therefore, to take a chance. As the retreating twilight filled the room with shadows, he began by telling Méndez that he was the bastard son of Felipe III.

Stunned, but nonetheless intrigued, Méndez sat in silence while William sailed through his adventures on the high seas and battlefields of Europe towards his plans for revolution and his 'Proclamation of Independence'—the first ever to be produced in the Indies and a document that not only promised racial equality, land reform, the removal of all barriers to trade with France, Holland, England and Portugal, but guaranteed that all who participated in the defence and liberation of New Spain would not only be freed but:

> . . . without any exceptions of condition or quality, whether born in Africa or already hispanicised, they would, henceforth, commensurate with their services and actions, be as likely as the Spaniards themselves to receive prizes, titles, *encomiendas*, Holy Orders, lordships, and offices at sea or on land, in the republic and in the government; for as they have shown art and industry in their cultivation of the land as labourers, they will, when free, possess all that is necessary to become lords.

It probably surprised Méndez to find that many of the papers he was being shown referred to the plight of the Indians and Negro slaves rather than the grievances of the military, but William was insistent that the moral justification for what they were about to attempt should be clear from the outset. With arguments heavily influenced by the *Defensio Fidei* and *De Bello et de Indis* (On War and the Indies) of Francisco de Suárez—the most influential exponent of the rights of people born in their native place to citizenship, to revolt in the face of tyranny and to the right to elect their own leaders 'by the consent of the community'— William attempted to convince Méndez that all men were born free and that nature did not confer on any man dominion over another. The principle reason for what he was about to attempt was not just the enslavement of Negros and *Mulattos*, but:

> . . . the complaints and tears of these poor natives, both Indian leaders and nobility as well as ordinary Indians and plebeians, that not only live dispossessed of the haciendas, possessions and lands, but are miserably tyrannised and condemned to forced labour as if they were not free men but slaves . . . and exposed to vassalage and vile taxes that forcefully obliges them, without payment for their corporal labours in the mines, tillage, drainage, haciendas, and sugar mills . . .

Echoing Suárez' contentions that there could be only two valid reasons for starting a war—to remedy an injury, or to defend the innocent—and that the overthrow of a legitimate ruler would be not only moral, but licit, if that leader had lapsed into 'tyranny', he attempted to justify what he was about to attempt, by stating firstly that 'tyranny' existed, and secondly that the war was defensive in nature:

> The same affliction and pain, as that of the Indians of whom I spoke earlier, is caused by the tyrannical enslavement of large numbers of Negros, Mulattos, Berbers and an infinitive number of other related groups whose natural rights are usurped, with little fear of God, by the Spaniards who reduce these people, that God has also created free, to the misery of slavery and servitude—the most fatal of punishments for those who had previously enjoyed a liberty more sweet and gracious than life itself. Despite the fact that they are as capable of the same glory as ourselves, they are looked upon as beasts, and poorly treated as captives and slaves.
>
> Also, as they are both Christians and members of the Catholic Church, who have been deprived of the very essence of life that is liberty, Divine Piety must necessarily be moved to pity their severe affliction and enslavement, and to sympathise with their arduous labours (which will serve to mitigate their pain-filled lives), and to liberate these kingdoms and subjects of this, and infinite other, tyrannies . . .

William then took the famous arguments of Las Casas and Vitoria to a new and, at least as far as Méndez was concerned, totally unexpected conclusion. The colony, he said, had not been *justly* conquered. The Pope had no jurisdiction in secular matters and the 1493 bull of *Inter Caetera*, in which Pope Alexander VI had divided the colonial world into zones of influence, was an irrelevance. As the natives had been forced into servitude against their will by 'tyrants' (there's that word again) who had ennobled themselves at their expense, the same natives ought therefore 'in truth to be lords over them, or, at the very least, equal to ourselves'.

In article twelve of his proclamation, therefore, William promised restitution 'to those natives who prove to have been defrauded of their lands from the Conquest to the present day'. The native races would then, as citizens and landowners, have the right to elect their own king, and once he had liberated New Spain from the mother country, *he* would have as much, if not more, right to that throne as any man.

This was the first time that William had mentioned becoming King, and he quite startled Méndez who, nevertheless, made no attempt to leave. The idea, however, was the obvious conclusion to his arguments. Independence without land reform and racial equality would merely hand the country over to the *gachupínes* and the Church (who owned most of the land). Genuine reform could never be accomplished without absolute power.

He had already, he claimed, recruited some four hundred men to his cause and he would soon be in a position to strike: all he was waiting for were papers confirming him as the new Viceroy and Marquis of Crópani. These papers were currently being prepared by an Indian counterfeiter and would be sent, following the landing of the second *Aviso* of the new year, to the Provincial of the Franciscans. Upon their arrival Salvatierra would be arrested as a traitor and Palafox, Villena and Cadereyta would all be returned to Spain. When things had settled down, he would hold elections.

The blue half-light of dusk slipped past them like a thief and still Méndez made no attempt to leave. Having lit the candles, William now handed him a five-page letter purporting to be a reply from the Portuguese King (the former Duke of Braganza). It detailed eighteen points on which they had agreed to co-operate. Braganza, William boasted, owed him a favour. Just two years previously, while waiting to sail for the Indies, he had accompanied the Marquis of Villena on a visit to Sanlúcar de Barrameda, where Braganza had been staying at as a guest of his brother-in-law, the Duke of Medina Sidonia. During that visit he had passed on some useful intelligence without which Braganza—whom he described as a 'simpleton'—could never have succeeded in breaking with Spain.

It was all very plausible, and Méndez appeared convinced; but it could never have happened. Apart from the occasion of his wedding, in 1632, Braganza had never set foot in Sanlúcar and, as Governor General of the Arms of Portugal, his presence would almost certainly have been noted. The conspiracy to raise Braganza to the Portuguese throne, furthermore, had not begun until October of 1640, a full five months after William had landed in New Spain.

Nevertheless, believing that he had hooked Méndez, William finally produced letters he claimed to have written to the Pope (justifying his revolution) and to Louis XIII (in which he complained bitterly about the Count-Duke). Both were dated 30 July. He also produced a copy of the report that had precipitated Villena's downfall, the prediction given to him by Saboyano, and told Méndez of Ignacio's experience with the peyote.

That was the last straw for Méndez. Biting his tongue he bade William goodnight and returned, anxious and troubled, to his apartment. It was to be a long and sleepless night.

The following day, William set about trying to mend his fences with Don Manuel Pedraza y Tapia and Don Francisco Solís y Corral—the young militia officers he had befriended shortly after his arrival in the capital, and with whom he had recently parted on bad terms. He invited them to his apartment for an early evening *merienda* of marinated tamarinds (prepared the night before), angel's hair (a sweetmeat in the form of threads), and four different types of Irish spirits. Don Sebastián de Isasi, who during the earlier argument had labelled him a madman, was not invited.

As William attended to his guests, Solís became much admiring of the receptacles upon which the food was presented.

'Where did you get these?' he asked, enviously pointing to a set of earthenware dishes fabulously ornamented with gold filigree—it being a commonplace of Castilian society that a gentleman exalted himself not just in the culinary delights of his table, but also in the manner in which they were served and presented.

'From Don Antonio de Vergara,' replied William, hinting at a degree of familiarity (perhaps even conspiracy) with the army general who had led Palafox's assault on the royal palace and whose escape from gaol had heralded the demise of Cadereyta.

As the evening progressed and the alcohol loosened their tongues, William also made some intemperate boasts concerning the ornamentation embossed on the silver salver on which he served them their drinks.

They were, he claimed, a means by which he could communicate with his friends at home in Ireland—where 'everybody wrote on pages of silver!' Whether said in earnest or in jest, Solís interpreted the remark as a reference to sorcery.

In the adjoining apartment meanwhile, a troubled Méndez was mulling over William's pronouncements of the previous night and debating whether or not he should tell someone. As a professional soldier the idea of a *coup d'etat* would not have been entirely abhorrent to him, but William's talk of popular sovereignty was another matter entirely.

Méndez was a *gachupín*. Born and reared in Espinosa de los Monteros, in the Burgos mountains of northern Spain, his outlook on life was entirely Spanish. The concepts of rule of law or sovereignty of the people, therefore, were about as alien to him as those of nationhood or independence would be to an *Indio* or *casta*. Such ideas undermined the very foundation upon which society was built—the divine right of the King to rule over his subjects. William's talk of racial equality and land reform, furthermore, was not the language of a *coup d'etat* as Méndez understood it; it was the language of class struggle. Destroying the racial hierarchy meant more than just a coup: it meant civil war!

Over the past few months the price of maize had more than doubled and discontent amongst the lower classes was fast approaching boiling point. Hearing the Irishman consorting with other members of the military (a wooden partition was all that separated their apartments) was the last straw. Worried, as much for himself as for the safety of the colony, he attempted, the following morning, to contact the civil authorities; but with little success. Everyone of consequence had travelled south to join in the celebrations. A judge of the *Audiencia*, Dr Andrés Gómez de Mora, was supposedly still about town, but Méndez was unable to find him. Tired and frustrated, he returned to his apartment determined to try again the following day.

(31)

'SEBASTIÁN,' WILLIAM ASKED tentatively, 'have you ever read a book called *The Secrets of Nature*?'

He had not.

There was a fine line between science and heresy, and an even finer one between 'modern science' and 'official science'. William was teetering on the edge.

The exact work to which he was referring is difficult to pin down, but between his arrival in London, where he had been introduced to the study of Natural Magic and the Secrets of Nature by John Greaves, and his departure from Madrid, where he had studied Natural Magic with Juan Eusebio Nieremberg y Otin, he could have read any number of books with this, or similar titles. The more renowned included works by Roger Bacon, Ramon Lull, Giovanni Battista della Porta and Philip Ulstadt. Indeed Niccolò Riccardi, in his imprimatur to Galileo's *The Assayer* (1623), also referred to Galileo as the 'discoverer of many secrets of nature' and a chapter by this name had comprised the final section of the *Curiosa Filosofia y tesora de Maravillas* ('Curious philosophy and treasury of marvels') by the aforementioned Nieremberg.

Europe, at this time, was undergoing a renaissance of interest in both astrology and medieval occultism, and books such as these had become extremely popular, especially outside of Spain. Many were, of course, banned by the Inquisition, but a collector such as William's former professor of occult philosophy, Don Juan del Espino (currently languishing in the gaols of the Inquisition of Toledo), could easily have procured any number of them, as indeed could the Count-Duke of Olivares.

Although famously dismissive of astrology and astrologers, the Count-Duke had nevertheless amassed a substantial collection of incunabula and esoteric books that were on the official index of forbidden and expurgated works. He had been allowed to collect such curiosities by virtue of special dispensations procured from the Inquisitor General and the Papal Nuncio, from whom he had also acquired a special licence to read the works of Erasmus, the rabbis of the Old Testament, and the Koran. When just a boy in Seville, it was widely believed that he had consorted with sorcerers, and similarly in Salamanca where he had been sent to study in 1601. He was also said to have been a friend of the infamous sorceress Leonorilla and to have provided positions in royal service for other known sorcerers such as the Mercedarian friar, Andrés de León, and the rationer of the Church of Toledo, Juan de Alvaro. He was even known to have financed the mysterious experiments of the Italian alchemist, Vincenzo Massimi.

In the social circles that William had frequented in Madrid, such interests were pursued with little fear of the Inquisition, and especially at the Colegio Imperial, where the Jesuits appeared free to study and teach whatever they wanted. Indeed, at a time when such practices were expressly forbidden by the Inquisition, the good fathers had openly taught the arts of magic, astrology and 'prediction' (*prónosticos*). Not only that, but these subjects were included amongst those listed as 'major' rather than 'minor' courses of study. The subject matter of any number of the aforementioned books, however, would have been looked upon with a much more jaundiced eye by the more obscurantist Mexican Inquisitors, and what William wanted to discuss with Sebastián appeared to venture far beyond the limits of acceptable science.

To Sebastián's surprise and discomfort, William began to tell him of a number of ways in which a man could make himself invisible. The first, he said, was to carry a small pin-head sized stone—which could only be found in the skull of a young raven—in one's mouth; the second involved beheading a black cat with a single blow, gouging out its eyes, placing chickpeas in the sockets and the brain cavity, burying the head and sprinkling it daily with water, and then carrying about one's person a grain from the plants that grew there.

Later that same day he began, for what appears to have been the first time, to discuss his revolutionary ambitions with Sebastián. In a moment of levity he asked the youngster to choose the post he would most like to acquire in the new administration.

'Collector of taxes,' replied Sebastián, half-seriously.

William laughed heartily.

'Choose another.'

Sebastián reduced his expectations and allowed that he wouldn't mind becoming a captain of the guard.

'When the time comes,' William promised, 'it will be yours for the asking.'

O N THURSDAY, 23 OCTOBER, after three days of searching, Méndez finally caught up with the missing judge, Dr Andrés Gómez de Mora. Accompanied by Don Francisco Gómez de Sandoval, and a certain Pablo Carracosa, he explained his fears of an uprising and told of the incident with the peyote.

A 46-year-old nobleman from Valladolid, Don Francisco had come to New Spain following the demise of his family's influence under the Olivares regime. He had known William since his arrival in the capital—in fact it had been William who had introduced him to Méndez. They had spoken many times, he said, but William had never discussed any of his 'diabolical intentions' with him. Everything he knew he had been told by Méndez, who lived in the same building. He did, however, voice a word of warning. The Irishman was extremely capable and there should be no doubting his intelligence. If he had said that there was to be an armed rebellion, then the matter should be taken seriously.

The judge, however, was reluctant to act. Newly married and barely a year into his appointment, he was understandably cautious of overreacting and whatever anxieties were racing through his mind remained concealed behind a mask of cold indifference. The new Viceroy, after all, had only just arrived and, from what he had just been told, there did not appear to be any immediate threat to the colony. The leaders of the Portuguese community were safely under lock and key. Who else was there to fear? A few Indians? Everything could wait, he insisted, until the new administration was in place. In the meantime they should try to retain the Irishman's confidence.

The following night, a mysterious Carmelite arrived at the Carrillo household looking for Sebastián. He brought a warning from a mutual friend in Puebla (most probably Don Jacinto Soria Naharro). Rumours were circulating quite openly, he advised, of his tutor's plans to raise himself to the throne of Mexico. If Sebastián did not immediately distance himself, he could find himself in serious trouble. He recommended that he evict the Irishman and endeavour to keep his distance.

Sebastián dithered: he was much to young and far too attached to William to bring himself to act. His conversation with the Carmelite, however, was overheard by one of his slaves, who promptly reported the details to someone who would—Don Francisco Gómez de Sandoval.

The propaganda that William had asked Ignacio to spread on his behalf had obviously spread far beyond the mining villages of Taxco. And if it had reached the Carmelites, then it would soon reach the ears of Palafox, who had travelled south to meet the new Viceroy. There was also every chance that Sebastián had already told William what the Carmelite had said, in which case the Irishman would be aware that he was running out of time. The implications were obvious. If William was to be stopped, something had to be done now.

On Saturday morning Gómez sought out Méndez and told him what the slave had overheard, prompting Méndez to return immediately to Gómez de Mora. But the judge was still reluctant to accept that the threat was either actual or immediate. He did, nevertheless, propose a compromise of sorts.

The use of shamanic inebriants had been outlawed by the Inquisition since June of 1620, when their use was declared to be 'a superstitious action condemned as contrary to the purity and sincerity of our Holy Catholic Faith'. If he wished to, the judge suggested as though it were a matter of little real importance, Méndez could take the matter of the peyote to the Inquisition. That should be enough to take the Irishman out of circulation for a while.

Méndez returned to his apartment to consider his next move. The matter could probably have waited a few days, but he was exhausted, vexed and frustrated. He wanted something done, and done immediately. Approaching the Holy Office, however, was a dangerous and drastic measure—one could never know for certain the direction such audiences might take—and up to now he had considered William a friend. It was a long and difficult night, but daylight brought clarity to his deliberations.

In the early morning of 26 October, Méndez left his apartment having convinced himself that the judge's advice had left him with no choice. Accompanied by Don Francisco Gómez de Sandoval, behind whose name he felt better protected, he headed straight for the headquarters of the Holy Office. Urgent in their demeanour, the pair demanded an immediate audience and after a brief wait they were taken to meet the Chief Inquisitor, Don Domingo Vélez de Asaz y Argos, and his corpulent sidekick, Don Francisco de Estrada y Escobedo—an inseparable brace of sybarites with a compulsive predilection for lining their pockets through bribery, theft and extortion. With a vested interest in the status quo that owed little to their devotion to either Church or Crown, Méndez could not have found a more sympathetic audience.

Certain factions within the capital, Méndez explained, were planning to depose the new Viceroy, and they were being led by the Irishman, Don Guillén Lombardo de Guzmán—a dangerous man who was nurturing ambitions of coronation.

Over the course of the next hour or so the Inquisitors heard of letters that William had sent to the Pope and to the Kings of France and Portugal. They heard of his claim to be the bastard half-brother of the King and of his intention to liberate the native and mixed-blood races in return for their military support. They also heard how Méndez had tried to convince the secular authorities to act, but without success, and how he had been advised to take the matter of the peyote and the Indian's 'conversation with the Devil' to the Inquisition.

Despite the fact that it was a Sunday—a holy day of rest—a tribunal of the Holy Office was convened during which William was accused of having committed sins against the faith, having had recourse to prohibited substances, having indulged in judicial astrology and having used 'remedies for the curing of superstitious illnesses which necessitated an implicit or explicit pact with the Devil'. Finally, and somewhat surprisingly given that it was essentially a civil matter, he was charged with 'conspiring against the King'.

Later that night, at about 10.30 p.m., a small posse of constables and familiars under the command of Captain Tomás de Soasnavar y Aguirre, the Chief Constable of the Holy Office, headed for the *Casa de los Condes de Carrion*. William was not at home but after a short wait they saw him arrive. He was armed. Soasnavar ordered his constables to wait a while longer. There was no need for anyone to get hurt. They would take him when he was asleep or unarmed: no gentleman, after all, wore his weapons about the house.

A short while later, as William left his room to get something to eat, they stormed the parlour and seized him, rousing the entire household in the process. There being little to be gained from a struggle (he'd left his weapons in his room), he surrendered peaceably. Rummaging in a wooden box that lay atop the Irishman's disorderly desk, they discovered several instruction manuals and maps that William had compiled on military tactics and fortification, and letters from such luminaries as the President of the Council of the Indies, the Cardinal Infante, the Count-Duke and Countess of Olivares, and the Secretary of State for War. There was also a letter from the King authorising William to recruit troops in Ireland, some pieces of romantic poetry and an astrological chart William had compiled for Sebastián. None of these, however, constituted evidence of treason and they next attempted to open a locked bureau.

William protested. Within that bureau, he shouted, were letters of a secret and sensitive nature. They should not, under any circumstances, be opened in public (inside were copies of letters that he had sent, or had been intending to send to the kings of France and Portugal, and copies of the letters he had written both in denunciation and in defence of the Marquis of Villena). Soasnavar nodded his assent and the entire bureau was carried unopened to one of the waiting carriages. The searchers did, however, open a small wooden Michoacán casket they found lying on top. Inside they found a forged patent naming William as a *Familiar* of the Inquisition—an unsuccessful reminder of his youthful naïveté. They also found a poem, written, allegedly, by the court dramatist, Don Pedro Calderón de la Barca y Henao, and entitled:

> A notice concerning the portrait of the prodigious youth, Don Guillén Lombardo de Guzmán of His Majesty's council, of His Highness' chamber, Field Master, and pupil of His Excellency the Count-Duke, which hangs in the palace of the Buen Retiro first amongst the portraits of the other noted gentlemen of our times.

These eight stanzas of six verses waxed lyrical about William's descent from three European royal families; his fluency in fourteen languages; his military prowess; his mastery of all the sciences; and the fact that both Felipe IV and Urban VIII had decreed that his portrait should forever grace the walls of the Escorial, the Vatican and the palace of the Buen Retiro. But could Calderón—a man generally considered to have been one of the greatest dramatists of the Spanish 'Golden Age'—really have been the author? Was it written, perhaps, tongue very much in cheek? Or perhaps many years earlier and added to by William to take account of more recent events?

Implausible as it may seem, it is not beyond the bounds of possibility. Calderón moved in much the same circles as William, had also been educated at the Colegio Imperial, and was a fellow veteran of the Army of Flanders. He had even fought at the Siege of Fuenterrabía. Most authorities, however, doubt that the poem could be the work of Calderón and it has been attributed by at least one to William himself; written, most likely, as a part of the self-serving propaganda that Ignacio was supposed to spread around Taxco.

By now a crowd had gathered and Soasnavar was anxious to avoid a scene. He ordered the last of the loose papers to be bundled into an old chocolate box and ushered everyone outside. No further search of the apartment was undertaken—not even of Sebastián's room—and to the chirruping of crickets and chattering of local gossips, William was bundled into a closed carriage and taken swiftly away.

As the crowd began to disperse Méndez approached Sebastián with an air of feigned innocence.

'Why,' he asked, 'had William been arrested?'

'I don't know,' Sebastián answered, 'but they say he wants to make himself King.'

Immediately following his arrest, William was brought to the *Casa de Picazo,* a private house on the Calle de la Encarnación that had been leased to the Inquisition and modified to serve as a prison—the Palace of the Inquisition having yet to be repaired following the floods of 1629. Here he was formally handed over to Don Pedro Jiménez de Cervera, the governor of the secret prisons of the Inquisition.

After a thorough body search he was tossed into a simple cell with whitewashed walls and two beds on a raised wooden dais. His only source of natural light, a small and solitary window that overlooked a small courtyard, was covered with a metal grille and wooden bars. He was given a small stove and a supply of coal to heat water and keep himself warm. At night, he was told, he would be given a candle and a chamber pot.

As was customary in the prisons of the Inquisition, he was warned not to communicate with the other prisoners, or anyone else for that matter. He was to consider himself in solitary confinement and was to maintain a 'modest and dignified silence'. He would be given some paper to enable him to prepare his defence, but the sheets would be numbered to ensure that messages were not passed to other prisoners or friends on the outside. If he behaved himself, he would be allowed a 'salary' of two reals per day.

Acts of treason, strictly speaking, were not the responsibility of the Holy Office. In Spanish society, however, Church and Crown were intrinsically linked—each affording legitimacy to, and requiring the obedience of the other. William's concept of popular sovereignty, therefore, not only threatened the Crown but the privileges, immunities, monopolies and tithes traditionally afforded by it to the Church. Indeed so abhorrent were such notions to the Holy Office that many years later it would place the Declaration of Independence and the Constitution of the United States on the Index of Forbidden Tracts.

In the eyes of the Inquisition, a conspiracy against the King was a conspiracy against the Church. Acts of insurgency, therefore, were nearly always denounced as heresy and the insurgents themselves as Protestants (a practice that would continue well into the nineteenth century). On this particular occasion, however, the Inquisitors were so unsure of their ground that they approached Palafox, in his secular role of Visitor General, to ask if he would take charge of the investigation.

He declined. He was, he claimed, personally acquainted with the Irish cardinal, Luke Wadding (to whom William had claimed to be related), and could not, therefore, be considered impartial. But why such reluctance? Why encourage the Inquisition to take charge of a matter that was so obviously beyond their expertise and jurisdiction? Surely the obvious path was to hand William over to the secular arm in order to face the greater charges?

While chatting to Méndez, it is true, William had claimed to have had the tacit support of some 400 men and, if the rumours concerning the social standing of his fellow-conspirators were true, a public trial might just have triggered the very revolt that his arrest was designed to prevent. But both Palafox and the Inquisition seemed more afraid of the Irishman's (or should that be Francisco de Suárez') ideology than his ability to lead a coup.

In the wake of recent political events and the continuing drought and epidemics, the colony had become a tinderbox of frustration and resentment. If allowed to distribute the type of pamphlets that Méndez had been shown, the Irishman could ignite no end of trouble. Even if he failed to catch the imagination of the resentful within the military, there was always the chance that the notion of racial equality and land rights would lend an air of legality and moral respectability to the explosive desires of the lower orders to right old wrongs. They would be faced then, not just with a change of regime, but perhaps the collapse of colonial society itself. At such times Church and State had to stand or fall together.

From the start of his imprisonment, the Holy Office appeared far more afraid of what William might say than what he might actually succeed in doing. Rebellions could always be put down: ideas were much harder to contain. Such was the distrust of sophistication and fear of intellectuals that the Irishman's arrest provoked, that it was followed soon after by a clamp down on the capital's scientific *tertulías* (traditionally informal gatherings that took their name from the Socratic discussion groups of Tertullian), which the Holy Office now viewed as centres of subversion.

The situation was further complicated by William's earlier collaboration with Palafox which, if it were to become public knowledge, could easily be construed as conspiracy and used by supporters of the deposed Viceroy to justify a coup of their own. Whatever His Excellency's motives for refusing to become involved were, they went a lot deeper than the possible embarrassment of an Irish Cardinal on the far side of the Atlantic.

$\mathcal{T}$HREE DAYS AFTER his arrest William was bound and gagged, bundled into a closed carriage, and driven to the Palace of the Inquisition (these days the Museum of Medicine). Here he was taken to a room shrouded with crimson curtains and heavy velvet drapes, and surrounded by statues of Saint Dominic and other sundry saints. Having genuflected and kissed the rings of Their Worship Inquisitors, Domingo Vélez de Asaz y Argos and Francisco de Estrada y Escobedo, he was invited to tell the truth, to keep secret everything he would see or learn, to declare his genealogy and name all others with whom he had communicated while in error.

Confident of an acquittal, he co-operated. Taking an oath upon the Holy Gospels, upon which he was made to place his right hand, he began his declaration. He was, he claimed, a 27-year-old nobleman from the Irish county of Wexford whose Catholic ancestry had been unbroken for almost 1,200 years. He had been baptised in the Parish of Saint Peter in Wexford Town, where he had also received the sacrament of confirmation from the Bishop of Ossory, David Rothe. He could not remember the names of his godparents, but he could remember his prayers and, having blessed himself, he began: *Pater noster, qui es in caelis, sanctificetur nomen tuum . . .*

Having reeled off his Pater Noster, Ave Maria, Salve Regina and Credo, he admitted that the last time he had received the sacraments had been on 2 August when he had gone to the Monastery of Saint Francis to receive the Portiuncula Indulgence. There he had attended Mass and confessed his sins to Father Hernando Pacheco. He was also, he claimed, the possessor of two Bulls of the Holy Crusade (a papal indulgence sold to raise funds for the Catholic Church). They could be found amongst the papers that had been confiscated during his arrest.

In declaring his genealogy he claimed his father to have been one *Don*

Richardo Lombardo, a 'Baron of Enniscorthy' who had led the armada of Don Juan del Águila into Kinsale and who had been gathered to God some ten years previously. His mother, who died in Wexford many years before his father, had been one *Doña Aldonsa de Guzmán alias Soton* (the presence of '*Guzmán*' in his mother's name was most likely an error by the scribe who, not knowing how William came to acquire the name of his benefactor, had assumed Gúzman to be his mother's maiden name). His brothers and sisters, he continued, were *Don Juan Lombardo, Don Heraldo Lombardo, Fray Juan Lombardo de la Orden de San Francisco,* and *Doña Cataliña Lombardo.*

His brother John (*Fray Juan Lombardo*), would later verify much of the above, with the exception of the first *Don Juan Lombardo,* whom he never mentioned at all, but whom William described as a 'Count of Ross' (New Ross?). At a later stage William would claim that his father had sired no fewer than seven 'legitimate sons' and that a 'brother' by the name of John had married a certain 'Isobel', the daughter of one Thomas Butler. It was this 'John', he claimed, who had inherited the Sutton lands of his mother's dower. Given the gap in ages between his parents, and the fact that Friar John would later name William and Gerald as his only brothers, it is perhaps not unreasonable to assume that this 'brother' was the sole surviving son of a previous marriage. The matter, however, is far from clear.

His paternal grandfather, William continued, was 'the great Patrick Lamport', 'defender of the Catholic faith at New Ross' and a 'defender of the province of Leinster' who had sustained 'at his own expense, and over a period of fifteen years, some 14,000 men and an armada by sea'. Patrick was assassinated sometime between 1616 and 1618 by paid agents of the English Crown.

The many services to the Spanish Crown of his maternal uncles, Clement Sutton (whom he described as a 'prince of the sea', possibly because this was the same Clement Sutton who had sailed with Sir John Crosby on the privateering ship *The Tiger*) and Edward Sutton, could also be found in the archives in Madrid; as indeed could the services of Edward's wife, Catherine Lamport.

Other sketchy details of his family were offered, but his claim to be a half-brother of the King was never repeated. He did, however, persist with his claim to be related, 'by another line', to Hugh O'Donnell (the Earl of Tyrconnell) and to have two aunts who had received the habit in the Calatrava Convent in Madrid. One, he claimed, was now an abbess called *Doña María de Jesús* and the other, whose name he could not recall, he believed to be a prioress. Then, in what looked suspiciously like an attempt to keep Ana and Teresa from becoming embroiled in the Inquisitorial process, he denied that he had either a wife or children.

In laying out the circumstances that had brought him to Mexico he claimed to have fled London following his composition of 'a book entitled *Defensio Fidei contra Carolum Anglie Regem*', a translation of which lay in the royal library at San Lorenzo and 'for which cause I left the [English] court with my tutor in order to pass into the protection of his Majesty'.

On his way to Spain, he continued, he had been captured by pirates in a raid off the French port of St. Malo. After only twenty days as a prisoner, the pirates had made him their 'general'; a position he held for almost three years. During this time his fleet met with:

> . . . the Armada of the French King at La Rochelle and when its general, the 'Principe de Rucoy', recognised my colours and my childhood reputation and personal Catholicism, without daring to engage in battle sent me an ambassador from the King, and asked for my aid against the rebellious heretics of that city . . . [and] when the said fleet arrived in view of La Rochelle, I engaged it in a tough battle in passing and, before the French fleet could weigh anchor, it [the English fleet] found five of its galleons sinking and, observing the power of the arriving French turned and fled. Such were the screams and weeping of the besieged inhabitants that they could be heard at sea.

He had also, he claimed, been a member of the retinue of the Cardinal Infante and had been responsible for the tactical improvisations that had led to the Spanish victory at Nördlingen, where he had 'commanded the troops with enthusiasm and skill, using a cavalry formation different to which the engineers were accustomed'. 'With His Highness surrounded by 20,000 French in Louvain,' he boasted, 'I attacked suddenly at night with 1000 Irish Catholics under my command and made them lift the siege and abandon their baggage, munitions and artillery'.

The Inquisitors were aghast, and accepted his testimony *cum granum salis*. Were they really be expected to believe all this? Was it really credible that hardened pirates would hand control of their ship to a thirteen-year-old or that an inexperienced teenager would be allowed to suggest battle tactics to the brother of the King? The genealogical part of his testimony, of course, was easily verifiable, but the rest of it seemed the stuff of legend, or picaresque fiction: the type of tale that leaves a man feeling as though his life has been only half-lived.

But fiction or at the very least gross exaggeration was exactly what much of William's testimony was; especially those areas he knew the Inquisitors would find next to impossible to verify. His claim to have actually commanded the pirate fleet in which he had served was unlikely in the extreme, as indeed was the claim that his grandfather had commanded an armada and 14,000 men. It is not beyond the realms of possibility that his grandfather had *financed* the activities of pirates, but a fleet of 14,000 men would almost certainly have brought his name to the attention of historians before now. As for the nighttime attack of 1000 Irish Catholics, this was possibly an error by the scribe who confused William's descriptions of the battle of Nördlingen with those of the Siege of Fuenterrabía, but in neither case was William actually in command.

At a later stage the matter of his genealogy would also be complicated by the testimony of his older brother, Friar John, who would name their paternal grandparents, not as Patrick Lamport and Helen Sutton, but as Nicholas Lamport and Catherine Synnot. He would also say that 'he had no other siblings' than William, Gerald and Catherine. For the time being, however, William's version was more or less accepted.

Over the next six days, William was questioned further on the papers recovered from his room, but his defence never varied. They were forgeries, he freely admitted that (he was hardly going to admit that they were genuine), but their purpose, he claimed, had been to help ingratiate himself with those Portuguese and Jews he believed to be plotting against the Crown. The papers, in any case, had been found in an unlocked box. No attempt had been made to conceal them. Had they been intended for the purposes of treason, then surely he would have hidden them? At every twist and turn, he insisted, his aim had been to uncover treason, not to initiate it. There were official papers in Madrid, he claimed, which could verify all of this, and much else besides.

During further questioning, in an attempt to copper-fasten his claims to a noble and Catholic pedigree, he claimed kinship with an Irish cardinal by the name of Luke Wadding. It sent the Inquisitors scurrying back to Palafox for advice. It was, after all, Palafox's alleged friendship with Wadding—the representative of the Irish hierarchy in the Roman Curia and a candidate, in 1620, for the papacy—that had been his excuse, three years earlier, for refusing to take charge of the investigation and ceding control of William's case to the Inquisition. But once again Palafox declined to intervene. All he would say on the subject was that it was vital that *everything* be kept secret. It was only a matter of time, therefore, before they found someone willing to refute the kinship.

Fray Miguel de Santa María (alias Michael Lombard of Waterford) admitted to having an intense dislike of both William and John Lamport—an admission that under the Inquisition's own rules of evidence should have barred him from testifying. Their claims to be cousins of the famous Irish theologian Peter Lombard particularly vexed him. They were not, he vehemently asserted, of noble birth; nor were they relatives of Wadding. They were merely the sons of a 'poor fisherman of humble lineage'. William in particular, he continued, was a lunatic whose mind had been deranged by an excess of mathematics and astrology. He was also 'a poet and in love, weaknesses that further contributed to his mental infirmity'.

The Inquisitors would later be forced to retract the claim that William was the son of 'a poor fisherman' and admit that his father had in fact been '*de oficio piloto* . . . a pilot by trade', a position that would have made him the third ranking officer aboard ship, usually with his own cabin and page; an educated man, in fact, and by the norms of the day as much a scientist as he was a sailor.

On 3 November, with Palafox and the new Viceroy yet to reach the capital, the Inquisitors, a number of whom were still suspicious of Palafox and his campaign of civil and religious reform, decided to wait no longer. Seeking advice on how they should proceed, they wrote

directly to the *Consejo de la Suprema y General Inquisición* in Madrid—
the central council that governed the operation of all the various Inquisitions throughout the Spanish Empire.

The Mexican Inquisitors allowed that William's crimes were more against the King than the faith. They were at pains, however, to highlight the difficulties that might arise should the secular arm be seen to interfere in the affairs of the Holy Office. Unable or unwilling to resolve the matter amongst themselves, the *Suprema* referred it to the Council of the Indies in the expectation, perhaps, that the King would solve it for them.

Salvatierra and Palafox, in the meantime, entered the capital to the usual formalities and festivities of welcome on 23 November, at which point Palafox finally relinquished the post of Viceroy. The uprising that William had hoped for never materialised and an uneasy calm was restored.

The Inquisitors, however, now found themselves plunged into an unexpected and unwanted quandary. William's arrest had not only embarrassed one of the most prominent families in New Spain, but also the Franciscans and the Visitor General. A protracted dispute over jurisdiction, furthermore, could expose the Holy Office to a secular investigation and, because of the vast fortunes they were currently amassing from their campaign against the crypto-Jewish community, that was the last thing they wanted. Unsure about what to do next, they decided to stall and let their superiors in Madrid sort out the mess.

(34)

THE LANDSCAPE OF the prison day was bordered on one side with morning ablutions, slopping out and breakfast, and on the other with the arrival of the candles, mosquitoes and rats. Day after day, week after week, the routine was so solitary and automatic that time soon lost all meaning and life gradually took on the dismal colours of the cells. Outside in the streets the scratching of brooms, the smell of cooking, the occasional muffled conversation or hearty laugh, and the rumble of passing wagons and *recuas* tantalised with echoes of normal life.

Remembering what one was missing, however, just made matters worse. It was enough of a battle to stay sane in what was effectively solitary confinement, without needless rumination on what might have been. There were only so many times that a man could relive his past, make plans for the future or fantasise about escape, before he began to dislike himself. If he was ever to come to terms with the dramatic change in his circumstances, a prisoner had to learn to detach himself from his past and concentrate his resistance on the here and now. He could do nothing to alter his circumstances: he could only hope to survive them. Tomorrow; next week; next month; next year; someday he would be free: but each day he would have to fight for the next.

As the months dragged on, the days would differ only in the places to which the imagination would wander. Deprived of any means of anchoring itself in the present, it would scurry off on interminable and directionless rambles. At such times nothing made sense: everything became jumbled. But it was generally preferable to reality, the intrusion of which was often impossible to avoid.

One morning the silence was shattered by the impassioned pleas of a woman known throughout the prison as 'The Cripple'. Doña Rafaela Xuárez begged anyone who could hear her to pray for her daughter, Blanca. Pregnant when she was imprisoned, Blanca's labour had proved difficult. Despite the presence of a midwife and a family slave, the child had survived for just three hours and the exhausted mother had fallen prey to an infection, causing her temperature to rise violently and her leg to swell up like a leather wine bag. So worried were the guards that a priest was sent for and the last rites were given. But in the end, the tormented supplications of Doña Rafaela were answered, and Blanca eventually pulled through.

Up until that moment William had kept a low profile and had more or less co-operated with the Inquisitors. He had tried not to get too caught up in what was going on around him and, like so many others, had attempted to consign traumatic events like these to the furthest recesses of his mind. He had, after all, no need to engage with them. His crimes were of a civil rather than a religious nature and with connections such as his he felt confident that he would not remain behind bars for long.

But every one of his fellow prisoners, having peered anxiously into the yawning chasm that was opening between the lives they had planned for themselves and what now lay before them, had constructed similar denials. They, too, believed that their imprisonment would be short-lived. The 'Jews' could even cite the precedent of 1635.

And yet William's predicament *was* different. He had not been accused of Judaism; nor was there any precedent for his situation. In convincing himself that he was in some way a special case, he had shielded himself from the suffering of his fellow prisoners. But it couldn't last. In such confined spaces he could escape neither their despair nor his compassion. Their suffering slowly became his suffering. It no longer mattered that they were Jews.

(35)

On 12 May 1643, in a sudden and unusual breach of protocol, the King decided to intervene in William's process. Bypassing the *Suprema*, he wrote directly to the Mexican Inquisitors by way of the Viceroy ordering them to 'abbreviate, finish and close' the case against the Irishman—which 'did not concern that tribunal [of the Inquisition]'—and to hand him over, along with all the papers connected with his case, to Don Andrés Gómez de Mora—a man rapidly becoming the most forceful of the *Audiencia* judges. Gómez, in turn, was ordered to return William immediately to Spain.

Four days after the Mexican Inquisitors had received this letter, which for some reason was not until 15 October of the same year, Gómez arrived at the headquarters of the Holy Office in Mexico City carrying a royal decree of his own and demanding to be provided with a list of the charges that had been preferred against the Irishman. His Majesty, it read, had ordered him to familiarise himself with the Irishman's process and to return him to Spain the moment he had been punished for his crimes against the faith.

The Holy Office, none too pleased with the interference, refused to meet with the judge and scribbled their response on the back of his letter: they would release only those papers that were not directly relevant to the inquisitorial process, and the Irishman *only* when specifically ordered to do so by the *Suprema* in Madrid. The same reply was sent to the Viceroy, informing him also that:

> in the matter of Don Guillén Lombardo de Guzmán, concerning whose trial we have on other occassions kept Your Highness informed, and against whom have arisen more proofs of his falsehoods and sorcery, and whom we now say is but the son of a poor Irish fisherman . . . we will hand over those papers that do not touch upon this Tribunal . . .

This was an astonishing state of affairs. The Inquisition was effectively attempting to place its authority above that of the King. William, it seemed, had become more than just their prisoner; he had become a symbol of their independence!

In the meantime, as was normal in cases of arrest by the Holy Office, William's problems began to take on a dynamic of their own—the fear of guilt by association being enough to convince many witnesses to tell the Inquisition exactly what it wanted to hear.

One witness who had sailed with William from Cádiz claimed that, while in the Port of Santa María, William had strutted about the place putting on airs and claiming such influence in Madrid that he had written letters of recommendation to all manner of nobility and royal secretaries on behalf of a man he had befriended in return for a small sum. The witness also claimed that on his arrival in Cádiz the Irishman did not even have a second change of clothes to his name and that when the laundress came to collect his washing he had to remain in bed for want of anything else to wear.

William denied these charges emphatically. The witness was 'a deceiving scoundrel and sacrilegious liar'. He had not been short of clothing in Cádiz, nor had he been short of money: in fact he had even advanced a small sum to the Chief Constable of the palace, who had also agreed to hang some clothes in his wardrobe for him, his sea-chest being full to bursting. The testimony of this witness, however, may have contained a grain of truth. With the long delay in Cádiz, and William not knowing from one day to the next when the fleet might be departing, he may simply have been too lazy to unpack.

An Irish priest with whom William had travelled from Cádiz alleged that William had left 'his little woman and tiny daughter' in total poverty and had travelled to the Indies 'stowed away with the cooks and lowest of servants'. Another witness alleged that every time he met William he 'found him absorbed in new fancies', but that he never paid any heed to the man as he judged him to be mad.

Testimony also continued to be harvested, of William's eccentric and unpredictable behaviour in Mexico. Juan de la Vayen described him as inconsistent 'in his words and his deeds' and remembered him speaking of an Indian who had promised to reveal to him a secret that would enable him to make any woman, or even the Viceroy himself for that matter, fall under his spell.

William later denied the implications of sorcery. There was no magic potion. The secret to wooing women and Viceroys alike, he protested, was money!

Don Francisco Solís y Corral also spoke of magic spells, and of a particular night when William, armed with harquebus, pistol, and sword, arrived at his apartment in such a fury that he repeatedly stabbed at the wall with his dagger and refused the offer of a meal saying that 'a man of his station could not dine outside of his home'. Solís believed him to have been involved in a duel.

William refused to accept that any such incident had taken place. Not one person in New Spain, he protested, had ever seen him carry a harquebus, and he was widely known to be a staunch opponent of duelling.

Asked about the note of condolences he had sent to William following the nomination of the Count of Salvatierra, Solís claimed it to have been written more in irony than sympathy. He also claimed that although he had felt that William's claim that his two letters to the King concerning Villena had been inspired in their turn by the Devil and the Holy Spirit had bordered on heresy, he had not denounced him to the Holy Office because it was obvious that William was not in his right mind. He did, however, admit that William had offered him a position in his administration—an admission that should have raised some suspicion of conspiracy, not to mention a secular investigation of the behaviour of those members of the military who had appeared willing to befriend, and perhaps even to explore the possibility of a coup with the Irishman.

But the Inquisitors did not pursue the matter; nor did they ever ask Solís why he had continued to socialise with William in the wake of so much 'evidence' of madness. Despite all evidence to the contrary, the Inquisitors continued to ignore his pathology and proceeded to judge him as sane. Out of their depth in such matters they stuck to what they knew best—heresy. The search for a wider conspiracy, therefore, never took place; perhaps because they truly believed it had never existed; perhaps because they considered William's arrest sufficient to prevent the spread of his radical ideology; perhaps it was simply payback time for the criticism he had attempted to send to the King. But they never sought, and William would never volunteer, the names of any accomplices.

Sebastián Carrillo was as adamant as he was contrite. He had always been impressed by the intelligence of his Latin tutor, 'Field Master General Don Guillén de Lombardo', but he had also observed in him a certain 'conceit and haughtiness' not to mention the occasional 'flash of madness'. His tutor was often immersed in papers of one sort or another which he 'pretended' to be important correspondence from Madrid, but which he had never been allowed to read. He also recalled William claiming to be the bastard son of Felipe III and the Countess of Ross, and more recently an occasion when William had told him of a number of ways in which a man could make himself invisible.

William did not deny discussing sorcery with Sebastián. He had, he said, merely been repeating some of the curiosities he had heard tell of since his arrival in the Indies. More of a dilettante than a scholar in these matters, he did not believe in such superstitions; he merely found them interesting.

Sebastián's testimony, however, was especially damaging in that it gave the Inquisition concrete evidence of heresy. But with the possible exception of his younger brother, nobody knew anything of this conversation. So why be so forthcoming?

Perhaps it had something to do with an astrological chart found amongst William's papers. Drawn for Sebastián at his own request, it bore witness to the close bond that existed between them. If the Inquisitors were to believe that he had no knowledge of the seditious papers found in William's room, then he needed to provide evidence of his good faith. His uncle, Don Gonzalo de Carrillo, was a *Licenciado* (a type of lawyer) of the Inquisition and Sebastián was not short of advice. At seventeen years of age he had his whole life before him. Now was not the time to be foolish. The advice was well taken. Sebastián survived the ordeal without a stain on his character—allowing him, in the years to come, to rise to the powerful position of Chief Assayer and Smelter of the Mexican mint.

Don Francisco Gómez de Sandoval remembered William claiming to be in regular correspondence with the King by means of a secret code, the cipher to which was known only to himself and the Count-Duke of

Olivares. When the blind Indian, Ignacio Pérez, was eventually found, he testified that he had encountered no-one, heard nothing and felt nothing on the night he took the peyote, other than the mother and father of all headaches. He also claimed to have taken the herb only out of fear of what William might have done to him had he refused. He had never, he swore, spoken of rebellion with anyone else. Everything he had told the Irishman to the contrary had been to humour him.

But Pérez, it must be remembered, was a member of the Aztec nobility and far from the innocent dupe he was claiming to be. The Inquisition, in fact, already knew from a conversation that had been overheard between Sebastián and the mysterious Carmelite from Puebla, that someone had been spreading propaganda in William's favour in the towns and villages outside the capital. Ignacio, nevertheless, was never charged. Considered legal minors and neophytes in the Christian religion, the native races lay outside of the jurisdiction of the Inquisition.

Other witnesses testified to William's belief in clairvoyance, his intention to commit bigamy, and the fact that he had reportedly left his wife and daughter in poverty or placed them in the care of a convent. Evidence was even presented that while a student at Alcalá and Salamanca he had become mentally ill—a claim he vehemently denied. He had never, he protested, attended either of these colleges. The only colleges he *had* attended, he insisted, were those at Santiago de Compostela and San Lorenzo de el Escorial. As for the allegations of having practised judicial astrology, he freely admitted to these, having made such charts in consultation with the tailor, Saboyano.

Many of the new charges against the Irishman were so ludicrous that it must have been obvious to the authorities in Madrid that there was much more to all this than met the eye; but there was no-one brave enough or bothered enough to challenge the Inquisition and they had found a bottomless well of 'witnesses' amongst the supporters of the deposed Viceroy and the enemies of Palafox. The general tenor of these testimonies was that William was not just self-deluding, but mad.

It is perhaps significant, however, that not a single witness to his alleged 'heresies' were ever asked why they had not reported them to the Holy Office earlier, as they were required to do by law. It is perhaps also significant that at least one Inquisitor (Estrada y Escobedo) is known to have been prone to intercepting witnesses and coaching them in their testimonies. As for those who were claiming William to be mad, they were the very same people who had recently accepted invitations to his home, had socialised with him in public, had sought all manner of favours and advice from him, and had sympathised with him when his promised title and promotion failed to materialise. One had even allowed him to participate in drafting a defence of the Marquis of Villena, and another had offered him shelter in his apartment when he turned up at his door in the middle of the night, allegedly armed to the teeth!

The Inquisitors, for some unknown reason, were strangely lax in their investigations and all manner of contradictions were left unchallenged. They were apparently willing to accept the allegations of madness at face value, but what they were not prepared to do was to allow him be examined by a physician (escape from the asylum of San Hipólito being far from inconceivable). Their greatest concern right now was not the Irishman's health, but his silence.

(36)

*W*HILE THE INQUISITION jousted with the King over whose authority was the greater, Palafox began to find himself embroiled in yet another dispute—this time with the Jesuits. The cause was the thorny subject of tithes.

As a religious order, the Jesuits were claiming 'benefit of clergy' and refusing to pay their fair share of diocesan taxes. So extensive, in fact, had their land grabbing become, that in many dioceses the amount of land on which tithes were actually payable had been reduced to the point where it threatened the salaries of the secular priests (who were paid directly from diocesan funds). Palafox was having none of it. The Jesuits' refusal to pay, he protested, was undermining his Episcopal authority.

And then there was the *repartimiento* (forced Indian labour). The local *corregidores* had the power to raise a labour force from amongst the Indians to carry out necessary 'public works'—a power that was frequently abused in order to provide slave labour for the haciendas, many of which were run by the religious orders. When Palafox's secular priests began to block the passage of Indians to the friaries, the dispute rapidly escalated into one involving the whole of the body politic. Each side had its supporters, but for the moment the pendulum was swinging in favour of the anti-Palafox faction.

The Viceroy now joined the Jesuits in harassing Palafox and, with the help of the Inquisition (who had come out in favour of the Jesuits), attempts were made to convict him of having conspired to overthrow Villena. Preoccupied almost exclusively with this new campaign, the Inquisition more or less forgot about William. His hopes of an early release were dashed, and worse was soon to follow.

Back in Spain Olivares' unpopular and disastrous policies had brought about such a steady exodus from court that, on Christmas Day 1642, just a single grandee took his place in the royal chapel. It was a snub that even the weak-willed Felipe could no longer ignore and, on 17 January, he gave Olivares leave to retire and banished him to the country.

With the Count-Duke gone, there was an immediate backlash against his dreaded *criados*. Most were persecuted, some even imprisoned. His second-in-command, Don Jerónimo de Villanueva, was arrested by the Inquisition and would spend the remainder of his life struggling to defend himself. With the possible exception of the King himself, William no longer had any friends at court. He was entirely on his own.

UNDER THE INQUISITION'S rules of secrecy, a prisoner was obliged at all times to maintain a 'dignified and modest silence'. Sheer force of numbers, however, made the rule difficult to enforce. Scribes were assigned to the dungeons to eavesdrop, prisoners were offered favours in return for informing on others, and spies were placed in the cells. Even if he knew to whom he was speaking, a prisoner could never be sure of who might be listening.

At a time when many cells were filled to overcrowding and even the torture chambers had to be occasionally emptied of their instruments and pressed into use as emergency accommodation, William continued to be held in solitary confinement. But he was far from silent. The very thought that in the other cells were other human beings, suffering as he was but unable to reach out to each other, outraged him. Despite the risks, he set out, not so much to break the rule of silence, as break through it.

Determined that they should at least *try* to empower themselves, he sought to awaken some small spark of resistance in his fellow prisoners by watching from his window until he saw the warden leave for the night, and then exhorting his fellow prisoners to converse. The Inquisitors, however, were soon wise to his antics, and shortly afterwards the unmistakable scratching of goose quills announced that scribes were now being assigned to the gaol at night.

For William there had to be at least one contest in which *he* was in control, in which *he* set the rules, and which *he* was capable of winning, and so he devised a primitive form of Morse code (one blow for A, two blows for B etc). The scribes might hear it, they might even decipher it, but it would be almost impossible to tell who was tapping without leaving their posts and alerting the sender by their movement.

One by one, slowly at first, the other prisoners began to grasp what

William was attempting and soon almost all were using the code. To protect their identities, they adopted aliases. Doña Francisca Texoso became 'Celia' and 'Malintzi', Francisco Botello became 'The Pestle' and 'The Innkeeper', and Tomas Treviño de Sobremonte became 'The Mountain Man' and 'The Congolese'. Collectively the Inquisitors became 'Hawks' or 'Pharaohs', and the Negro slaves that worked in the prison, 'Crows'. William himself adopted the pseudonyms of 'Charcoal', 'The Astrologer', 'The Cockatrice' and 'Don Antonio de Castro'.

The code was mind-numbingly tedious, time-consuming and easily intercepted, but the need to communicate with other human beings was far greater and most, especially those held in solitary confinement, were willing to accept the risk. But though the take-up was feverish to begin with, the tapping gradually fell silent. Days, and then weeks, would pass when nothing newsworthy would happen and, as the prisoners struggled to find topics that were worthy of the effort, the code gradually fell into disuse.

In search of an alternative more amenable to small talk and ordinary social interaction, many now began to converse in Portuguese and other more obscure idioms that might better baffle the scribes. Merchants like Francisco Botello and Tomas Treviño de Sobremonte conversed in Nahuatl (the native tongue of the Aztecs), while Rafaela Enríquez and her daughters Ana and Blanca, having been reared in the company of Negro slaves, spoke in Bantu. For much the same reason the use of Balanta was also common.

Conversing in African languages, however, was not entirely without risk. A prisoner's slaves were generally confiscated along with the rest of his or her property and put to work in the dungeons. Being no less susceptible to bribes than the wardens, they were often the source of betrayals. There was no form of communication, therefore, that did not carry some degree of risk.

Conversations, nevertheless, continued to take place and privileges continued to be bought. Simón Váez Sevilla dined on linen table cloths and from a dinner service of fine china; Rafaela Enríquez slept on a red-ebony bed; Juana Enríquez paid a warden with cash, silk and a diamond ring for news of her son, and Inés Pereira sold her pearls to another in return for not revealing her conversation with Gaspar Váez Sevilla.

Valuables would also change hands in the pursuit of useful intelligence and the envy and wrath that this provoked made informers of former friends and drove others to a preoccupation with loyalty and treachery that led them to the brink of madness and beyond.

Under the rules of the Inquisition a prisoner was not entitled to know the names of his accusers. The names or testimonies of the witnesses who had condemned him, therefore, became invaluable tools in his defence. But as an entire community had been imprisoned, any number of whom were privy to secrets that could be traded for leniency or release, communication had become much more than an act of self-affirmation, it had literally become a matter of life and death.

When eventually charged with breaking the rules of silence, William protested that it had been the Jews who had taught the code to him. He had, he said, only communicated with them in order to expose their sins. He even testified against a number of them (Francisca and Inés Texoso), though his behaviour in this regard was hardly exceptional. So widespread and frequent were the rounds of condemnation and counter-condemnation that it was almost impossible to keep a secret. Someone, somewhere, would eventually break their silence and those whose lips had remained sealed would eventually be identified by the Inquisitors and punished for their reticence.

It was about this time that a letter to the King, that William had written prior to his arrest, was recovered by the Inquisition. Despite the fact that it was technically an act of high treason to do so, it was opened, read, and torn up in front of him. In this letter William had written of the criminal irregularities he had discovered in the arrests of suspected Jews and the rapacious theft of their belongings. The Inquisitors were livid. His 'libels', they warned him, were tantamount to a 'mortal sin'.

Shortly afterwards, William was denounced as a Jew by Doña Isabel de Silva. A warning shot, it seems, had been fired across his boughs.

As the investigation of the religious charges against William neared its completion, the Inquisitors found themselves facing the prospect of having to release him. Whether they still believed they had something to fear from him, or whether they needed him as leverage in their battle with Palafox, remains a mystery. Whatever the reason, and despite the King's orders to the contrary, they not only decided to hold on to him but even to confiscate the coded letters he was attempting to send to the King.

In an uncoded plea which accompanied a coded letter that he was attempting to send to the King, William appealed to Felipe to recognise his past service and that of his family and have him transported immediately back to Spain, as his 'personal loyalty and political employments concern nobody but Your Majesty'. If he had a case to answer for any crime against the faith, he wrote, he would gladly do so before the *Suprema* in Madrid, but it was of the utmost importance that the ciphered letter be deciphered and that he be taken back to Madrid. The countercipher to this letter, he advised, 'will be found in the Count-Duke's pugilar, [which was used] for his secret correspondence with me on Your Majesty's behalf'.

The Inquisitors did not forward either letter to Madrid. They did, however, relax the conditions of his imprisonment, and for the first time since his arrest he was allowed to share his cell. The arrival of Tomás Núñez de Peralta, and later of Francisco López de Fonseca, was a welcome development. But company brought its own problems.

Like every other human being faced with a sudden and tragic change in his or her circumstances, the initial reaction of many prisoners was to trivialise the seriousness of their predicament. There was nothing unusual in this: it was a natural defence mechanism that gave them time to adjust to the crisis and to rally their defences. In refusing to face reality, however, a prisoner was led ineluctably towards an inflated sense of his own importance and behaviour that, in more sober moments, would be a cause of severe embarrassment. Given his state of mind at the moment of his imprisonment, William's was always going to be a little bit beyond the ordinary.

One night at about 10 p.m., the distinctive crackle of harquebuses was heard in the alley outside the prison. Nuñez rushed to the window to see if he could ascertain what was happening.

'Two of the Inquisition guards,' he muttered.

'You should probably know,' said William, 'that an entire company of guards have been paid to watch these cells, purely on my account. They are afraid the armada I am expecting will yet arrive and, knowing that I have been imprisoned, will come to rescue me.' On another occasion he claimed to have been sent to Mexico to spy for the King of France, and on another that three kings had intervened in his case to explain away the presence of the papers found in his writing desk.

His account of his arrest, as told to a fellow prisoner, also had him quenching a candle to protect the modesty of an illustrious female 'guest' and vociferously demanding that she be left alone. No such lady, however, was mentioned in the extremely detailed account of the arrest made by the officials involved, nor was any such lady ever detained for questioning. She, too, was most probably a figment of William's imagination, and his chivalrous attempts to protect her little more than a story like all the others, designed to impress his cellmates and reinforce his pretensions to grandeur.

William's self-exaltation grated on his fellow prisoners and some were inclined to laugh at him. There were others, however, who had nurtured their own lies and self-deceptions and dared not gainsay him lest they be forced to recognise the same frailties in themselves. Like shipwrecked sailors they clung to what they could and more or less accepted the bargain that in sharing each other's company they must also share each other's suffering. Difficult as it may have been to do so, not to would be so much worse.

But it wasn't easy. The inevitable differences in temperament and class, not to mention the interminable boredom and a lack of privacy that extended to the most personal and solitary of physical reliefs, were wont to provoke even compatible cellmates to extremes of mutual aversion and violence. To reap the benefits of company, therefore, one needed to make an enormous investment in tolerance and compassion.

As a good Catholic, however, William had little tolerance for religious difference. He may not have believed, as many others of his generation still did, that the Jews were the murderers of the Divine Saviour; but as a student of theology and canon law he still looked upon other faiths and religions as heresy rather than differences of theological opinion. On a human level he could empathise with his fellow prisoners and share in their suffering, but on a theological level he found it difficult, at first, to shake himself free from the intellectual shackles of the '*unam, sanctam, catholicam et apostolicam Ecclesiam*' and embrace the underground tradition of '*cada uno se puede salvar en su ley* . . . each can save himself in his own law'. To the devout Catholic, the Jews adhered to a faith that had been rejected by God, and their beliefs, therefore, were an affront to Christ Himself.

But rather than inhibit them in the practice of their faith, imprisonment actually inspired many of his fellow prisoners to even greater extremes of religious devotion and, faced on a daily basis with such overwhelming evidence of their piety, he found himself moved towards a grudging respect for their beliefs and a recognition of their shared humanity. Much as he might have liked to believe otherwise, they weren't so different after all.

(38)

*I*N THE AUTUMN of 1643, following an unsuccessful attempt at suicide, Antonio Caravallo was placed in a cell with his wife, Isabel de Silva. Regaining his wits, he claimed his marital privileges and left her pregnant. On 8 August 1644, she gave birth to a daughter.

There are few more emotionally traumatic events to be experienced in prison than that of childbirth, and the cries that heralded the child's arrival in the world could not have failed to send memories of Teresa flooding back into William's mind. She would be eight years old by now, and most probably asking some very difficult questions about her absent father.

Events such as these were far more effective than the conventional forms of torture, in that they reached a place far behind a prisoner's psychological defences, and the Inquisitors knew only too well how to maximise their effect. But with William they stirred him, not to greater extremes of melancholy, but to a renewed sense of purpose.

By imprisoning him amongst a persecuted community with whom he had far more in common than he was perhaps willing at first to recognise, the Inquisitors had unwittingly handed William the chance to heal. They had given him, not just another cause to champion, but something with which to justify his imprisonment.

His outrage and sympathy, however, did not, apparently, extend to those prisoners his Catholic conscience deemed to have been justly imprisoned, especially one Lorenzo Torquemada—a deranged Franciscan who had been imprisoned for claiming he could see through walls. William denounced him to the Inquisitors as a sorcerer. This brief moment of co-operation notwithstanding, however, William, having lost his battle with the government, now began to dig deep into his reserves of resistance to find a new target for his rage—the Holy Office itself.

(39)

O N 19 April 1644, with the Count-Duke in exile, and all manner of jockeying for position going on around him, the King took time out from the business of empire to write to Salvatierra, ordering William's immediate detention and return to Spain 'in the event of his being set loose by the Inquisition'. Just four days later he agreed, albeit reluctantly, to allow the Holy Office to have its way in the difficult matter of the Irishman. In February of 1645, by way of an afterthought, he added a request that, if they still felt they could not release the process papers into his hands, they might send them to the *Suprema* in Madrid.

The Inquisition had won: they had defeated and humiliated the King. Who, or what, was responsible for this remarkable royal *volte-face* remains a mystery, but it is probable that Felipe did not want the matter to grow into a heated dispute with the Catholic hierarchy, whose support he badly needed to keep his fragile empire intact.

The Mexican Inquisitors moved quickly to bring the investigation to a conclusion and William was summoned to an audience. A list of over seventy charges was read to him, the reading and answering of which took almost two days. And yet again, despite the matter being outside of their jurisdiction, charges of treason were levelled. He had, they alleged, conspired to raise an army of no fewer than 'two thousand paid men'.

The papers found in his room, William countered, had been part of his work as a double agent and intended for the purpose of flushing out Portuguese rebels. The story of the peyote, too, was an obvious untruth: the drug was a mild one that could never have induced the symptoms claimed by Pérez. He had heard said that some people took this herb in order to predict the future, but he himself did not know for certain whether or not they did, or how exactly it was taken. As for his supposed belief in astrology, sorcery and clairvoyance, he merely found such curiosities to be interesting.

On 21 October, an advocate was finally assigned to William. His name was Don Juan Bautista Martínez de Cepeda. But he was of little use. In the prisons of the Inquisition advocates were not permitted to speak to their clients in private and their every word was recorded by a notary. Nevertheless, not even Martínez seemed to recognise in William any signs of madness, and he never once attempted to have him seen by a doctor, as might have been expected in such cases. To Martínez William seemed as sane as the next man and, realising that the charges on which the Inquisition could legally proceed were relatively minor, he advised his client to make a full confession.

He refused.

A little over two weeks later, the testimonies of some twenty-nine witnesses were finally read to William omitting, as was customary, any information that might identify them to him. After three years of imprisonment, the possibility of release was at last presenting itself. The threat of an uprising had long since receded and his continued detention served no discernible political or moral purpose. All it would take to secure his passage back to Spain was an admission of guilt. The punishment would be public and humiliating, but at least the nightmare would be over.

Well, not quite. While most of his fellow prisoners would have said, done, or signed anything to ensure their release, William had too much to lose. There was nothing for him to go back to if found guilty. Even for the modest transgressions of faith with which he had been accused, a guilty verdict would prohibit him from ever working as a physician, apothecary, lawyer or tutor to the young—in effect condemning him to a life of penury and shame.

There was also the risk that, as part of his penance, he would be exposed to the universal scorn, derision and humiliation that accompanied the public wearing of the *sambenito* (penitential habit). He could also find himself stripped to the waist and paraded through the city carrying the insignia of his offence. For a man of his rank and station, the value of honour surpassed that of life itself and he was determined to walk out of this pernicious purgatory with his honour and reputation intact. The struggle to clear his name had sustained him thus far. Pride demanded a victory.

All of a sudden, however, the Inquisitors dramatically changed tack. Word had filtered through to them that Palafox was planning to target *them* in his latest drive against corruption, and they were determined to strike first.

(40)

$\mathcal{B}$ARELY A YEAR had passed since Don Juan de Mañozca succeeded Palafox to the Archbishopric of Mexico. A small bespectacled Basque with a burnished lunar pate, tiny ears and a prominent jawline that sported an unfashionable grey thicket of Byzantine proportions, he was as conservative in his philosophy as he was in his grooming. He brought to his new office an inveterate prejudice against Creoles and an inexhaustible enthusiasm for hunting heretics.

Frail, disillusioned and bilious of humour, Mañozca thought that he had found in New Spain the perfect shelter from the kinds of reform that Palafox had recently begun to impose upon him and from the winds of change that were blowing, much too strongly for his liking, through the Church in Europe. The two had initially been quite close but they had drifted apart when Palafox began to describe the Mexican Inquisition as a 'corrupt body interested only in seizing money from rich Jews and neglectful of its duties in the areas of public morals'—a criticism as much of Mañozca's impotence as *visitor* or inspector of the Holy Office as it was of the nefarious activities of the Inquisitors themselves. Mañozca was envious, moreover, of the fact that the colony's clergy and laity persisted in looking to Puebla for leadership. The bitterness had seeped into his bones and his health had begun to fail.

With Palafox's relationship with the Holy Office deteriorating daily, the Inquisitors began to probe for links between William and their troublesome gadfly. In no time at all they uncovered a forgotten copy, written in 1642, of one of William's letters to the King. The donor, much to their surprise, had been Palafox's secretary, Gregorio de Segovia.

On 7 November 1645, the Inquisitors summoned William to an audience. Had he, they inquired, conspired with Bishop Palafox to bring about the downfall of the Marquis of Villena?

William was quick to appreciate what they were up to, but to admit to having 'conspired' with Palafox, a man he still greatly admired, would have been to condemn them both. Not only did he deny having been part of a conspiracy, he denied ever having been in contact with Palafox at all; at which point the Inquisitors produced the letter.

William was shaken. How could he be expected to remember every letter he had written, let alone one written three years ago? All he knew for certain, he declared, was that *he* was not involved in any conspiracy.

How then, his interrogators continued, could a copy of his letter have come into the hands of the Bishop of Puebla? Surely the bishop had opened it in order to copy it?

'It would appear to me,' William speculated, 'that he opened it in his role as King's counsellor.'

But the Inquisitors were not buying that.

'Not even a King's counsellor,' they countered, 'could open a letter addressed to His Majesty without committing an offence of lese-majesty, and it is hard to believe that he would do so without your permission.'

But William would not budge.

Persisting with the accusation that he had in fact conspired with Palafox to bring about the downfall of Villena, the Inquisitors next alleged that his visit to Churubusco had been undertaken rather to find further evidence against the Viceroy than to assist him with his defence. But William denied this also. He had never accused the Viceroy personally, he claimed, only his officials.

For the next two days the Inquisitors tried time and again to manoeuvre William into implicating Palafox, but each time he repeated his claim that the one and only time he had spoken to Palafox concerning the coup was *after* the event, and even then solely concerning the organisation of the militia, which Palafox was quite entitled to do as Viceroy. At no time during this period of questioning was William's mental state ever considered to be an issue—even though the testimony of witnesses taken at the time of his arrest should have rendered his evidence against Palafox worthless.

Unable to break him down, the Inquisitors gave up trying and allowed him to set to work on his written defence. On 14 November 1645, his advocate was finally permitted to present these fifteen and a half pages of tightly written renunciations, and they were subsequently passed on to two Jesuit theologians for examination. But hard as they tried, they could find nothing of a heretical nature in them, just the occasional minor error in quotation.

At this stage, after three years of investigation, the process against him appeared to stall. With the Holy Office trammelled up in the struggle between Palafox and Salvatierra, William had become little more than an irritating itch that could wait to be scratched.

(41)

SALVATIERRA MUST HAVE wondered if things would ever be any different. Palafox had returned to the capital to resume his investigations and officials of every rank and station were complaining of a witch-hunt and clamouring for protection. Finding himself in an almost identical predicament to his predecessor, he believed his authority too would soon be at risk if he did not call a halt to the gallop of the meddlesome Visitor General.

Villena, of course, had tried and failed. But the odds, this time, were stacked in Salvatierra's favour. Realising that the death of the Count-Duke of Olivares (in July of 1645) had robbed Palafox of his influence at court, he set about coercing a reluctant city council to send written excoriations of him to Madrid. Everyone of consequence, he claimed, was opposed to the Bishop of Puebla.

Palafox, for his part, alleged that the Viceroy was so hen-pecked that the control of the colony actually lay in the hands of his wife and her ladies. It was an inflammatory remark, intended to wound, and not entirely a lie: the Countess of Salvatierra *was*, in fact, helping to direct the Inquisition's propaganda campaign against him.

With each side demanding the recall of the other, a stalemate of sorts evolved during which Salvatierra decided to wait for an apposite smoke-screen behind which he could act with impunity. But as he dithered, his authority was slowly undermined by an avalanche of satirical verse directed against himself, his wife and the Inquisition. And worse was soon to follow.

Following orders from their generals in Europe, the Jesuits and Franciscans were forced into an uneasy peace with Palafox, and Salvatierra was deprived of their support. He managed, nevertheless, to retain the allegiance of Archbishop Mañozca, whose intense dislike of Palafox was common knowledge about the palace. The truce, such as it was, was fragile.

In 1646 Father Pedro de Velasco, a man closely associated with the anti-Palafox faction within the Society of Jesus, became Provincial of the Jesuits in New Spain. Under his direction, the Jesuits entered into a conspiracy with the Inquisition to rid themselves of Palafox by forcing him into a confrontation with the Holy Office.

The first move was made by the Mexican Inquisitors. Supported by the Jesuits and the Dominicans, they declared criticism of the Holy Office to be an offence against the faith: a move they hoped would either stifle Palafox or enrage him. The Jesuits, with their usual venomous eloquence, also began to slate Palafox from the pulpit. They were led, on this occasion, by William's old messenger, Juan de San Miguel.

'Salvatierra,' he railed, 'is a Galician coward, too scared to seize Palafox and throw him out of here.'

Preoccupied almost exclusively with Palafox, the Inquisitors began to neglect their spiritual duties in the prisons. Nourished by their absence, a growing spirit of defiance began to grow amongst the Jewish prisoners and on 26 March 1646, those whose windows overlooked the street began to ridicule and scoff at the first of the Holy Week processions that passed below. The derision was led by Duarte de Torres, Solomon Machorro, and man known only as 'one-eyed Medina'. Despite warnings from the guards, the abuse resumed on the Tuesday, prompting the guards to close the shutters.

By midday on Holy Thursday the entire prison population was suffering. With the shutters closed the humidity became unbearable and deprived of their only source of natural light many of the prisoners became unhinged. In an effort to goad him into entering one of the cells, they hurled an endless string of insults at one of the guards. But he refused to take the bait.

At about 10 p.m., after the guards had left for the night, the prisoners began an inexorable tumult of yells, howls and banging of plates that disturbed, not just the peace of the prison, but that of the entire neighbourhood. It continued until five o'clock the following morning. The following night it happened again, and once more on the Saturday, before the threats of the warden finally quelled the clangour.

But if the Inquisitors had little time for their Jewish prisoners at this time, they had even less time for William. Compared to their battle with Palafox such matters paled into insignificance. There was also the small matter of Archbishop Mañozca's continuing investigations into Inquisitorial misconduct, not to mention the internal strife and petty jealousies that followed the appointment of the archbishop's cousin, Juan Sáenz de Mañozca to the post of Inquisitor; an appointment that was never fully accepted by his new colleagues and which earned him the enmity, in particular, of Inquisitors Estrada and Gaviola. Such was the discomfort he felt in his new role that he was soon writing letters to the *Suprema* critical of his new colleagues, so endearing himself to Gaviola that he was soon living in fear of his life. With no sign in sight of an end to the hostilities, William must have despaired of his process ever being brought to a conclusion. The only person who could help him now, he realised, was the King. He needed to find a courier.

Sharing William's cell throughout the fourth year of imprisonment, were Gaspar Váez Sevilla and Juan Francisco de León Jaramillo. Váez, the 22-year-old son of Simón Váez Sevilla, was pretty much a model prisoner, but Léon had already been caught attempting to smuggle messages to his mother in a small box of peach preserve and openly conversing with María de Campos—conversations which had been overheard by the prison spy, Gaspar Alfar (alias Gaspar de los Reyes).

A 45-year-old conman who had been imprisoned in August of 1641 for having administered the sacraments without having been ordained, Alfar rarely wasted an opportunity to ingratiate himself with the wardens. Indeed such was his relationship with them that, on occasion, he had been let out of his cell to assist them during staff shortages. For this small consideration, he boasted, they had allowed him to have his way with Catalina Enríquez and Isabel de Rivera.

To help him spy on his fellow prisoners, Alfar had recruited a 21-year-old Negra slave of William's previous cellmate, Tomás Núñez de Peralta. Her name was Antonia de la Cruz and she brought candles to the prisoners each night and gave massages to those who needed them (a treatment frequently prescribed by the prison doctors for a wide variety of psychosomatic illnesses). Already accustomed to subterfuge—having regularly carried notes between Ana Xuárez and another of William's former cellmates, Francisco Lopéz de Fonseca (written on a tobacco leaf and concealed in the sleeve of a recently washed shirt)—

Antonia was ideally placed to spy, not just on the prisoners, but on her fellow slaves.

William would have known only too well at this stage that attempting to get a written message to someone on the outside was a dangerous proposition. But he was desperate. In January of 1647, on half a sheet of writing paper that he had been given by the warden Pedro Ximenes, he began a letter to Palafox. 'As I have done on your behalf,' he wrote, 'I hope Your Excellency will now do for me, and put my case before the King.'

The plan was that León, who was due to be released at the forth-coming *auto de fe,* would smuggle the letter to Puebla. The pair had initially got on quite well: so well, in fact, that William even told him of the time he had stolen a copy of the Koran from the library of Forbidden Books at San Lorenzo. But things did not go to plan. Before William's letter could be completed, the pair had a falling out and León informed the Inquisitors of its contents and told them how William still intended, when released, to start a revolution with the aid of the colony's Negro slaves, *Mulattos* and *Mestizos,* and to put to death those Inquisitors who would wish the same fate on him. It must have seemed to William as if Fate was toying with him: opening doors merely to taunt him with their closure.

(42)

*T*HE PERPETUAL DREAD of torture was one of the most potent weapons that the Inquisition had at its disposal. It induced a terrible sense of helplessness and humiliation and, like a powerful poultice, drew fear from its hiding places and into the forefront of consciousness. Prisoners were frequently consumed with speculation as to how they might cope when their turn came around, and their fears often proved far more potent than the torture itself, which could awaken an inner strength in some prisoners that few would have guessed had existed beforehand.

The trials of one such prisoner made a lasting impression on William. Her name was Isabel Tristán and her stubborn defiance had won her the undying admiration of all of the other prisoners. Over the course of 1647 she was subjected to an instrument of torture they called '*el potro* . . . the colt'. Stripped of all but the minimum necessary to shroud her private parts, her extremities were tied to a bed-like frame with leather straps which, when tightened by the turn of a wheel, bit into her flesh causing excruciating pain. Few expected so delicate a creature to survive her imprisonment, let alone a visit to the torture chamber, but throughout it all she maintained an heroic and hermetic silence. By the end of the year she had suffered such horrible dislocations and muscle tears that she had permanently lost the use of her legs. Within the prison, songs were composed in her honour.

Isabel's bravery contrasted starkly with the blabbering of the highly strung Juana Enríquez, wife of Simón Váez Sevilla, who worried herself into anxiety attacks at the merest thought of being tortured. By giving voice to her fears, of course, she guaranteed their realisation and in the end she told the Inquisitors everything she knew, and more.

From the confines of his cell, William could not have failed to hear the rattling of keys in the locks, and the sobbing of prisoners as they were taken, with varying degrees of resistance, to be tortured. Their suffering would have become another part of his own and he must often have lain in wait half-expecting to be next. But nobody ever came for him.

Almost one in three prisoners were tortured at some time or other and if there really had been a conspiracy, then William's refusal to name names should have guaranteed that he was too. But not only was William never tortured, a blind eye was even turned to his conversations with the Franciscan priests who occasionally came to say Mass, hear confessions, and anoint the dying. There was still an apparent acceptance amongst the wardens that the Irishman was a special category of prisoner (the King himself having taken a personal interest in his process) and for the time being they endeavoured to treat him as such. Their patience, however, was frequently tested.

Determined, it appears, to take control of any aspect of his confinement that might be moulded into active resistance, William refused to wash, shave or cut his hair. It did little for his appearance, but it presented the mosquitoes with significantly less bare skin upon which to gorge themselves and annoyed the hell out of the wardens and Inquisitors.

Back in 1646, on the occasion of one his rare visits to the prison, the Chief Inquisitor, Don Domingo Vélez de Asaz y Argos, became somewhat vexed at the Irishman's dishevelled appearance and ventured to suggest that he might better improve his spirits if he paid a little more attention to personal hygiene and grooming. The very least he should do, Argos suggested, was cut his hair.

'Why don't *you* cut it,' barked William, 'seeing as you're used to cutting heads.'

There were few prisoners of the Holy Office who would dare to be so contumelious with an Inquisitor, let alone one as dangerous as this. For much of his recent career the walking skeleton had been lining his pockets with the confiscated goods of those he had sent to the stake and such was the delight he took in the application of torture that he would occassionally allow members of his family to eavesdrop at an open trapdoor. As lacking in conscience as he was in flesh, Argos was incapable of shame. That particular day, however, the hoary old reprobate was in an uncommonly generous mood and he let the matter pass.

'Death to Argos!' William bellowed after him as he shuffled away, 'DEATH TO ARGOS!'

ON 6 MARCH 1647, the patience of the Inquisitors was finally rewarded. Palafox excommunicated the Inquisition: the Inquisition, in return, excommunicated Palafox. The power struggle descended rapidly into farce and within weeks Villena's former chaplain, Father Gutiérrez de Medina, was leading the Inquisition into Puebla. He was accompanied, to the surprise of many, by Palafox's former secretary, Melchor Xuárez, who, having fallen out with Palafox, had managed to secure for himself a position as secretary to Archbishop Mañozca—no mean feat, in the current climate, for a Portuguese *converso*.

With Palafox on the run, the Inquisition marched into Puebla in triumphant and extravagant procession. The Jesuits celebrated; the *Mulattas* danced; raucous music was heard once more in the taverns, and the prostitutes returned to the plazas. In the campaign of intimidation that followed, many of Palafox's supporters were arrested and imprisoned. The following month, the Archbishop of Mexico, Juan de Mañozca, wrote to the King alleging that a conspiracy had existed between Palafox, the Marchioness of Cadereyta and the Irishman, William Lamport, to overthrow Villena.

On 10 August, still in hiding at Chiapa, a nervous Palafox wrote an impassioned plea to the King and the Inquisitor General complaining of various libels that Archbishop Mañozca and the Inquisitor, Juan Sáenz de Mañozca y Murillo, were publishing with the assistance of the Countess of Salvatierra. The Holy Office, he claimed, was doing untold damage to the reputation and authority of the Church in New Spain and his every word on the matter could be proven 'before any judge that Your Majesty and the Supreme Council might care to nominate'.

There was little more that Palafox could do right now but lie low and wait. In the prisons of the Inquisition not even a bishop would be safe from torture and there was no knowing what nonsense he might confess to in such circumstances. He could only hope that his friends in Madrid would come to his rescue before his reforms were completely undone, or he himself was captured.

That October, his patience bore fruit. Word arrived from Madrid that Salvatierra had been 'promoted' to Viceroy of Peru, where he was to replace William's old sponsor, the Marquis of Mancera. He was to be replaced temporarily in New Spain by Bishop Marcos de Torres y Rueda, who had been ordered to hold the fort until the arrival of the new Viceroy. Under no circumstances, Torres was told, was he to interfere in the internal politics of the colony.

Torres, alas, was as impetuous as he was rapacious and, on 15 May 1648, he began a purge against Palafox's enemies, and his own. Over the year that followed he and his extended family lined their pockets to the tune of more than half a million pesos. But just when it was looking as though the Inquisition might finally leave Palafox alone, the Chief Inquisitor, Don Domingo Vélez de Asaz y Argos, passed away. He was succeeded by Juan Sáenz de Mañozca y Murillo—a man who had recently thwarted the Bishop of Oaxaca's investigation into Inquisitorial misconduct and whose hatred of Palafox was rivalled only by that of his first cousin, Archbishop Mañozca.

William's links to Palafox were never going to help his case under the new regime and an Irish friend by the name of John Fizgerald ('Juan Geraldo—Irlandés') returned to Spain to see what could be done from there. But Mancera was in Peru, Olivares and Camassa were gone from this world, and Jan-Karel della Faille was absent on a military tour of Catalonia, Sicily and Naples. Fitzgerald did, however, manage to track down Ana and Teresa. Despite the serious nature of the charges, the scope of the Inquisitorial investigation, and the unusual duration of his imprisonment, this was the first they had heard of William's difficulties. Ana was devastated: Teresa did not remember much of him.

Upon his return to Puebla, Palafox proceeded to open up a second front on the issue of education—an activity in which the Jesuits effectively held a monopoly—by founding college seminaries at San Pablo and San Juan and putting them under diocesan control. The new colleges soon eclipsed the Ignatian establishments and the resulting dispute became extremely bitter.

Drunk on his recent successes, Palafox now wrote to the Pope requesting that the Jesuit order be done away with in its current form. It was the last straw for many of the bishop's old supporters in Spain and it had the unfortunate effect of embroiling the European Jesuits in a battle they had thus far been happy to keep out of. Madrid wanted calm in New Spain and Palafox, having exhausted everyone's patience but his own, was finally recalled to Madrid.

Freed from other distractions, the Inquisitors finally returned to the matter of the Irishman and on 10 February 1649 they notified him of the publication of a new body of evidence relating to 'crimes' he had committed while in prison. A few days later, his advocate resigned and William was asked to nominate another. He chose Dr Juan García de Palacios. Ignorant, perhaps, of the truth of his client's predicament, García brought a naïve enthusiasm to his defence. The charges of treason, he argued, were outside the jurisdiction of the tribunal, and the more recent charges were inadmissible, having been made by Jews and drunkards (the rules of the Inquisition forbade the acceptance of the word of a Jew over that of a Christian).

It was an old ploy, and a moot point. The prisoners may have been practising Jews but, having received the sacrament of baptism, they were also, technically speaking, Christians. His demands that William be set free, therefore, yielded nothing.

Having been notified by now of his recall to Madrid, Palafox began to concentrate what little time he had left in New Spain on completing the cathedral in Puebla—a building he hoped would stand as a monument to his reforms, and to his memory. Believing the work to be an attempt by Palafox to perpetuate his influence after his departure, Mañozca decided to pre-empt the opening ceremony of the cathedral in Puebla, by staging a gigantic *auto de fe* in Mexico City. By removing all of his 'Jewish' prisoners in one fell swoop, he would considerably ease the administrative burden of the Holy Office and bring the whole of the city and surrounding countryside onto the streets. Palafox's celebrations would seem puny in comparison.

A tribunal of the Inquisition was convened and William was sentenced to be punished and released at the forthcoming *auto* as a 'penitent suspected of a pact with the devil'. After seven years of incarceration and investigation, the only thing they could prove against him was the incident with the peyote and despite all evidence to the contrary, he was adjudged to be sane.

Discussion now centred on what exactly his punishment should be. Several options were discussed: a public whipping of 200 lashes; ten years penal servitude as a galley slave; and a lifetime's exile from Madrid, Seville and the Indies. Archbishop Mañozca, however, was quick to highlight the dangers inherent in setting such a man loose at all, and managed to swing the opinion of the Inquisitors quickly in line with his own. For such an erratic and dangerous character, it was argued, the oath of secrecy would be a poor guarantee of his silence.

The Inquisitors finally concluded that William's association with Palafox might expose the Holy Office to the wrong sort of attention and their discussion briefly turned to how best to ensure his silence upon his eventual release. Unable to reach a conclusion, they referred the sentence back to the *Suprema* (who rejected it as excessive). There were times when the enormous distance from Madrid had its uses.

The impending *auto* increased the already soaring tensions in the prisons of the Inquisition and the blackmail threats of wardens and slaves assumed a more immediate importance. But bad and all as such threats were, when they came from one of their own tightly-knit community, they were potentially cataclysmic; and not just for the victim, but for *all* of the Jewish prisoners in the *Casa de Picazo*.

Gonzalo Díaz was a *Mestizo* Jew with a history of blackmailing fellow prisoners when financially embarrassed. Seeing the *auto* as a chance to make some ready cash, he pushed his luck too far and so outraged the richest and most powerful of the prisoners that they badgered his estranged half-brother, Manuel Díaz, into doing away with him. After the assassination, Simón Váez Sevilla and Isabel Tristán bought enough false testimonies (with promises of payment when released) to allow Manuel to escape without punishment. Sadly for Isabel, no amount of testimony, bought or otherwise, could save *her*. She was sentenced to burn at the stake.

William's feelings at this time had to have been mixed. He had escaped being included in the *auto*, which could only mean that the *Suprema* had still not decided how to deal with him. His cellmate,

Gaspar Váez Sevilla, on the other hand, had been reconciled to the faith and was due to be released. A little envy was not entirely out of order. Gaspar, after all, and despite every oath he had sworn to the contrary, was a practising Jew. William was a devout Catholic.

On Saturday 10 April, an extraordinary and wistful silence fell over *Casa de Picazo*. Not even the guards were inclined to talk: the unimaginable anguish of those sentenced to burn the following morning having struck everyone dumb. Even the cells seemed smaller, as though the enormity of the occasion were pressing as much on the walls as on their emotions. Every leaden footstep seemed to sigh and the clank of keys and drawing of bolts screeched like nothing that had ever come from the torture chamber.

The following morning, five hundred carriages of noble families and a great concourse of some 30,000 people descended on the Plaza del Valour for a celebration billed as the greatest ever to be held outside of the Iberian Peninsula. A double row of coaches lined the route of the procession; the occupants having spent the night in them to guarantee the best viewing positions. Forty Jews were tried on the day, thirteen of whom were burned at the stake. Twelve of these were reconciled to the faith and garrotted first; the one exception being Tomas Treviño de Sobremonte, a man whose wealth had made him a particularly attractive victim to the Holy Office.

'Pile on the wood,' Treviño cried as they tied him to the stake, 'after all its my money that's paying for it!'

After the public humiliation of the *auto*, Simón Váez Sevilla and his family were released, with the exception of his daughter Leonor, who had died in prison. They fled immediately, and against the express orders of the Inquisition, to Campeche, where they were reunited with an old friend, Don García de Valdés Osorio, who was now Governor of the port. With a passionless *adíos*, they gathered what was left of their wealth and set sail for Spain.

Palafox's celebration took place in Puebla on the following Sunday. It began at 6 a.m. and lasted the entire day—with intermittent encores over several of the succeeding days. The festivities were attended by 1,200 clergy, Palafox's magnificent (and exclusively white) choir, and a vast gathering of lay worshippers. But magnificent though the spectacle was, it paled in comparison to the multitudes that had thronged the streets of the capital for the previous week's *auto*.

The following Thursday, the Archbishop of Mexico died, leaving power, in the absence of a nominated successor, in the hands of the Creole government—the very situation which Villena, Palafox, and William had been despatched to New Spain to prevent. Life had come full circle for the Bishop of Puebla, and he set sail from Veracruz on 6 May 1649. Despite the prayers of his many supporters, he would never return.

Just over a month later, the *Audiencia*, led by its president, Mathías de Peralta, and the judge, Andrés Gómez de Mora, began to restore those pro-Salvatierra officials who had been sacked by Bishop Torres to their posts. They also sent a special task force to Puebla to forcibly remove the royal shields that Palafox had placed either side of the altarpiece, on the grounds that he had illegally placed the royal arms of Aragon, the province of his birth, in a place of priority over those of Castile. The same was said of the quarter-red cross with green tree that he had included on the shields. This symbol, unknown to local heraldic experts, was believed to have some connection with his family.

Palafox's departure left William isolated and desperate: a fallen pawn in an abandoned game. The possibility that he might implicate Palafox in the downfall of Villena was by now an irrelevance and the threat of revolution had long since passed. Nobody believed he could resurrect it and even if he could, all it would take to stop him would be to return him under armed guard to Spain—exactly what the King had demanded of them in the first place. Keeping the Irishman under lock and key served only one purpose: it guaranteed his silence and prevented the one thing the Inquisitors feared above all else; a secular investigation of their activities. By attacking their reputations in the letters he had attempted to send to the King, William had irrevocably altered the nature of his plight.

(44)

SOLOMON MACHORRO HAD not come to the Indies to enrich himself; he had come in search of his father. Had he heeded the pleas of his mother he would still be enjoying a dull but comfortable life in the Italian port of Livorno. That another piece of maternal advice should be responsible for trapping him in his current nightmare was the cruellest of all ironies.

Amongst the first to be denounced by Blanca Rivera and her daughters back in May of 1642, thirty-year-old Machorro was generally recognised as the spiritual leader of the Jewish community in Mexico City and he had already been the victim of some horrendous bouts of torture. In August of 1649 he was moved into a cell with a strange Irishman he had heard had tried to start a revolution.

Solomon (alias Juan Pacheco de León) had his own peculiar regimen with which to pass the long hours of daylight. Every day without fail, at 5 a.m., midday, 3 p.m. and 7 p.m., he would don his black felt hat and long black cloak and spend up to fifteen minutes in not-so-silent prayer. He was also forever washing his hands. After four months of solitary confinement, however, William was not about to complain.

It took some time for the pair to get the measure of each other; each being well aware by now of the folly of rushing headlong into relationships from which he might later want to withdraw. But both were in need of the solace that came from sharing their suffering, and mutual suspicion soon gave way to respect and friendship—a relationship that would not have been possible earlier in William's imprisonment. The simple honesty of their exchanges proved a soothing balm for the torments of William's despair and renewed his reserves of optimism.

Years of sharing his living space with Jews had long since forced William to confront the various anti-Semitic myths upon which he'd been reared and, despite Solomon's odd behaviour, he soon discovered that they had much in common. Solomon, too, had served time at sea, had been captured by pirates in his youth, had acted as a tutor to the children of a wealthy patron and had been betrayed to the Inquisition by those he had considered his friends. A dark-skinned Andalucian from the mountain village of Antequera, he had been taken at the age of two to Italy, where his father, David (alias Antonio Fartán y Narváez), had found work on the estates of the Grand Duke of Florence. Although reared as a Jew and sent to a Hebrew school, his curiosity led him, sometime about the age of ten, to take an interest in the faith of his predominantly Catholic peers. Worried that he was in danger of conversion, his parents apprenticed him to his uncle Abraham and shortly after his thirteenth birthday he was taken on a trading voyage to the Levant.

Somewhere off the coast of Izmir, Abraham and Solomon were captured by pirates and taken to Algiers, where they were held captive for almost four years. After their release (a ransom presumably having been paid), Solomon returned to Livorno to be re-united with his mother, Luna, and his brother and sister, Isaac and Raquel.

Whenever he enquired about his father, Solomon's mother would tell him only that he was absent on business. Fearful that the son she had given up for dead might be tempted to follow after him, she refused even to reveal his whereabouts. But when the months came and went with no sign of her husband returning, she finally relented, and allowed Solomon to set out after him.

Upon his arrival in Cádiz Solomon heard that before sailing to the Indies his father had left word that should his son ever come looking for him he was to follow after. Then again, he also heard rumours that he was dead. Unable to determine the truth of the matter, he sailed for Veracruz where, in July of 1639, he discovered the rumours of his father's demise to have been true. Alone in a strange land, and with no resources worth speaking of, he headed for Mexico City (possibly in search of relatives—his grandmother was believed to be the godmother of the merchant Tomas Treviño de Sobremonte), where he quickly acquired friends, protectors, and disciples!

Through his friendship with Blanca Enríquez, Solomon managed to install himself in the home of Simón Váez Sevilla (her son-in-law) as Hebrew tutor to his son. Within two years he had turned himself into the capital's unofficial rabbi and the Váez household into something of a synagogue. Uneasy with the influence that the young Andalucian was wielding over his wife and son, Simón advanced him some money and set him up in business in Querétaro, a small market town about 180km north of the capital where Solomon's grandmother was believed to be still living. Sadly for Solomon, it was to prove not nearly distant enough. On 22 May 1642, following his betrayal by the loose-tongued Rivera women, he was arrested by constables of the Holy Office.

Before leaving Italy Solomon's mother had warned him that, should he ever be arrested by the Inquisition, he should tell them that he had been born in Spain and baptised a Catholic. Upon his arrest, therefore, he followed his mother's instructions to the letter and told the Inquisitors that his knowledge of Jewish rites and ceremonies had been learnt from the late Blanca Enríquez. Eighteen months later, however, he yielded to the contrary advice of some fellow Jewish prisoners and changed his story and claimed to be Italian born and bred.

In 1648, impatient at the lack of progress on his case, he returned to his original story and, in a vain effort to convince the Inquisitors of his sincerity and contrition, confessed to various ritual fasts he had undertaken while in prison. The Mexican Inquisitors, tired of his indecision, wrote to the *Suprema* requesting a search of the Church records of Antequera and Seville for a record of his baptism. Nothing was ever found.

The tragedy of it all was that had Solomon not claimed to have been baptised but openly admitted to being a Jew, he would not have been in such hot water. As a Church court the Inquisition had no real jurisdiction over Jews: only when a person had been baptised did he become capable of heresy. The problem now was that the Inquisitors took a very grave view of being lied to. Failure to make a complete confession, in fact, completely nullified the positive effects of confessions already made. By the time he was moved into William's cell, he was a desperate young man who would have said or done anything to secure his release.

As a self-styled expert in Canon Law, William was only too willing to help, and he sat down to write a theological opinion on Solomon's behalf:

I, Don Guillén Lombardo, declare that while in my company in the month of August past in this year of forty-nine, Juan de León put the following questions to me concerning the validity in other jurisdictions of a declaration made by a person who knows full well and infallibly that he has been baptised, but neither knows where he was baptised nor possesses a baptismal certificate. Should he, for want of said baptismal certificate, be re-baptised, or could he be compelled to produce a baptismal certificate or to declare definitively where he was baptised ?

To the above I replied that if the said person knows for certain that he has been baptised, it shall be thus for all eternity, whether or not he can produce a certificate or testimony to either the baptism or its location, for assuming that he does not know exactly where it took place, he cannot be forced to do the impossible (*nemo at impossibile tenetur*), nor can any man say he has been baptised, nor where he was baptised, if he has not been told, for no man has the use of reason as an infant and a baptism is considered valid on the word of the godparents even if the child is not aware of his having been baptised.

Thus a baptism shall be valid even if the exact location of its occurrence cannot be determined. In fact, certificates or witnesses to a baptism are not customary in the greater part of the Catholic Church, and even heretics, as is commonly known, are baptised even if they do not know where it took place but know that it has, and in the early Church all that was required to join the unbelievers to the believers was the oral declaration of the cleansing sacrament of baptism to the faithful (*confesio oris baptismatis lavacri fidelibus*).

Although Our Lord Jesus Christ, through Saint Mark, ordered the Apostles to go forth and bring the faith to all, and preach that he who believes and is baptised will be saved and that he who does not believe will be condemned (*Ite predicate Evangelium a mi creature qui crediderit et baptizatus fuerit salvus crit, qui autem no crediderit condemnavitur*), he left no precept which obliges a Christian to produce written proof of baptism, from which I infer that baptism is both inner and external knowledge and that it is certain that he who says and believes that he is baptised, shall be deemed baptised, for that indeed satisfies the need for certification and human witness.

In addition, I replied that even though one might lack a baptismal certificate, once baptised one cannot be baptised again, for that would be to repeat a sacrament, which is forbidden under grave penalties by our Holy Mother Church and by the Canon Laws from which I quote in this context. But while under certain conditions of doubt it can be repeated, where there is no doubt it cannot, from which one can say that the said person's declaration that he knows infallibly that he has been baptised is valid, even if he is ignorant of the place or location in which it took place and cannot produce a baptismal certificate to prove same, and thus the said person cannot receive the sacrament of baptism again. This is my opinion which, in the absence of any evidence to the contrary, is in keeping with our Holy Catholic Faith that is truth infallible. And as Juan de León asked me for my written opinion, I have signed it with the authorised form of my name.

Don Guillén Lombardo.

When the case was finally heard, on 19 October 1649, William's opinion was included among the process papers and Solomon attempted to quote him as an authority in his defence. The Irishman's arguments, however, had little, if any, positive effect.

On the night of 28 June 1650, the sound of music and fireworks in the streets outside the secret prisons heralded the swearing in of the new Viceroy, Don Luis Enríquez de Guzmán, the Count of Alba de Liste. Ten days later, when the celebrations abated and the Inquisitors returned to their duties, Solomon was hauled from his cell and condemned to a public whipping and eight years as a galley slave on the oars of His Most Catholic Majesty's navy—effectively a death sentence: few men ever survived such brutality.

Two days after sentencing, Solomon was again taken from his cell and brought to the Church of Santo Domingo to make a formal act of abjuration and sign the Deed of Penance. The following morning he was stripped to the waist, paraded through the streets of the city on an ass, and subjected to a punishment of 300 lashes. Returned to his cell, he was given a further two days to recover before being escorted to his final audience, this time to sign the Deed of Secrecy. Having been warned of the penalties that he would suffer should he ever break his vow, he was handed over to the secular arm, who took him away to the hot and humid dungeons of San Juan de Ulúa, to await what Cervantes once described as 'a kind of civil death' in the *gurapas* of the King's navy.

Following Solomon's departure, William found himself once again in sole possession of his cell. It was not the first time he had seen a cellmate released, but this particular leave-taking appears to have hit him especially hard. The Inquisitors, unhappy with his interference in Solomon's process, determined never again to allow William to share his cell with a Jew. It would be some time, in fact, before they would allow him to share it with anyone.

In the perpetual twilight of the dungeons, night now separated day only in the intensity of his isolation. He got up each morning and dressed himself; but there was nowhere to go to or come back from other than where his mind would take him. Deprived of all means of anchoring itself in the present, his mind would scurry off on its own in search of somewhere to escape the boredom. At such times, nothing made sense. Everything became jumbled and his dreams and reveries left him feeling drained and insensible. The diamonds in his eyes lost their lustre and his ruddy complexion faded to a vanquished pallor, covered for the most part now by a tangled brown mane that was brindled with silver. Sleep was his only companion and her visits became more and more irregular. Every colourful delusion he had harnessed to his denial had been bleached by the reality of his abandonment and from time to time he cried uncontrollably.

(45)

SHORTLY AFTER HIS thirty-fifth birthday, two letters addressed to William found their way to the headquarters of the Holy Office in Mexico City. They came from his daughter, Teresa, and from Ana de Cano y Leyva. They had been carried to Mexico through the good offices of the Franciscans.

Teresa's letter, which was written for her by her tutor, was short and awkward: just a single page of twenty-seven lines in which she struggled heroically to find something comforting to say. Her mother had told her the terrible news, which had upset her beyond measure. She spoke of the devastation of 'feeling in the soul something I will not be able to relieve'. She wanted him to know that she was now twelve years of age and being well looked after. She did not remember much of him 'on account of the very young age at which you left me', but she had heard stories of his many successes from her mother. She addressed him with the formal *usted* rather than the familiar *tú*, and in a childish hand she signed herself, 'Your daughter, Doña Teresa.' It was dated 16 January 1650.

Ana's letter was dated one month later and, as befits a letter she hoped would be passed on to William by the Inquisitors of the Holy Office, it was suitably pious and deferential: the one month gap between mother's and daughter's letters perhaps reflecting the seriousness of the situation and the difficulties to be overcome in the wording. Expecting that it would be read by strangers, Ana betrayed precious little that could be described as being of an intimate or personal nature, and at times it read like a character reference (at one point she referred to William as 'the son of such good parents').

But despite the formality, the letter was not totally devoid of emotion. She explained that she had been unaware of William's predicament until quite recently and the news had made her ill. Fondly remembering the joy of their life together, she spoke of the 'ties of love' that still bound them to each other. 'May God grant me' she wrote, 'the grace to serve Him, and may He protect you and permit me to see you again.' Written more in the hope than the expectation that it would ever reach William's hands, she implored God to allow him 'to live a little more with [his] *mujercita*' and to protect her husband more than her. Bidding what was to prove a final *adiós* to her 'husband for life', she signed it 'your beloved wife, who desires your life and to see you'. Nostalgic and sincere, her words were not those of a deserted fiancée, and her frequent attempts to underscore the fact that they were married (she had no way of knowing that William had denied the fact) suggest that she truly believed it to be the case.

William would later claim to one of his fellow prisoners that 'he had intended to send for the aforementioned lady of the palace in order to marry her, because neither she, nor he, could marry another'. In saying this he most likely had in mind the legitimising of a private exchange of oaths that had taken place illicitly (at least in terms of Canon Law). In calling William her 'husband', on the other hand, Ana was possibly adhering to the natural law view of marriage: a view that had existed for centuries prior to the Council of Trent and was only slowly yielding to the demands of the *Decree Tametsi*.

It is not known if William ever received Teresa's letter, or even Ana's for that matter, but shortly after its arrival, and for perhaps the first time since his confinement, he began to seriously entertain the notion of escape. From the iron grille on his cell door he broke away a sharp piece of iron and hid it in the lining of his doublet. But before he could use it to loosen the bars on his window, he was overcome once more by depression. Becalmed in a sea of sadness, he appeared to his gaolers to drift into abysms of boredom, fatigue and self-obsession far deeper than anything he had exhibited before.

(46)

*I*F SOLITARY CONFINEMENT could be said to have any positive effect, it was that it allowed a prisoner the time and space to examine his life with real clarity. Those who could do so without regrets, however, were few and far between, and the fruitless retracing of his life in search of a plan left William with an aching desire to explain himself. A Franciscan visitor to the prison, who was shortly to return to Spain, was persuaded to smuggle a letter to Teresa. She would be fourteen now—an age when many young women became available for marriage.

It was hard to imagine Teresa as a young woman. The clear light of remembrance had faded to a crepuscular glow, but what little remained of her features were those of a four-year-old child. Nevertheless, there was a vacuum that had to be filled; words that could no longer remain unspoken.

The simplest of physical tasks now intimidated him with the effort required and he lost the will to block the progress of his mind to places he had no real desire to visit. His hallucinatory fantasies dragged him helplessly through a mire of emotional turmoil and he began to complain of 'terrors' and of 'diabolical visions'. Paralysed by his despair, he became a total stranger to the sensation of pleasure, lost his appetite and self-esteem, and struggled to imagine a future any different from the present. The only thing keeping him from suicide, it seemed, was his outsized pride.

Watching him decay, his gaolers were moved to pity: he was, after all, a pious Christian, and his alleged crimes had been more against the Crown than the faith. The Inquisitors were still refusing to allow him be seen by a doctor, but perhaps something else could be done. In a crude attempt to procure a remedy for his despair, they pleaded for him to be allotted another cellmate 'that he might find some relief from his melancholic passions'. It had worked before, it might just work again.

$\mathcal{D}$IEGO PINTO BRAVO was a 42-year-old blacksmith whose hair and beard had turned prematurely white and fell lank over the greater part of his face. He was not a Jew. His one and only crime, he claimed, had been to believe in the supernatural visions of his sisters-in-law. Short, leather-skinned and heavy-boned, he was just the man that William had been waiting for.

From the moment he entered the cell, Diego's relationship with William was underscored by a wariness that owed as much to a gulf in social class as William's fear of informers. Seven years earlier he would have felt dishonoured by such company, but things were very different now. Ever so slowly, the clouds began to lift and he began to make some cautiously defensive overtures towards his new cellmate and to approach a reasonable simulation of friendship.

Perhaps it had something to do with the solace he found in being able to communicate meaningfully with another human being; perhaps it was simply that Diego was willing to listen; but the days no longer passed in interminable delirium and, purging himself of the fears and insecurities that solitary confinement had imposed upon him, he began to open up. In no time at all the pair were exchanging stories of the bizarre journeys that had led them to this loveless and joyless sepulchre: stories that for a few brief moments transported them beyond the suffocating confines of their cell.

Diego was married to María Romero, daughter of Juan Romero Zapata, a peasant labourer who, following the death of his wife, had taken clerical vows with the intention of eventually becoming a priest. Natives of Cholula, the family consisted of twelve boys and four imaginative, impressionable and troublesome young girls; Nicolasa, Josefa and María (twins), and Teresa.

Forbidden the passions of chivalric literature, the girls took to immersing themselves in the lives of the saints, finding an acceptable substitute for the romantic adventures of *Palmerín* and *Amadis* in the stories of Catalina de Siena and, most especially, Mariana de Cruz—a woman whose virtue was so pure that she abstained totally from food, drink, and conversation with men. In no time of all they were dreaming, like Teresa of Ávila, of 'having the freedom to preach, confess and deliver souls to God'.

The family's odyssey began in earnest when Josefa made an apparently miraculous recovery from serious illness through the intercession of Luis Beltrán, a recently canonised saint. Envious of the attention that Josefa was receiving from a father she believed was not particularly fond of her, Teresa contrived to suffer an equally serious illness and achieve a miraculous recovery of her own, this time through the intercession of Nicholas of Tolentino—a healer renowned for his visions of Purgatory. The father, a man later described by the Inquisition as '*un hombre satírico . . .* a satyr', was quick to recognise the commercial possibilities.

Though all of Juan's daughters were talented in their deceptions and could convincingly feign raptures that would last for days, Teresa was a consummate actress and a class apart from the rest. Receiving more attention from her father than she had ever received before, she went to greater and greater extremes to please him. She feigned paralyses, raptures, and visions of Thomas Aquinas, Nicholas of Tolentino, Teresa of Ávila, Peter of Alcántara, the Blessed Virgin and Jesus Christ. She told people she wanted to go to China to be martyred for the faith, claimed the ability to divine the fate of the dead, and invented a second purgatory known as the *penacularia*. When receiving Holy Communion she would take the Host in her hands, display it to those who surrounded her and place it on her tongue, where it would apparently dissolve into blood and dribble from her mouth. Every once in a while she would also bear the marks of the stigmata.

As the gifts and donations began to roll in, Juan decided to take the show on the road. Dressing Teresa in the robes of a Carmelite nun, he took the entire family first to Atlixco, and then to Puebla, where they remained for some time, the girls now calling themselves 'María of the Incarnation', 'Nicolasa of Saint Dominic', 'Josefa of Saint Luis Beltrán', and 'Teresa of Jesus'. From Puebla the family eventually headed to Tepetlaoxtoc, where the whole affair almost blew up in their faces.

Having earned the scorn of their Creole neighbours—for appearing to mix too freely with Indians—the family's reputation took a further hammering as a result of Teresa's affair with an Indian youth which, when discovered, was touted as 'rape'. They survived the general opprobrium by generally ignoring it, only to be run out of town in the wake of a near riot that followed Juan's eviction of an Indian family he had cheated out of their home.

Forced to flee Tepetlaoxtoc, the family made their way to the capital, where the girls resumed their 'visions' and the mask of holy idiots. Showered with compliments and gifts by some of the wealthiest families in the city, they began to enjoy a lifestyle that only a few years previously they would have thought permanently beyond their reach. Josefa, in particular, became so individually wealthy that she was soon able to dress in fine clothes and travel in her own coach. She even attracted a disciple—a Spanish priest by the name of José Bruñon de Vértiz—who proceeded to publish two books based on her sayings before switching his allegiance to María, to whom he became spiritual advisor.

Bruñon, an ingenuous old cleric who hailed from the Spanish city of Pamplona, genuinely believed the girls to be living saints and so jealously guarded their virtue that at one stage he even attempted to persuade Diego from enjoying marital relations with his wife (who had managed to persuade the old priest that she was God's secretary and spokesperson) on the grounds that it would spoil her spiritual purity. As for Teresa, the young Indian was still on the scene, and she was already with child.

Despite countless attempts by the family to induce an abortion, Teresa's pregnancy continued apace. For much of the time it was easily concealed beneath her long and shapeless habit, but in the later stages she dropped completely out of sight. In the basement of the family home she gave birth to a boy and named him Nicolás, after Nicholas of Tolentino, the saint who had miraculously 'cured' her.

Shortly after the delivery, Teresa being unable to feed Nicolás, the child was secretly taken by his father to a wet-nurse on the outskirts of the capital. About a week later, by which time Teresa was up and about

231

again, he was brought back and deposited on the doorstep of a neighbour. Under the pretence of having adopted an abandoned child, Teresa was able to raise him without any undue scandal. But the fraud could not go on forever and, in the early autumn of 1649, Teresa and her son were finally detained by the Inquisition, who suspected them of belonging to the heretical sect of the *alumbrados* (enlightened ones).

The arrest came as something of a relief. The responsibilities of child rearing had changed Teresa's outlook on life and she had become weary of the charade. When questioned about her visions and raptures, she admitted that they were fraudulent and implicated the rest of her family in the deception. Pregnant at the time of her arrest (evidence, the Inquisitors said, of her 'dangerously licentious' nature), she gave birth to a second son in prison and named him Juan, after the child's father.

Following Teresa's confession, Diego was arrested along with his wife and her sisters. His protestation of being an innocent dupe, however, was ignored by the Inquisitors. They believed it impossible that he could have been any less involved, or informed, than the rest of them. And when he refused to incriminate either Teresa or Nicolasa (the two sisters the Inquisitors were most interested in), he was gaoled for his trouble.

Diego's physical attributes opened the door to new possibilities. Schemes abandoned as being too much for one man could quite easily be accomplished by two, as long as both were fully committed to the enterprise. The realisation prompted William to set about turning the blacksmith's head against the Holy Office and his rough gnarled hands to the delicate task of escape.

'Where do you think you are right now?' he asked Diego one day.

'In a tribunal of mercy,' replied the blacksmith.

'Wrong,' thundered William, 'You are in a place devoid of faith, law, reason and even of justice. Here there is nothing but cruelty, torture, floggings, galleys and penitential habits.'

Using the only tools at his disposal, fear and intimidation, he bombarded Diego with harrowing accounts of cruelty, neglect and executions, not to mention numerous heavily embroidered stories of his own past glories. Over time, as the simple blacksmith listened to his exaggerated genealogy and grandiose scheming, William just about grew to trust him or, at the very least, to trust in his ability to manipulate him.

Sometimes in response to questions, sometimes unbidden, he began to share more and more of his past and hardly a conversation would pass between them that was not punctuated with some vainglorious anecdote of his time at court.

He was, he told Diego, a secret agent of the Count-Duke of Olivares who had been sent on a mission to New Spain following an unfortunate affair with a lady at court—a lady he had intended to send for when he received the title promised him by the Count-Duke. Such was his fortune, he boasted that a valuable collection of clocks and jewel cases had been confiscated from his apartment following his arrest, along with a rare perfume said to contain all the scents of the world in one. Also taken were some slaves, a coach, some mules, a good walking mare, bracelets, paintings, a bed of red ebony, a much admired set of chairs and writing desks, a number of boxes of soap, a gilded plate, some fine china, linen, a plethora of expensive shirts and a different change of clothes for every day of the week, all of which were worth a small fortune to the Inquisition (a prisoner's belongings were always auctioned 'to pay for his upkeep').

On another occasion he alleged that, shortly before his affair with Ana de Cano y Leyva, he had worked for one of the royal councils in Madrid and while there had once taken it upon himself to intervene in a dispute between the their Royal Majesties over the fate of an imprisoned nobleman that the King wanted executed but the Queen did not. According to Diego:

> A certain person was imprisoned . . . and either sentenced, or about to be sentenced to death. The King wanted that he should die and the Queen that he should not, and on this point the entire palace was in such a state of agitation that he [Don Guillén], dreading some great tumult, arranged with the Nuncio that the Pontiff should write to His Majesty that he should send the prisoner to him, as he had cases outstanding in the Roman Curia. The said Don Guillén had also written to His Holiness on this matter, and he had responded by writing to the King requesting the prisoner and putting him [the King] under threat of excommunication if he

did not send him. This excommunication was notified by the Nuncio to His Majesty, who then sent the prisoner. In this manner the dispute between the King and Queen had been settled by the device which he [Don Guillén] had contrived. This Don Guillén had discovered later, when the Count-Duke showed him the letter that the Pontiff had written to him.

A copy of the Pontiff's reply, William maintained, had been confiscated with the rest of his papers (no such letter, however, has ever been found) and when his role in the matter was made known to the King and Queen, he received, or so he claimed, the grateful thanks of both.

William also led Diego to believe that the blue-green velvet cross embroidered on his doublet was the insignia of the *Habito de San Patricio*—a prestigious order, he claimed, that was awarded only to those who had performed great deeds in the service of the faith. The honour had been bestowed upon him because of a pamphlet he had written in London. Only two people had ever been admitted to this order—the other being King Sigismund of Poland (the son of a Swedish king whose adherence to the Catholic faith had cost him his hereditary right to the Swedish throne).

The bravura and self-delusion that had helped William hang on to some semblance of self-worth during the early years of his captivity had by now crystallised into sincerely held beliefs. Having convinced himself, it was no great task to convince others and the apparent acquiescence of his audience only helped to reinforce the distortion. But Diego, a simple and illiterate peasant, knew nothing of what had gone before, and was as enthralled by the Irishman's stories as he was intimidated by his wit. So, when William eventually spoke of escape, he uttered little in the way of protest.

Not since 1624, however, had anyone escaped from the prisons of the Mexican Inquisition. Should they be caught it would mean much more than a whipping, it would mean the stake. But *that* was something William kept very much to himself. They would be quite safe, he declared, if they could reach a Negro *palenque* (literally, 'palisade') in the far south. Here they would find refuge with some rebel slaves who had kept a little piece of Africa alive in their hearts and did not return run-aways to the Spanish—or at least that was what he had been told by one of his previous cellmates, Francisco Lopéz de Fonseca.

Slave revolts had, in fact, been common in New Spain since the early 1560s, especially in the areas around Veracruz, where escaped slaves fre-quently joined together to form communities called *palenques* and, from the safety of their bases in the lush and inaccessible mountains further inland, survived by raiding colonial settlements. Unable to suppress them, the Spanish had been forced, in 1608, to sign a truce with their leader, a Ghanaian slave by the name of Yanga. Under the terms of the truce, Yanga's band of eighty men and twenty women gained their emancipation, and their new settlement, San Lorenzo de los Negros, was granted the privilege of becoming the world's first 'free town'.

In return for these concessions, Yanga betrayed the remainder of his race and agreed to return all runaway slaves captured after September 1608. But despite the treaty, new *palenques* continued to appear and dis-appear and William was pinning his hopes on one he believed to exist at San Antonio, in the jungle-covered hills that lay inland from Veracruz. From here, he claimed, he 'would despatch to His Majesty an account of the injustice that the Viceroy had done to him in not arresting the Inquisitors and asking them to account for the three or four million pesos they had confiscated from such an infinity of prisoners' (an accu-rate estimate as it turned out—the *auto* of 1649 alone having seen Inquisitorial confiscations amount to almost 3,000,000 pesos).

One night, in November 1650, after he had finished his supper, William pulled a sharp piece of iron from the lining of his doublet and told Diego the time had come. For three nights running he sealed the windows of the cell so that their activity could not be seen from outside, laid straw about the floor beneath the window to cushion the fall of debris, and set about uprooting the wooden bars from their base (fol-lowing the departure of the Jews the Inquisitors had ceased to assign guards to the prison at night).

With an interminable stream of interrogation, flattery, insults and bribery (he promised Diego that he would help set him up in a shop sell-ing government-controlled tobacco), he chipped away at the simple blacksmith's reluctance and harried and hectored him into helping with the more physically demanding tasks. With Diego's assistance he removed a piece of iron from his bed and fashioned it in the brazier to make a crowbar. A piece of iron was fixed to a bone to make a primitive bore; a hinge was fashioned into a plane; and the corner plates of a wooden chest were straightened to make brackets. With these simple tools he modified two floorboards to fit through the window and cut grooves into the sides to which they could later attach linen stirrups to form a ladder.

'There is not a man in this world,' he laughed as he braided strips of torn shirts, sheets and pillowcases, 'can compare with me when it comes to this particular task.'

Over the days that followed, William asked the wardens to purchase some silk, cotton, chiffon gauze, thread and silk points for him. He also managed, despite the general prohibition on such things, to procure some paper, upon which he began to compose a letter to the Viceroy; a letter he hoped would lead to the imprisonment of the Inquisitors and the confiscation of their belongings. The Inquisitors, he told Diego, 'would drop dead from the fear' of what he had discovered of their 'abominations, turpitude and wickedness'.

With the chiffon gauze he mended his cuffs and his collar; with the silk and cotton he repaired his clothes. And when he had darned enough to allow them to disguise the fact that they were prisoners, he trussed the mended clothes into two small bundles and asked to have his beard trimmed and his hair cut. The guards saw nothing unusual in his new-found concern for his appearance and attributed his improving spirits to the companionship of his new cellmate—a companion who was already entertaining thoughts of betrayal.

(48)

O<small>N THE EVENING</small> of 12 December, William and Diego had a dry run. The whole exercise, they found, could be completed in less than eight hours. If they started at 8 p.m. they could be free before dawn.

'With this escape, Diego,' William enthused, 'we are going to attempt something heroic, just, and Christian.'

The following day, the incessant carillon that traditionally accompanied such momentous events announced the death of Archbishop Mañozca. It delighted William no end. 'One enemy less,' he exulted.

He woke next morning seized with an idea. The deceased Archbishop, he told Diego, had been sent to him in a vision to seek his forgiveness and assist him with his escape. He had even given him a sign: with a hand of fire he had left his mark upon the wooden dais of his bed.

Diego recognised the mark—scorch damage from their exertions with the brazier a few nights previous.

William now went scurrying about the cell gathering the scraps of cigarette paper he had hoarded of late and amending the pamphlets he was making from them to include details of their miraculous escape. They had, he wrote, been carried from their cells by grace of God and the ghost of the late Archbishop. Having conspired to conceal the 'abominable horrors' perpetrated by the Holy Office, His Excellency now wished to atone for his sins.

Shortly afterwards, Diego requested an audience with the Inquisitors. He loved his wife dearly and was not about to leave prison without her: he was also deathly afraid of being excommunicated. Finding what he thought was an ideal opportunity to procure some leniency for them both, he told Don Francisco de Estrada y Escobedo about a pamphlet that William was currently writing about his 'vision' of the late Archbishop and of the corruption of the Inquisition. He also told him of William's plan to escape on the night of 24 December.

Estrada was delighted. An attempted escape was tantamount to a refusal to repent and as such carried the death penalty. As long as he was caught, the Inquisition's problems with the Irishman would be solved. But even if he managed to evade capture, the Irishman's escape would still prove tremendously embarrassing for the new Chief Inquisitor, Juan Sáenz d Mañozca. Since 1642, when Mañozca reported Estrada to the Suprema for laziness and incompetence (thereby scuppering Estrada's hopes of promotion), there had been bad blood betwen the pair and so he offered Diego a deal. Both he and his wife would be allowed to escape in return for the details of William's plans. The blacksmith would leave with William, and his wife would be secretly released afterwards. Only William would be returned to prison. Nobody would ever know of the agreement, and it would be up to Diego and his wife to make good their escape. In the meantime, William was to be allowed to continue writing his pamphlets.

With one foot already in Guanajuato, where he was heading for the Christmas holidays, Estrada then oversaw the drafting of a proclamation detailing the escape, not just of Diego, but also of his wife, María Romero. But whatever else William may have been at this time, he was not a fool. In fact he was already several steps ahead of them.

Two days later, taking his dream for an omen, William fashioned a penitential cilice from a piece of matting and fell to his knees. Hands clasped in supplication and face turned to the wall, for eight days straight he prayed and fasted. On Friday 23 December he finally accepted some tortilla and, ceremoniously sprinkling it with ashes, declared his fasting to be at an end.

On Christmas morning William told Diego to prepare. They would escape that night. It was a public holiday. The prison would be unguarded and the streets deserted.

Diego was caught between sword and fire. An audience with Estrada would not be possible until he returned from Guanajuato and he dared not raise the alarm for fear of retribution. He had little choice, therefore, but to go along with the plan and hope that the swag-bellied Inquisitor would honour his part of the bargain.

At the hour of the siesta, William took himself off to bed. He slept through most of the afternoon and even through the arrival of the warden,

Hernando de la Fuente, who arrived shortly after dusk to bring the prisoners their supper and candles. After the Angelus, Diego roused William and for the next two hours they waited.

At 8 p.m. they began. Forcing the grille from the window and dismantling the wooden bars, Diego scrambled down into the small courtyard below. Before following, William passed him their makeshift ladder and tools, two bundles of clothes and the brazier. Heading in the direction of the orchard, they found their access barred by two heavy wooden doors and an iron gate. Lighting the brazier, they began to heat their improvised tools and to remove the locks.

At every stage of the operation, William took care to sweep away the debris and put the equipment back into a canvas sack. His embellishments cost him time, and the use of his left hand (burned while shifting the brazier), but he had his reasons. On gaining entrance to a fruit and vegetable garden belonging to Inquisitor Mañozca, he paused to wrap his wound in a piece of clean linen while Diego buried the tools—the absence of which, William believed, would create the illusion of a supernatural escape.

Using the first of the two planks they had brought from their cell, they now attempted to scale the garden wall. It was too short. For a moment it looked as if they were going to have to dig up the tools and join the planks together, but William spotted a stone trough above which the wall was fortuitously crenellated. Between the merlons one plank was just about sufficient.

Having changed his clothes, William scrambled onto the wall. Tying one end of the linen rope round a merlon, he lowered himself into the narrow alley on the other side. Diego followed after him, his heart fluttering like frantic sparrow. Under a clear sky and an incandescent moon, they scurried along the Calle de la Perpetua, dumping the old clothes as they went. Within minutes they were upon the vast expanse of the Plaza Mayor.

There was not a lantern or torch to be seen anywhere. The only sounds to break the stillness were the ripple of water against the Puente de Palacio, the occasional echo of '*agua va*' as a shower of excrement splattered the cobbles in some distant street, and the seditious whisper of William's pamphlets as he fixed them to a door at the northwest corner of the palace. Turning to Diego, he explained that he had one more task to complete, told him what to say should a night patrol come by, and asked him to wait.

The palace gates being unattended it was easy enough to break in and William had already entered the first building when he was spotted by a halberdier of the Viceroy's guard. Sent to fetch some playing cards by the butler of the Viceroy's son, José de Villafuerte was returning to the royal apartments when he spotted movement in the shadows. He drew his sword.

'Who goes there?'

William stepped forward into the light, revealing himself, in Villafuerte's words, to be 'drably dressed, of reddish colouring, and with a sharp voice—like a parakeet'.

There was no need to be alarmed, William reassured him, he was just a messenger from Havana with urgent letters for the Viceroy (at this time Luis Enríquez de Guzmán, the Count of Alba de Liste). The letters were important, he explained, and must be placed only in the hands of the Count.

William had made several attempts to get letters to the King while in prison. None had succeeded. By placing his latest in the hands of the Viceroy he believed their delivery would be guaranteed. Hoping for a generous tip as the bearer of what he assumed must be important news, Villafuerte took possession of William's sealed bundle of seventeen pages and began to walk away.

'Immediately,' William growled after him.

'IMMEDIATELY!'

The halberdier quickened his pace and headed in the direction of the royal apartments.

'For the Viceroy's hands only,' he repeated, and waited until he saw him enter.

Villafuerte went straight to the living quarters of the Viceroy's eldest son, Don Juan Enrique, and tried to bargain with his pages to allow him to deliver the papers to the Viceroy in person. They refused. At the very least, he pleaded, one of them should wake the Viceroy. But the pages were not about to wake the most powerful man in the Indies to deliver a suspicious letter. He could leave it with them if he wanted.

Afraid of losing his tip, Villafuerte placed William's letter between his doublet and jerkin and went about delivering the playing cards. He would try again in the morning.

As soon as the halberdier had disappeared from view, William rushed back to where he had left Diego. He found the blacksmith nervous and anxious to get going. Crossing the plaza to fix two of his pamphlets to the giant wooden doors of the Metropolitan Cathedral, he looked up at the clock. It was almost 3 a.m. They were still ahead of schedule.

He should have been thinking of Veracruz; he should have been miles away by now; but William wanted so much more than his freedom; he wanted to smash the shroud of secrecy that shielded the Holy Office from public scrutiny and to publicly advertise what he knew of its corruption and cruelty. He wanted to wake the righteous from their innocent slumber and open the eyes of the wilfully blind. He wanted people to know, not just what had been done to him, but also to the likes of Isabel Tristán. He wanted to name names:

> . . . the insidious traitors, Domingo de Argos (deceased), Francisco de Estrada alias Cuadros, Juan de Mañozca, and Bernabé de Higuera, with their monstrous secretaries and accomplices . . .

So preoccupied was he with his pamphlets that William barely noticed his surroundings. Turning to leave, his attention was caught by a giant stone crucifix. Almost ten metres high, it was engraved with a skull and cross-bones on the side facing the Plaza and on the opposite side with the arms of Saint Peter and the diadem and keys of the Papal emblem. He turned inquisitively towards Diego.

'Who put this here?'

'Archbishop Mañozca.'

The cross had been discovered a few years previous in an overgrown cemetery in Tepeapulco. Believed to have been sculpted by Franciscan missionaries about the time of the *Conquista*, Mañozca had ordered it brought to the capital and had commissioned some additional ornamentation—not least of which was his personal coat of arms.

'I venerate you,' whispered William sarcastically in genuflection, 'even though you were erected by a thief!'

Heading at last towards the Plaza del Empedradillo, William fixed another of his tiny lettered pamphlets to the 'Saddler's Cross' before scampering down the Calle de Tacuba and the Calle de los Donceles towards the Calle del Esclavo. From there they headed by way of the Calle de la Pila Seca and Calle de San Lorenzo to the Calle de la Concepción, their intended destination being a house in the predominantly Indian neighbourhood of Santa María de la Redonda.

At several prominent locations along the way, William stopped to fix his pamphlets to the walls with pieces of chewed bread. It drove Diego to distraction. Every minute's delay seemed like an hour and with every stop his courage leaked a little more. As they neared the house they were seeking, it deserted him entirely. Confronted by a group of irate Indians who had taken them for thieves, Diego took to his heels and fled. He did not stop running until he reached Guanajuato (350km away). William, meanwhile, managed to convince the irate Indians that he was not a thief and to take him to the house that he was seeking.

Francisco de Garnica would never forget the cold December night he first set eyes on William Lamport. Fast asleep in his bed alongside his wife, Beatriz, he was awoken by a commotion in the street below and a banging on his door that also roused from their slumber his two unmarried daughters, Madalena and Catalina (twenty-two and twenty years old respectively). Going to his window he saw a small crowd of Indians holding a man hostage.

'Oy, Señor Garnica, it's me, Olivera.'

Intrigued by the familiarity with which the stranger spoke, Garnica came down for a better look. But this was not Olivera: in fact it was not anyone he knew at all. Before Garnica could give the game away, William asked if he could have a word in private.

The stranger spoke with the manner and bearing of a gentleman, but he did not look like one. His chestnut-brown hair was cut uncommonly tight, his skin was as pale as alabaster and he was cadaverously thin. One hand carried a bundle of old rags, the other was bound with a makeshift bandage. His apparel, all of which had seen better days, consisted of a bright red cloak, a green silk doublet and hose, and two shirts against the cold. But one can always tell a bird by its flight and this was no jackdaw.

Shielding his wife and daughters behind him, a suspicious Garnica motioned his strange visitor inside and led him towards a small luminous whitewashed patio. As William passed the ladies in the doorway they were struck by his 'very bright eyes'. A faint whiff of perfume confirmed them in their assumption that, despite his pitiful and sickly pale appearance, he was a man of some consequence.

'Do you know a man by the name of Diego Pinto Bravo?' William enquired as they entered the courtyard.

Garnica did know a man by that name but he was currently being held by the Inquisition and he did not believe it could be the same man.

'No . . . I'm afraid not.'

Recognising his difficulty, William told him of their escape and Garnica returned immediately to the Indians to tell them that everything was fine. Satisfied, the mob returned to their homes.

Garnica, a master tailor, was a timid man. He was not wealthy, but he was happy and comfortable with his lot and nervous of getting involved in anything that might upset it. His 'guest', on the other hand, had to be a close friend of both Olivera and Pinto to have been given his address, and if they were prepared to trust him then, for the moment at least, so was he. He offered William a bed for the night and, half-expecting Diego to turn up at any minute, set about preparing something for them to eat.

As he devoured his food—his first decent meal in over eight years—William explained how he intended to hang around the city for a few days to see if the Viceroy would act on his charges and how he would leave within sixty days in order to be crowned 'King of Mexico'. He even invited Garnica to accompany him on the journey to San Antonio, where he planned to link up with some runaway African slaves.

The tailor declined. He was frightened out of his wits. Where the hell was Pinto?

*A*T SIX O'CLOCK the following morning, the warden, Hernando de la Fuente, returned to the *Casa de Picazo* to bring the prisoners their breakfast of bread and hot chocolate. He was full of festive cheer.

'*Buenos Días,*' he bellowed.

No-one answered.

There was a palpable tension in the air, and Hernando knew instinctively that something was wrong. When he reached the Irishman's cell, he discovered why. Leaving his Negro slave, Luis, in charge of breakfast, he ran immediately to find the Chief Inquisitor, Juan Sáenz de Mañozca y Murillo.

At roughly the same moment, William's seventeen-page letter was being handed to the Viceroy, Don Luis Enríquez de Guzmán, the Count of Alba de Liste. Don Luis had only read about half a page when he realised the seriousness of the matter and immediately sent for the guard who had delivered it.

'How did you come by this letter?' he asked the anxious halberdier.

Villafuerte recounted, as best he could remember, the events of the previous night.

A couple of hours later, a small crowd began to gather outside a corner shop on the Calle de Tacuba. They were soon joined by Father Juan Fernández Morera, a priest of the cathedral on his way to Mass.

'This can only be some sort of dishonesty,' he shouted, pointing to one of William's pamphlets, 'it must be taken down immediately.'

Jerónimo de Herrera, a local cocoa merchant, whipped out his knife and carefully removed the pamphlets (he hadn't had a chance to read them yet). He showed them briefly to the shop-owner, Pedro de Mesa, then took them home with him.

After Mass at the cathedral had ended, Father Morera called to Herrera's house to examine the pamphlets in more detail. Another priest, a certain Father Nicolás, was reading them aloud as he entered. When he reached the paragraph where William accused the Inquisitors of corruption, Morera lunged forward, tore the pamphlets from his hands, and ordered Herrera to take them to the Holy Office before they found themselves languishing in the secret prisons. Herrera, however, had not quite finished with them yet and after the priests had left he decided to hang on to the pamphlets for a while and to share their contents with his friends and acquaintances.

Mañozca, meanwhile, having satisfied himself that the prisoners were not hidden somewhere within the grounds of the prison, sent a messenger to rouse Don Bernabé de Higuera y Amarilla and returned to the Offices of the Inquisition to await his arrival. A young presbyter was awaiting his return. In his hands, Pedro de Salinas held the pamphlets that William had fixed to the doors of the cathedral.

If he was incensed before, then Mañozca was positively apoplectic now. The town was alive with stories of two prisoners whose escape from the secret prisons appeared to confound the laws of God and nature, and positively buzzing with news of the exposés they had posted throughout the city. In every barber-shop and sacristy, in every tavern and *tertulia*, the talk was of little else. No-one had ever challenged the Holy Office in such a manner before: William had even gone so far as to claim that the late Archbishop was rotting in hell while the Jewish merchant, Tomas Treviño de Sobremonte, was singing with the angels.

By midday, scattered by wind and curiosity, the majority of William's epistles had been carried throughout the city, lighting small bonfires in the minds of those who read them. It would not be easy to determine who had seen the pamphlets, or to put a stop to the murmuring and *sotto voce* insolences, but the Inquisitors were determined to try. An edict was drafted to be read aloud at High Mass the following day. It declared possession of his 'libels' or knowledge of their contents to be a grave sin. Transgressors, it threatened, would be excommunicated.

A messenger was then sent to look for the printer, Antonio Calderón, or more precisely his mother, Paula de Benavides, who had run the family business since the death of her husband, Bernardo, two years previously. Despite the fact that it was a public holiday she was ordered to produce 200 copies of the edict and to have them ready for distribution by 8 a.m. the following morning!

That same morning, after Garnica had left for Mass, William asked his wife, Beatriz, to fetch him some paper and ink, as he had some urgent correspondence to attend to. He also requested a sealing wafer, but there were none to be found in the house and she offered him some blue sealing wax instead. It was not what he wanted, but it would have to do.

Beatriz thought William arrogant and unstable, and feared that he would bring nothing but trouble. His presence also worried her husband, who reserved an especially malicious imprecation for Olivera and Pinto for having landed him in this mess. He had not asked for this dangerous guest; nor was he particularly welcome. All day long it played havoc with his nerves.

At nightfall Garnica went looking for his good friend, Alonso de Benavides, and found the amiable coachman at a card game in Juan Perez' fruit and vegetable shop on the prestigious Calle de los Donceles. As they ambled back to the coach house, Garnica explained that he was sheltering a guest who needed a place to lie low for a few days. He was a poor man, a friend of a friend who had become involved with a married woman and was fleeing from her husband and relatives. He did not think it prudent to have such a man alone in the house with his wife and daughters.

It seemed an innocuous enough request, that is if Benavides and Garnica are to be believed. Such was the furore created by William's escape that it could only have been a complete idiot who did not suspect that he was being asked to harbour a fugitive: this would have been especially so if Benavides was in any way related to the same Paula de Benavides who at this time was busily printing Inquisition edicts condemning all who might assist the fugitives. Nevertheless, Benavides agreed to help.

'Cristóbal.'

A light-skinned youth came running.

'Gather your things from the alcove and take yourself to one of the coaches. I have a guest coming who will need your mattress.'

Upon his return, Garnica told William that he was to be transferred to Benavides' house. It would be safer all round. There were far too many people who had seen him arrive and one loose tongue would bring the constables of the Holy Office storming down upon them.

William was far from happy with the arrangement. Benavides lived on the Calle de los Donceles—uncomfortably close to the Palace of the Inquisition. But he had little choice in the matter. Pulling a borrowed hat down to his eyebrows to conceal his face, he arrived minutes later at the coach house to find the apprentice, Cristóbal de Escobar, making up a bed with fresh sheets. William was surprised to find a youth with no obvious Negro or Indian features working as a servant.

'Are you Spanish?' he asked him.

'Hardly,' replied Cristóbal, 'there are no *Mestizos* in Spain.'

William smiled.

'One day we will change these things. One day I will be serving you.'

Early next morning, ironically the day of the Holy Innocents, Garnica called on William to see how he was getting on. The Irishman was not in good spirits. He cursed Benavides for not having brought him his breakfast and called him a 'horned Indian' (a contemporary metaphor for cuckold). Garnica admonished William for the abuse of his friend—a friend who without question had agreed to shelter a complete stranger in his home.

William's temper calmed when Cristóbal arrived with some toast and hot chocolate, and for the next two hours Garnica sat with him as he recounted his experiences in prison and his plans for the future. Garnica then left for High Mass at the cathedral—Benavides and his wife having already left for the Temple of the Incarnation.

At every one of the forty-seven churches in Mexico City, Mañozca's edict was announced with gargoyled fury from the pulpit. A copy was also nailed to the doors. In both instances the prisoners were named. Had Benavides and Garnica been uncertain before, then neither could claim ignorance now. They knew exactly who they were sheltering, and why.

After she returned from Mass, Doña Inés de los Reyes (Benavides' wife) was visited by her godfather, the surgeon Juan de Hoz. He told her of rumours that were sweeping the city concerning the breakout of two prisoners from the secret prisons of the Inquisition. They had, he said, escaped in a flying ship constructed by means of necromancy and manned by all manner of demons.

By midday Garnica's nerve had failed him completely and he went to tell the Inquisitors what he knew. One and a half hours later, his testimony having been transcribed and witnessed, the Inquisitors ordered him to take the constable, Pedro López de Soto, and a posse of minor officials to William. So as not to attract any undue attention they were to split into small groups and travel by separate routes.

At about 2 p.m., Cristóbal heard a commotion in the courtyard. Looking out of the kitchen window he saw a large group of men enter the house with swords drawn. They went straight to the alcove under the stairs where they found the Irishman eating his lunch.

William jumped to his feet.

'This business will end at the stake,' he shouted menacingly, 'and I swear I will not go alone.'

Despite the bravado, he was easily overpowered and a letter he had just written to the new Visitor General, Don Pedro de Galvéz, was confiscated. Bound, gagged and bundled into a carriage, he was hauled immediately back to prison.

Along the road angry citizens, recognising the insignia of the Holy Office, assailed the carriage. Some even drew their swords.

'DOG!'

'HERETIC!'

'JEW!'

Back at the prison, William was locked in the ante-room of the torture chamber. To prevent him from committing suicide, his hands were fettered and his feet were placed in stocks.

A troubled Benavides, meanwhile, was making his way home from the Temple of the Incarnation, where he had remained for the duration of two Masses. As was his custom on Sundays, he headed for Juan Pérez' shop to purchase a *chirimoya*.

Pérez knew Benavides' habits as well as he knew the ticking of his parlour clock. They had sat for many years across the same card table and knew each other better, perhaps, than they knew their own wives. Pérez could almost divine the exact moment of his friend's appearance and was standing in the doorway as he turned the corner.

'There has been a commotion at your house,' he called out, 'and the Inquisition have taken a man away.'

Benavides raced home to find his wife still standing in the middle of the street in a state of shock. He took her straight to the headquarters of the Holy Office to tell their story before they were compelled to do so. The Inquisitors, however, were otherwise engaged, and the pair were asked to return the following day.

Immediately following William's arrest, the Inquisitors called on the Viceroy, ostensibly to seek his assistance in capturing the escapees, but also to ascertain how much he knew. Cool and courteous, Alba admitted to having received some seventeen sheets of allegations. He would hand them over in due course, he said, *after* he had read them. But though he promised his assistance in helping to recapture the prisoners, his admiration for their ingenuity led the Inquisitors to believe that he intended to send the pamphlets to the King. It sent them into goitres of rage and, threatening Alba with excommunication, they eventually bullied him into handing them over.

William's pamphlets caused a scandal in the city like none other before it. They made public the unspoken and privately held convictions of many, and destroyed a number of important reputations. Almost overnight he became a legend and the 'supernatural' nature of his escape was on everyone's lips—so much so that, on 31 December, Mañozca felt it necessary to issue a new edict declaring possession of the pamphlets a sin punishable by excommunication. The detail in William's accusations left little room for doubt and those who read them by and large believed them. As for the grandiloquent pedigree that accompanied them, this too was probably taken at face value:

> I, Don Guillén de Lombardo, by the grace of God, pure, perfect and faithful Catholic, Apostolic, Roman, firstborn of the Church and heir to her purity in direct descent for more than fourteen hundred years, as recorded in the archives of the Vatican, Simancas, Toledo, Escorial, Santiago, and His Majesty's Council of State; Seafaring General, *Colegial Mayor* at His Majesty's College in San Lorenzo, promoted to the College of *San Bartolomé* in Salamanca, natural courtesan in the kingdom of Castile, Fieldmaster and pensioner of the kingdom of Naples, Simple Beneficiary of Ávila, Baron of Enniscorthy,

Confidant of his Majesty, Chief Quirite of Saint Patrick, Defender of the Faith by Apostolic vote, Marquis of Crópani by royal decree of His Majesty according to the advice of the Count-Duke etc., etc; son in legitimate marriage to the illustrious and catholic Baroness Sutton and Richard Lamport, heir to the royal blood of the Kings of Lombardy . . .

In many of these pamphlets William claimed that prior to his arrest he had written a letter to the King concerning the imprisonment, on spurious charges of Judaism, of seventy of 'the most powerful families in the kingdom'; of the illegal seizure of their belongings; and of the havoc that such action was wreaking on the commercial life of the colony. This letter, which he had given to the Carrillos' servant, Sebastián de Almeida, had found its way into the hands of the Inquisition and had been unlawfully opened. Finding themselves accused of corruption and treason, the Inquisitors had sought to frame him:

. . . and in this detestable deceit they plotted with such precision that on the Saturday morning they induced a certain Felipe Méndez to false testimony and on the Sunday night they stripped me of my honour, liberty and possessions . . . on the pretext that I had ordered a blind Indian to take the drink they call peyote in order to ascertain if a certain appointment was coming to me from Spain. This, oh ye Catholics of Spain, is the shadowy pretence with which for so many years now they have tried to silence a firstborn of the Church and conceal under a mantle of Jesuitism the abominable fraud with which they are blinding the simple common people . . . and they are now intent on killing the man that heaven protects like Daniel, to prevent his exposition of the sacrilegious abominations of these Priests of Baal with their gluttonous hunger for sacrificial victims . . .

William also accused the Inquisitors of simony, of being motivated more by greed than piety, and of treason. He called them, amongst other things, homicidal assassins, hypocrites, thieves, apostates, gamblers, dogmatists, and keepers of concubines. He questioned the very notion that justice could be expected from men so intent on lining their own pockets:

> . . . the haciendas they seize, are for themselves; and a fortune that is guaranteed at 300,000, in an instant is not worth ten . . .

Mohammed and his brothers, he railed, were angels in comparison to the Mexican Inquisitors, whose instruments of torture were more horrendous than any invention of Nero and whose excesses were greater than those of Diocletian. Under such torture many prisoners had been compelled to falsely accuse themselves of all manner of heresies or 'die as glorious martyrs'. Good Catholics had admitted to being Jews; fathers had testified against their sons; daughters against their mothers. If Christ himself had been present, he too would have been denounced. Prisoners were even instructed by stealth in heretical practices, the knowledge of which would be later used against them:

> . . . they killed some with hunger, nudity and penury; others with torture, dungeons, dampness, solitude, shackles and secret whippings, in such a manner that over the course of nine months one poor woman was on a daily basis, and at times twice daily, flogged with irons and did not die; as God is my witness, . . . they drove others to such despair that they would hang themselves; and denied the sacraments to those who were dying lest they should describe these heretical treasons to their confessors;

The posting of his pamphlets to the door of the cathedral was a bizarre act and the echoes of Wittenberg in 1517 were not lost on the Inquisitors. His intended audience, however, the Indians who were first to gather in the plaza each morning, read them more in curiosity than in anger. It was a peculiar feature of the passive and submissive nature of the indigenous races that while they might react against bad government, they would never consider defying the King. They remained as they had always been, fatalistic and acquiescent. For them there had always been a King. It made little difference to the quality of their lives whether he was Aztec, Spanish or Irish!

(50)

*A*S SOON AS he was re-arrested William set about trying to salvage something from the debacle. On the morning of 29 December, he requested an audience with the Inquisitors and, 'with much urgency and tears' (their words not his), he pleaded for an amanuensis. He wanted to retract what he had written in his pamphlets. His request for an audience was initially refused, but such was his insistence that he was eventually, and reluctantly, granted one with Juan Sáenz de Mañozca.

Perhaps Mañozca was still seething at the contents of William's pamphlets, perhaps it was simply that William had once again refused or forgotten to genuflect upon entering the audience hall, but Mañozca ordered the guards to drag William to the ground so that he could humiliate him further. With his foot pressing down on the Irishman's neck, and oblivious to the fact that his actions were being recorded by the scribe, he began to recite, or rather to paraphrase the 91st psalm:

> *Super aspidem et basilicum ambulabo: et leonem conculcabo et draconem* . . . I will walk upon the asp and the basilisk: and will trample under foot the lion and the dragon.

And yet still William insisted that he be allowed to make a retraction. To shut him up Mañozca allowed him a quill and some paper, and had him returned to his cell. And so began *The Penitent Christian—The retraction of Don Guillén Lombardo of the criminal complaint fulminated in this city of Mexico on the 25th of December 1650.* Prefaced by twenty-two octaves of verse composed in honour of the *Illustrious Señor Inquisitor General and Supreme Council of the Holy and General Inquisition of Spain,* it began with a classical flourish in the style of Luis Góngora y Argote (perhaps the most popular poet in Spain at this time, and a man whose works had been greatly favoured by the Count-Duke of Olivares):

Great Alcides and, from Olympus pure,
Steadfast Atlas, who on your shoulders carry
That felicitous Colure of the eternal globe,
And from the fixed Pole aim at the fallen Arcturus
Orion's rage to forestall.
Listen attentively, one moment, to my song,
My flowing prose and my damburst of tears . . .

By admitting his guilt and seeking a reconciliation with the Holy Office, William hoped to avoid the stake. It was obviously a ruse, but it would be difficult to prove him insincere. Twelve days later, having completed the poem, he sent the Inquisitors the text and requested an audience. Both were ignored.

The same, unfortunately, could not be said of his accomplice. Having travelled over 350km on foot to Guanajuato, Diego arrived to find Estrada vexed beyond reason. William's pamphlets had changed everything. Despite their secret pact, Estrada booted the unfortunate blacksmith back to the capital and, several weeks later, before he could be questioned in any great detail about his part in the escape and why he had travelled to Guanajuato, Diego was found dead in his cell. Physically strong and exceptionally fit, his death was sudden and mysterious—though he was not the first potential embarrassment to the Holy Office to die in custody.

On 1 February 1651, William requested some paper and books with which to settle his 'quarrel' with the Inquisitors. Amongst them were included the religious treatises of the Jesuit theologian Gaspar Hurtado (professor of theology at the Colegio Imperial between 1633 and 1636), the old reliable *Defensio Fidei Catholicae* of Francisco de Suárez, and some books on Canon Law. It is not known if he ever received them, but it is unlikely. The Inquisitors were much too preoccupied with discovering just how many people had seen, taken or spoken of his pamphlets.

It was, of course, much too late for rectification or mercy. His pamphlets had hit the Inquisitors where it hurt most; their reputations. They were still feared by the general public, but it was a different kind of fear. They still received the outward courtesies of respect, but it was a different kind of respect. The tongue said 'Your Worship', but the eyes spoke 'Hypocrite'.

Still too powerful to become the subject of derision, they neverthe-less found themselves looked upon, not as princes, but as petty tyrants, and ran around in an agitated delirium trying to control the spread of this strange virus that was eating away at their sanctity and turning the world against them. They returned to the Viceroy and demanded the hand-over of William's letter to the King. Unwilling to directly oppose them, Alba agreed to their demands, only to find himself approached shortly afterwards by an eminent theologian, infected by the same insid-ious contagion, who had spotted an opportunity for revenge.

Juan Bautista de Herrera, or 'Herrera the Wise' as he was more pop-ularly known throughout Mexico, was a 59-year-old Mercedarian friar (an order, ironically enough, that had originally devoted itself to the ran-soming of captives). Once Palafox's diocesan representative in the capi-tal and a professor of theology at the Royal and Pontifical University of Mexico, he had, during Palafox's struggle with the Jesuits, publicly berated Archbishop Mañozca for his calumny and had been imprisoned and removed from the chair of theology as a result. He had been wait-ing quite some time for an opportunity like this, and he was not about to let it pass.

Herrera convinced the Viceroy to write to the King informing him of William's escape and of the content of the Irishman's letter. Having been selected by his order to represent them at the Chapter of Saragossa, he was shortly due to depart for Cádiz and would personally guarantee it delivery.

But merely embarrassing the Inquisition was not enough to assuage Herrera's bitterness; he wanted to savour it as well and before he depart-ed he paid one last 'courtesy' call on Mañozca and Higuera. Showing them the sealed bundle of papers he had been given to deliver, he allowed them to glimpse just enough of William's name to leave them seething. The last thing Mañozca needed now was censure from the Viceroy.

On 14 March, in an audience with the Inquisitors, William's reserve deserted him once again. He questioned the legality of his imprison-ment and the impartiality of those who would judge him. He called them 'heretics' and, in an obvious reference to their recent war with Palafox, 'excommunicants'. As a result of this outburst the Inquisitors, in August of the same year, instructed the warden, Cristóbal Mañoz de Mancilla, that the Irishman was not to be brought before them again. He went immediately to advise William of their decision.

'Well if they are so ignorant that they cannot understand me in Latin,' William replied, 'then next time I'll speak in Castilian. I can't wait to see their faces when I tell them what idiots they have been.'

Some days later Mancilla entered William's cell to bring him his dinner. He was barely inside the door when he spotted a scorpion and he crushed it beneath his boot.

'This place is full of scorpions,' remarked William.

'It's the humidity,' replied the warden, oblivious to the sarcasm.

'Not those,' William corrected, 'I was referring to those upstairs— the Inquisitors.'

As all hope slipped slowly from his grasp, William began to allow himself slip into deeper and deeper bouts of depression. An enormous emotional weight was crushing him and for hours on end he would sit vacant and motionless, swaddled in a cocoon of despair. He tried to find some solace in prayer, but even this could not stop the tears, and he dearly wanted them to stop.

The Viceroy's letter to the King, received in Madrid on 20 April 1651, provoked a response that was less than complimentary to the sender. Alba explained that he had originally intended to hand over only one of William's sheets of allegations and to send the rest to the His Majesty, but had been persuaded otherwise by the Inquisitors who claimed that in matters of faith even the person of the King was subject to the Inquisition.

The letter infuriated Felipe. Once again the Mexican Inquisitors had challenged the authority and privileges of the Crown and Felipe was not about to allow them to be trampled upon on foot of unjustified threats of excommunication. In a letter dated 31 December of the same year he excoriated Alba for having ceded his authority to the Holy Office. At the very least, the King argued, before handing over letters that had contained allegations of Inquisitorial misconduct in the matter of confiscations, and touched upon various other matters pertaining to the common good, Alba should have made copies of them. As for William, Felipe had little to say other than that the Irishman appeared to have had made 'poor use of his studies'. There were no denials of any of the Irishman's claims.

The King was William's last hope, but Felipe appeared reluctant to do anything that might destabilise the colony or encourage the Spanish Inquisition to enter the dispute—something that could easily happen were he to attack their Mexican brethren. He needed help to resolve the matter but the only man he could trust to manage so sensitive an affair, Don Pedro Medina Rico, was already engaged in an investigation in Cartagena, and would not be free for another two years. Felipe had not forgotten the Irishman, but he would have to wait.

On 21 June, the *Suprema* wrote to the Mexican Inquisitors demanding, most likely at the behest of the King, that William's process be wound up as quickly as possible, that he be watched to prevent suicide, and that he be given a companion and some books to read. Refusing one book after another he eventually accepted *The history of the triumphs of our holy faith, The model wife in the life of Santa Lugarda, The symbols of the Faith* and a volume of Pedro de Rivadeneyra's *History of the persecution of the Society of Jesus* that covered the persecution of Catholics in England. The books were, of course, no substitute for company or conversation, but despite the debilitating effects of his depression and the soporific heatwave that was currently enveloping the city, they did at least succeed in resuscitating his sense of crusade.

In the meantime, in November of 1651, the man into whose custody Felipe had wanted William released, Andrés Gómez de Mora, was arraigned on charges of corruption alongside the president of the *Audiencia*, Matías de Peralta, and both were suspended from their duties without pay. The Visitor General, Don Pedro de Galvéz, had swiftly become at one with the *Palafoxistas* and was revelling in taking action against those who had precipitated the bishop's downfall. William was now totally without allies in New Spain.

(51)

ON 14 AUGUST 1653, the morning after the traditional celebrations of the *Conquista*, Don Francisco Fernández de la Cueva, the eighth Duke of Albuquerque, was named as the 22nd Viceroy of New Spain. But even though it continued to be a source of conflict between the Mexican Inquisition, the *Suprema* and the Council of the Indies, the new Viceroy showed not the slightest interest in intervening in William's process.

The fleet which carried Albuquerque and his family to New Spain did, however, carry an unusual instruction from the Inquisitor General in Madrid. Afraid that Palafox's continued absence might give rise to some form of cult following, the *Suprema* banned, under pain of excommunication, the production of all portraits of the former Bishop of Puebla and ordered the surrender of all existing ones. For many of Palafox's friends it was a dangerous time and, rather than risk making representations on William's behalf, they melted away like shadows under clouds.

The Creole resistance movement, such as it was, was equally disinterested. Led now by Don Antonio Urrutia de Vergara (the merchant whose escape from gaol had led to William being sent to Mexico in the first place), their resistance was confined these days to commercial rather than political activity. Urrutia, in fact, had become so wealthy and influential in the intervening years that Albuquerque quickly came to consider *him* as the single greatest threat to his attempts to stamp out corruption.

As for Albuquerque himself, he was, ironically enough, the type of Viceroy that Palafox would have approved of—a zealous reformer and strong governor. He abhorred the state in which he found the colony and was especially robust in his attempts to stamp out alcoholism and delinquency.

Paradoxically, not only did Albuquerque dislike Palafox, he even chose to align himself with his enemies, and in particular with the Inquisitor Juan Manuel de Sotomayor. Even had he known of William's predicament, which does not appear to have been the case, it is unlikely that he would have been inclined to believe anything other than the spin which Sotomayor would have put on the matter. Only one thing had changed since Palafox's departure, and that was the burgeoning thirst for vengeance of those Inquisitors the Irishman had publicly accused of corruption.

(52)

$\mathcal{D}$ON PEDRO MEDINA RICO, the Visitor of the Holy Office, finally arrived in Veracruz on 30 July 1654. Tired and weak, he had little enthusiasm for the task ahead and was in no fit state to take on the wrath of the Mexican Inquisitors. As an Inquisitor himself, he was hamstrung by divided loyalties, but even he could not help being shocked by the laziness of his colleagues and frustrated by their disorganisation and hebetude—a state of affairs most graphically illustrated for him by his investigation into the death of Doña Catalina de Campos.

Theoretically it was the duty of the Inquisitors to visit the prison twice monthly in order to exhort the prisoners to full confessions. Between 1643 and 1647, however, not a single Inquisitor had set foot inside the *Casa de Picazo*. The secret prisons were like a cactus to their consciences and their neglect had encouraged such a culture of lethargy among the guards that on the day that Doña Catalina's corpse was discovered it had already been half-eaten by rats. The guards, who were supposed to bring her food and candles each day, had apparently failed to notice that she was dead. And then, of course, there was the little matter of the Irishman!

Just four days after his arrival in the capital, Medina Rico went to visit William in his cell. Complaining bitterly about the criminality of the Mexican Inquisitors, the Irishman asked for a pen and paper and was given them. Some days later, and for the first time since his re-arrest, his shackles were removed.

The report William compiled was sent to the King with Medina Rico's blessing. The Mexican Inquisitors, however, were none too happy with this development and refused to allow the Irishman any further access to writing materials. But having allowed him to start, there was no way on earth that William was going to stop.

Teetering on the edge of insanity, the only thing that had kept William from falling was pride. But pride alone was never going to be enough. If he was ever to stop himself being swept away on the random torrents of the imagination that were stealing away all semblance of order and control from his miserable existence, then he had to find something upon which he could focus his attention and re-take control of his mind.

And so, trimming a quill from a chicken feather, he started, on his bedsheets, the *First book of the Royal Psalter of Guillermo Lombardo or Lamport, Irishman of Wexford, appointed King of Nearer America and Emperor of the Mexicans.* Saturated with classical allegories his compositions covered a wide range of subjects from romance to religion, philosophy to politics. When his ink supply—salvaged from cotton fibres in the bottom of his inkhorn—finally ran out, he replenished it with the juice of limes and oranges and from candle smoke collected in drops of honey or unrefined sugar-loaf, which he then diluted with water.

From the time he left Wexford, some thirty years previously, the greater part of William's life had been spent in the company of Jesuit tutors or Jewish prisoners. He had, as a result, become as intimately familiar with the psalms of David as he had with the licentious poetry of Ovid. The seven penitential psalms would have been especially familiar to him, and in particular the lachrymose *Domine ne in furore* (traditionally chanted during Lent). He appears to have found great comfort in these ancient cries of anguish and to have recognised in David's struggles with Saul and his attempts to create an independent Israel, something of his own struggle with the Holy Office and his plans for an independent Mexico.

For the first time in his life he was writing entirely for himself and the result was a veritable deluge of intensely personal revelations, confessions, apparitions and miracles. Every morning he would begin a new piece in his head and chip steadily away at it until he felt it worthy of transcription—at which point he would commit it in tiny lettering to his bedsheets. The psalter not only helped to pass the time but to mark its passing (his psalms frequently celebrating the feast days of the liturgical calendar) and it opened, as was perhaps to be expected, in a penitential vein:

I have sinned, O Lord, I have sinned;
I will confess to you with all my heart:
Since I have transgressed against thee
with all my strength, sunk in my wickedness.
But truly I only hope for your immeasurable mercies:
And my deadly illness asks only for health . . .

(Psalm No. 1)

. . . Yes I have sinned. Too much, O Lord!
In your presence tears have cascaded down my face,
My eyes are red from weeping
And my heart breaks with the pain.
And, still sad, and still weary,
I will wipe my tears from my face . . .

(Psalm No. 55)

Consumed with anger and self-loathing, and desperate to renew a connection to his God that was weakening daily, he began once more to over-indulge in acts of religious devotion. He started with acts of penitence and abnegation—for hours on end he could be found kneeling in prayer and his bouts of fasting would last for days—and progressed to self-mortification with a canvas whip and nails.

This period of contrition and demolition, however, did not last for long and he was soon back to his old self, waxing ironical on the virtues of his gaolers and dipping in and out of other, more secular, influences. On an almost daily basis, in an effort to transcend the horrors of what he perceived to be nothing less than a living death, he challenged the fertility of his imagination, the breadth of his classical education, and the power of his memory, and skilfully adapted to his own religious and messianic ends the epistles of Horace, the twelve books of Virgil's *Aeneid* and, not just the *Metamorphoses* of Ovid, but also the profane *Ars Amatoria*:

'Oh Thou, sublime Master of Divine Love,
remind me with your light,
the rules and the art of loving . . . '

(Psalm No. 154)

The works of Juvenal were also frequently quoted, as were, less frequently but no less knowledgeably, the works of Cicero, Juvenal, Quintilian, Prudentius and Pliny. 'The eloquence of Cicero,' he boasted at one point, 'I have in excess, and of Seneca's sententiousness I am not lacking': a comparison that appears to have been a deliberate attempt to invoke a parallel between his own predicament and that of Seneca—a man who, in the public mind at least, had worked himself to death in public service and brought about his own destruction by his inability to reconcile the demands of his conscience with his duty to his Emperor. In fact one cannot help but wonder if that extraordinarily apposite line from Seneca's *Madness of Hercules*—'*Virtutis est domare quae cuncti pavent . . .* It is a virtue to subdue those before whom all go in dread'— could in some way have inspired the resumption of his epistolary crusade against the Holy Office:

> Here, my God, is the holy Inquisition!
> Here its sacred house, its sacred walls,
> And here the holy tribunal where sits
> The holy Minister for Injustice . . .
> My Lord, my God, let me declaim the
> Cruel atrocities of the impious.
> They have rendered a hovel of God's temple,
> Made of it a den of thieves.
> With the plough they have sown your fields
> With deceptions for your heirs.
> From the dark belly of their viscera
> They extract a harvest of sacrilege,
> And like bats have sucked our blood
> With the blood of Our Lord.
> Thus dwellers of dark caves they have made of us.
> Thus have they buried us.
> And still we live.
>
> (Psalm No. 44)

His output was extraordinary. For almost two years hardly a day passed that he did not write something. It was frustrating and difficult work, requiring an almost superhuman degree of self-discipline, but it provided him with something upon which to nourish his intellect and a means of keeping his mind on a tight leash. It did little, however, to relieve the loneliness:

> There is no-one with me now.
> Only the mice.
> My bed is their bed,
> My plate their plate.
> And the worms,
> And venomous crawling scorpions.
> One wounded me once with its deadly sting.
> But never have I felt alone
> In my remove from the world:
> I had companions, Thank God!
> The heartfelt prayer requires silence,
> The man that prays, solitude.
> Yet here I see the shadow of the tomb.
> I am living buried in life,
> Alive in a living death . . .
>
> (Psalm No. 182)

Though his psalms and hymns were generally of a religious or confessional nature, time and again he returned to the abomination of slavery—his work frequently betraying the influence of Suárez and declaiming phrases borrowed from the fathers of what, in modern times, would come to be known as 'liberation theology'.

Delivered in 1511, and quoted by Bartolomé de las Casas in his *Historia de las Indias* (1560), the famous Christmas sermon of Fray Antonio de Montesinos was probably the first public denouncement in the Americas of the enslavement and oppression of the Indians. Although speaking on different subjects—Montesinos on the maltreatment of the Indians and William on the subject of slavery—the influence of this sermon can be clearly seen in both the structure and content of William's 'Psalm No. 652'. Both open with an exhortation to their audience to justify their treatment of their slaves and indentured servants; both continue by asking how the killing of such people can be justified; both appeal to a sense of common humanity and both end on the threat of divine retribution:

Tell me, by what right and by what justice do you hold these Indians in such cruel and horrible servitude?

By what authority have you waged such detestable wars on these people who were living meekly and peacefully in their own lands, where you have laid waste to infinite numbers of them with unheard of havoc and murder? Why do you keep them so oppressed and fatigued, without giving them enough to eat nor curing them when they are ill so that, by the excessive work you inflict upon them, they die, or rather, are slain, in order that you might daily extract and acquire gold? . . .

Are they not men? Do they not have rational souls? Are you not obliged to love them as you love yourselves?

How do you remain in such a state of profound and lethargic slumber? Be certain that in the state in which you find yourselves you can no more be saved than the Moors or Turks who lack and do not want the faith of Jesus Christ.

Tell me, my faithful Americans who claim to follow God, Why do you buy and sell men as though they were beasts?

Why do you kill in slavery those who confess in the name of Christ? Why do you, contrary to the law of God, buy Ethiopians, though you yourselves would not wish to be bought by them? By what right do you take another man's liberty, which is more precious than gold? Is it not sinful to retain stolen goods?

Were they not born free like us? And just as it is wrong for them to to take us captive, is it not also wrong for us to reduce them to cruel servitude?

Unjustly are they sold to you, and unjustly do you purchase them: a great crime have you committed against God, and you must restore the freedom of free people, lest their blood and their slavery cry out to God against you and ensure that the blows of heaven will rain down upon you and your children.

Glory be to God . . .

The threat of divine retribution was expanded even further in Psalm No. 680, in which William claimed that God had given the colony of New Spain to him to hold in trust for all who had the good fortune to live there:

> The Lord will rid us of the Babylonians and turn their statues into ashes,
> He will strike terror amongst the children of Nembroth.
> He will ostracise the wicked-hearted and those who cast scorn upon the humble,
> And He will scatter the bloodthirsty and the iniquitous.
> Those who bear false witness against their neighbour shall be confounded,
> And those who violate the rights of the poor, destroyed.
> Oh! My fellow Spaniards, cast aside forever your arrogant claims to sovereignty
> And despise not my humble Indians and my poor Ethiopians.
> For they are the children of God and like ourselves the work of His hands.
> The Lord is the protector of the weak and He will avenge them their wrongs.
> Honour them, and the Lord will grant you honour and benediction;
> You shall enjoy the abundance of this land He has given me for all.

But whether styling himself as David or Seneca, William had now begun to see himself as a hero of classical proportions, bathed in supernal light and persecuted for his righteousness; a statue, if you like, in search of a pedestal. He understood exactly what he was facing, and while yet to abandon hope entirely, was writing now, not to any person in particular, but to Posterity. As he wrote in one of his earliest psalms (No. 36), he lived in the fear that 'like a bubble in water, my story is being lost from the memory of man'. The 'psalter', to all extents and purposes, had become his valediction; a preparation, perhaps, for what he suspects must inevitably come.

(53)

On 7 December 1654, William was provided once again with a companion—a Basque by the name of Andrés Iriquoz. His latest bout of solitary confinement, however, had left him intolerant to social interaction and the pair did not get on.

A newcomer to the prison, Iriquoz did not understand the unspoken bargain that allowed prisoners to co-exist in peace and was lacking in the patience and understanding that might have been forthcoming from a long-term inmate. Unable to recognise or empathise with the Irishman's suffering, he found his mood swings so annoying that before the day was out he had informed the guards of a book that, for the past two years, William had been writing on his bedsheets. The sheets were confiscated, the Inquisitors informed, and Iriquoz was removed to another cell.

By the time it was transcribed, William's psalter, which filled 234 pages, was found to consist of some 918 psalms and hymns. More commonly known as his *Regio Salterio*, it was an astonishing achievement, especially given his state of mind, the conditions under which it was written, and the effort it must have taken to keep it hidden for so long. To the Mexican Inquisitors, however, it represented, not the heroic struggle of one man to cling to his God and to his sanity, but the clearest evidence yet of demonic possession and so, on 8 June 1655, they handed the psalter over to two Jesuits, Matías de Bocanegra and Marcos de Irala, for examination. But once again no concrete evidence of heresy could be found.

The Inquisitors were never going to admit that William was mentally ill. To do so would be to risk his being taken from their jurisdiction. Despite the fact that in one of their earlier letters to Madrid the Mexican Inquisitors had mentioned that 'the prisoner shows signs of being mad' and the Inquisitors in Lima who had examined some of

William's pamphlets had declared him to be 'a heretic with indications of madness', they still refused to allow him be treated as a mental patient and continued to try him as sane.

In her book *Psiquitría e Inquisición . . . Psychiatry and Inquisition*, the eminent Mexican psychiatrist and ethnohistorian, Dr. Ernestina Jiménez Olivares, notes that:

> despite this evidence of pathological paranoia . . . neither successive fiscals nor advocates, nor even the Inquisitors, nobody!, neither by way of simple humanitarian sentiment, or the most minimal of Christian charity . . . asked that he be examined by a doctor, and his process continued to be aggravated by all the insults and accusations that he made against the Holy Office.

On 23 September 1655, Cristóbal Mañoz de Mancilla made his way to William's cell accompanied by an assistant with the intention of cleaning it out. What happened next was a matter of some dispute, but the warden claimed that the sight of the open door proved too much for the Irishman, who threw himself upon them in such a blind fury that, in the violent set-to that followed, he suffered a stab wound to his side.

William recovered consciousness to find a trickle of olive oil running off his brow.

'Ego te absolvo ab omnibus peccatis tuis.'

The surgeon, Dr Juan Correa, had thought his wounds so grave as to send for a priest to hear his confession and give him the last rites.

'At least now,' William muttered faintly to his confessor, 'I will not be judged by any Inquisitor or Secretary.'

William's version of events, not surprisingly, differed from that of the warden. He had, he claimed, been the victim of an assassination attempt. It was only by his own bravery, and not a little luck, that he had survived. The Inquisitors had been trying to silence him.

But if this had been an assassination attempt, then it was a particularly crude one, especially in the light of the more mysterious death of Diego Pinto Bravo (presumably poisoned). It also required the complicity of far more people than would seem prudent at a time when the Inquisition was under such close official scrutiny. Nevertheless, given the degree of panic that Medina Rico's investigation seems to have inspired, his explanation is not entirely unbelievable. Having escaped once before, his death during a second attempt would at least appear plausible.

William's bruises healed in weeks, but the stab wound to his left side took a lot longer and by the time it had closed his skin covered little more than his bones. Such was the magnitude of the despair into which he plunged following this beating that over a twelve-month period he allowed himself to be shaved just twice, changed neither his clothing nor his bedding, which rapidly became filthy, and began once more to cover his skin and his food with ashes. He also consistently refused to use his chamber pot, causing the floor of his cell to become submerged beneath a stinking faecal sludge. On occasions he would even smear his face with his faeces, claiming that it was a well-known cure for the eye complaint from which he was currently suffering.

The smell alone made official intervention inevitable. The Inquisitors ordered that he be forcibly cleaned, and this time the guards came armed with sticks and whips. With the help of some Indians they had him tied up and brought to another cell and, according to the testimonies of those who took part in this operation, William resisted their attempts to remove him with such fury that they were forced to restrain him by beating him with sticks and flogging him with leather straps.

Whenever he could, the disgruntled warden also cut William's food allowance. Instead of his usual breakfast of chocolate he gave him drinks of maguey juice; and for dinner instead of meat, a meagre ration of sweet peas, kidney beans and some tiny white fishes from Lake Texcoco that weighed little more than an ounce. The evidence of the warden's neglect, however, was writ large upon William's skin and when Medina Rico witnessed his concertina ribs he ordered, on several occasions, that he be given bread, meat and wine—even though the cost would exceed his daily allowance of two reals.

But that was more or less all that the Visitor of the Holy Office did for William. Neither his nakedness, hunger, nor the overwhelming evidence of mental illness that was daily brought before him, could move him or his colleagues to mercy. Exhausted by poor health and the overt hostility, legalistic procrastinations and blatant non-co-operation of the Mexican

Inquisitors (of which he had complained often to Madrid), he had wearied of the struggle and the unpleasant isolation his investigations had imposed upon him. Once again William was left in limbo: lost, but not entirely forgotten.

Despite his reluctance to be publicly critical of his Mexican colleagues, Medina Rico still managed to correct a number of obvious falsehoods in the reports of William's process and to send copies of his confiscated letters to Madrid. Such was the panic that his investigations provoked that, in July of 1655, the Mexican Inquisitors even attempted to pressurise William's confessor, a Dominican by the name of Rodrigo de Medinilla, into breaking the seal of the confessional. Just one of Medina Rico's initiatives met with the general approval of his peers, and even that came as something of a surprise.

In an attempt to reconcile the outstanding inconsistencies and tie up the remaining loose ends in William's process, messengers were sent to Zacatecas and the Monastery of Guadalupe, where William's brother John was currently missioning. Assuming that John would offer them little, they travelled more in hope than expectation. What they returned with, in June of 1656, surprised even the flinty-hearted Mañozca.

When called to testify before the Inquisitor Eugenio de Saravia, John's comments were angry and bitter. He told of how 'his father had devoted himself to William and his studies at the expense of his property', of his visits to William in Madrid and of how he had reproached his brother for not marrying Ana, to little effect. He even went so far as to say that Ana was Portuguese, a dangerous thing to volunteer in the current climate and potentially catastrophic for both Ana and Teresa. Asked if he knew anything of the 'Order of Saint Patrick' that William claimed to be a member of, his reply could hardly have been more cutting.

'I imagine,' he said, 'that no such order exists, and that it is all lies.'

He went on to explain how William had been 'restless, audacious, astute and untruthful' as a child. His brother, he declared, had been a 'mendacious youth' whose natural audacity had often led him to 'attempt things that should never be attempted'.

'What type of things?' the Inquisitors probed; 'Could you be more specific?'

But John could not remember anything specific.

(54)

$\mathcal{T}$HE SCANDAL HAD never really gone away. Fifteen years had come and gone, but the Irishman continued to be a controversial figure. Throughout the capital his name was frequently whispered in private conversations, not least amongst the Franciscans.

William was not the first man ever to have escaped from the secret prisons of the Inquisition (a certain Martín de Villavicencio y Salazar had escaped in 1624), nor was he even the first Irishman to find himself in this predicament (a Protestant Corkman by the name of John Martin alias 'Guillermo Cornelius', who had served with the English pirate John Hawkins, was burned at the stake in 1575). William was not even the most *famous* adventurer to land in New Spain—his escapades paling in comparison with those of Catalina de Erauso who, having escaped from a Basque convent in 1599, proceeded to dress and live as a man, serve with distinction in the Spanish army in Peru and Chile, survive a shipwreck and numerous attempts to murder or execute her, and to kill her own brother (amongst others) in one of her many duels. Like William, she too had enjoyed the favour of the Count-Duke of Olivares, had been introduced to the Pope, and granted a pension from Felipe IV of Spain. She had also, during her visit to the Vatican, been made an honorary citizen of Rome. At the time of William's arrival in New Spain, in fact, she was earning her living as a muleteer in Veracruz under the name of *Don Antonio de Erauso* and it is entirely possible that she travelled with the viceregal mule train that brought William to Mexico City in 1640.

No, the factors that had caused William's legend to endure had little to do with any of his adventures prior to his imprisonment, and everything to do with the pamphlets he had posted throughout the city on the night of his escape. In daring to publicly excoriate the Inquisitors of the Holy Office he had acted out the fantasies of many who were too fearful to speak out themselves.

His greatest champions, not surprisingly, tended to be of Irish extraction and, in March of 1657, a Father Derek Nugent (alias Fray Diego de la Cruz) became enmeshed in a discussion with a number of fellow Franciscans concerning an *auto de fe* held several months earlier. Gabriel de Amaya asked after the fate of two prisoners who had escaped from the dungeons of the Inquisition seven years past. Had they, he wondered, been released?

The Irishman, Nugent answered, had not, and while he did not know for certain where he was, he had heard it said that the Count-Duke had ordered him returned to Madrid. For the benefit of those unfamiliar with the story, Nugent then proceeded to explain how his countryman had escaped from the secret prisons of the Inquisition, broken into the Viceroy's palace, and placed details of Inquisitorial corruption in the hands of the Viceroy. He also proffered the opinion that William had perhaps been more of a Christian than the Inquisitors who had imprisoned him. Fray Nicolás de Santiago did not agree and in a fit of pique he reported Nugent to the Holy Office.

Time had neither assuaged the fears of the Mexican Inquisitors, nor had it tempered their wrath. Still struggling, after all these years, to undo the damage created by William's pamphlets, they were determined to aggressively stamp on any attempts to revive the issue. Nugent's careless words, therefore, cost him ten years in prison and helped to convince Medina Rico that the reputation of the Holy Office could never fully be repaired as long as the matter of William Lamport remained unresolved. One way or another, and before he began his campaign of reform, the mettlesome Irishman would have to be put out of harm's way.

(55)

*A*FTER THIRTEEN YEARS of isolation, William had cried himself dry. Pleasure no longer seemed to hold any real meaning for him and even sadness appeared to have forsaken him. He had entered a world of shadows where all manner of hirsute and masked demons had begun to invade his cell. So real, in fact, had they become to him, that at times he even looked forward to their visitations and regarded many of them as his friends.

The most frequent and enduring of his visitors was a 'guardian angel' who came to him in the form of a sixteen-year-old boy. Dressed predominantly in scarlet, and always wearing white boots, he entrusted him with various revelations—the mere mention of which was treated by the Inquisitors as further evidence of 'demonic possession'.

His belligerence and irascibility also increased daily. Utterly contemptuous of the authority of the Inquisitors, he refused to kiss their rings, to genuflect before the altar in the audience hall or show sufficient respect to the various statues or religious paintings therein. In consequence, every dream, vision, or divine revelation he dared to mention, saw another chapter added to the weight of evidence against him. By the end of October 1659 it amounted to a staggering 228 charges! Death was stalking him, and there was nowhere left to hide.

Time was running out too for Medina Rico. His health was deteriorating daily and, not wanting to die in the Indies, he began to consider a change of strategy. He had little sympathy for either the Irishman or the Mexican Inquisitors: his only concern was for honour and reputation. He allowed himself, therefore, to be brought round to the opinion that William's release would be seen as an admission of guilt and would set back his programme of reform by decades.

The opportunity to resolve the issue, however, did not present itself until June of 1659, when an examination of William's *Regio Salterio*, completed by two Spanish theologians friendly with Mañozca, found the psalter to be 'sacrilegious, defamatory, injurious and contumelious towards the Holy Office'. They also found the author to be 'seditious, reckless and scandalous' in his questioning of the divine right of kings, the right of the Holy Father to interfere in temporal matters, the legality of the rights of conquest granted to Spain by the Pope in his bull of *Inter Caetera* and his insistence on the right of the oppressed to overthrow tyrants by force. Most dangerously of all though, they found him to be 'suspect in the faith' and his psalter to be the work of an 'unrepentant heretic'. Such findings could mean only one thing—the stake.

In dire need of a public relations exercise to repair the damage that William's exposés had inflicted on the reputation of the Holy Office, Medina Rico turned to the Inquisitor's panacea, the *auto de fe*. No ceremony short of coronation could re-affirm in the public consciousness the dual legitimacy of Church and Crown, or allow the Inquisition to parade before the public in their most brilliant plumage and pious grandeur. The crowds that were bound to gather would present them with an audience of such magnitude as would take years to reach by any other means.

On 1 October then, with all the pomp that Mexican society could muster, a ceremony of proclamation took place:

> The Holy Office of the Inquisition hereby makes it known to all faithful Christians presently residing in this City of Mexico and beyond, that a General Act of Faith will be celebrated for the exaltation of our Holy Catholic Faith on the 19th day of November in the principal square of this city. In order that all faithful Catholics might assist in the ceremony and thereby avail of such indulgences as have been conceded by the Sovereign Pontiff to those who participate, it is hereby ordered that this news be proclaimed and brought to the attention of all.

Having escaped inclusion in the *autos particulares* (private ceremonies for less serious crimes) of 1646, 1647 and 1648, and the last great public *auto* of 1649, the Inquisitors were determined that William should not escape this one, and he was summoned to answer the outstanding charges. But he knew what he was facing and refused to co–operate. He was no longer willing, he declared, to respond to the charges of 'demons'.

The outstanding charges were thus added to the sum of those already 'proven' and on the morning of 30 October a tribunal was convened to decide William's fate. Consisting of seven Inquisitors, a minimum of four votes was needed to execute him. One by one, each was polled for his opinion.

The Visitor of the Holy Office, Don Pedro de Medina Rico, despite his earlier doubts about the validity of the charges, proposed that William be handed over to the civil authorities for 'relaxation' (the Holy Office's euphemism for execution). Juan Sáenz de Mañozca y Murillo agreed. The matter, he said, should be concluded as quickly as possible. There was no need to consult the *Suprema*.

Don Francisco de Estrada y Escobedo was broadly consentient with Medina Rico, but he cautioned that the decision should nevertheless be referred to the *Suprema* for ratification (in effect a vote against). His views were echoed by Don Bernabé de Higuera y Amarilla and Dr García de León Castillo.

With Don Francisco Calderón y Romero voting with Medina Rico, the decision was tied at three apiece, and the casting vote came down to the last to be polled, Don Juan Manuel de Sotomayor. He too was in favour of relaxation . . . but only after ratification had been received from the *Suprema*.

William, it appeared, had escaped again.

Alas, it was merely the overture. Unhappy with the decision of his colleagues, Mañozca proceeded to put unbearable pressure on the most vulnerable of them, 62-year-old Bernabé de la Higuera y Amarilla. A pusillanimous laggard who had fathered at least two children by two Negra concubines with whom he had lived for almost twenty years, and whose scandalously ostentatious lifestyle was funded primarily by loans he had never any intention of paying back, Higuera was extremely susceptible to blackmail. On Thursday 6 November, when the tribunal was recalled, he voted with Mañozca.

At forty-four years of age, Death finally laid his gelid fingers upon William Lamport and he was sentenced to be burned alive at the *Auto*

General de la Fe of 19 November 1659. As part of the same sentence his children and grandchildren, by the male line, were prohibited from ever 'wearing about their person, gold, silver, pearls, precious stones, coral, silk, camlet, fine cloth and from riding horses or carrying arms'. They were also barred forever from 'holding dignities, benefices or offices, either ecclesiastical or secular, or any public office or honour'.

On Tuesday 18 November, the city erupted in a fever of festivity. The canals were choc-a-bloc with canoes and the streets were lined with carriages. Apart from William, those sentenced to burn included a vagabond by the name of Pedro García de Arías; a mystical hermit by the name of Juan Gómez; a man in his mid-sixties from Bayona by the name of Sebastián Alvarez who believed himself to be Jesus Christ on account of a line in chapter five of the Book of Apocalpyse which stated that only the Saviour was worthy of understanding Sacred Scripture; a Portuguese healer from Faro by the name of Francisco López de Aponte who suffered from an unfortunate neuropathy that made him insensible to pain and allowed him to tolerate torture to such an extent that it led the Inquisitors to believe he was possessed by the devil; and Don José Bruñon de Vértiz alias 'The Knight of the Miracle'—the Spanish priest who had been spiritual advisor to the Romero sisters, and in particular to Diego Pinto's wife, María.

Arrested alongside Diego Pinto in September of 1649, Bruñon had spent almost seven years struggling in vain to learn the nature of the charges that had been laid against him. He'd grovelled, testified and confessed; he'd done everything that was asked of him until the struggle unhinged his mind and, following his denunciation of the Holy Office as 'a congregation of demons' and the Jesuits as the 'most detestable enemies of God', he was charged with demonical possession. He died on 30 April 1656 without ever learning of what he had been accused and, though his body had long since been removed from the prison and buried in unconsecrated ground, he was condemned alongside the others and sentenced to be burnt in effigy. Apart from Bruñon, and Pedro García de Arías (whose abjuration had earned him the mercy of strangulation), all of the others were sentenced to be burned alive.

Early that afternoon, the famous Green Cross (the symbol of the Inquisition) was draped in a black mourning veil and solemnly paraded from the Chapel of Santo Domingo to the Plaza Mayor. The finishing touches were still being put to a pair of wooden platforms as it arrived. The first was to hold the 'convicts' and their confessors; the second, and larger of the two, the civil and ecclesiastical authorities. To the accompaniment of hymns and burning of incense, the Green Cross was placed on the latter.

As evening fell, the prisoners to be 'relaxed' were taken from their cells and officially informed of their fate. Shortly afterwards the bells began to toll. Labourers stopped and blessed themselves in the fields, Dominican friars in white woollen gowns and black hooded cloaks led the recitation of the five glorious mysteries, and young boys in white cassocks sang antiphons at the cathedral. The Plaza Mayor became a sea of tightly woven blankets and flickering *anafres*, and every possible vantage point was secured and jealously guarded. Hymns were sung with festive gusto and, around the platforms, the Viceroy's musketeers fired volleys of celebration that continued well into the night.

Shortly before 9 p.m., the clergy arrived in the dungeons to hear the last confessions of the condemned; a frail and disinterested Medina Rico tottering along in their wake. He urged each prisoner to clear his conscience and assigned two confessors each to those facing the stake. Assigned to William were Jacinto de Guevara (a Dominican) and Francisco de Armentia (a Mercedarian).

The current occupant of the university chair vacated by 'Herrera the wise' during Palafox's dispute with the Inquisition, the presence of Armentia raised more than a few eyebrows and it is possible that he had volunteered himself for the task. Only a last minute confession could help William now. If his confessors could at least extract that from him, then there might be some hope of procuring the mercy of strangulation.

But William would not capitulate. He had committed no great crime against the faith and back in Madrid men had been forgiven greater crimes against the King. This was not justice, it was murder; and he was not about to dignify it with either his consent or a confession. Accusing his confessors of being 'possessed by a hundred legions of demons', for four hours straight he drove them to distraction; repaying, as one witness recalled, 'their holy zeal and Christian charity' with 'such insults that they believed him to be possessed by some devilish fury'.

The good friars were accustomed to ministering to the dying; but this was a different kind of death. Their presence here made them Death's accomplices and the last minute confessions they so zealously sought were as much for themselves as for the condemned. But with William they struggled. Such was the power of his memory and the breadth of his education that, since the time of his first written defences, he had been able to quote from memory all manner of religious and biblical texts in their original Latin and Greek, and with such uncanny accuracy that the qualificator of the Holy Office himself had been unable to find any errors. Unable to match the Irishman's mastery of Holy Scripture and Canon Law, the efforts of the friars threatened to become violent and a third priest was sent in to calm them.

It was now almost on the stroke of midnight and, despite the braziers, the dungeons had become bitterly cold. Father Francisco Corcheno Carreño entered the cell to find William cowering in a corner, his blanket wrapped tightly about his shoulders. With a studied solemnity he sympathised with William on the duration of his imprisonment and enjoined him to repent his errors and die as a Christian. Eternity was beckoning: it would soon be too late for a confession.

But William was adamant.

'I have erred in nothing.'

'Seventeen years of imprisonment and not even one act of impatience?'

'No!'

'Cast your mind back Don Guillén, do you not recall breaking out of the secret gaols of the Inquisition—a truly grave sin—or writing defamatory libels against priests and other ministers of the Church and posting these libels in public places? Were these the actions of a Christian?'

'One can interpret these things in many ways Father; but yes, I am a Christian.'

William then turned his face to the corner and began to gesticulate at the walls as though talking to some invisible cellmate.

'I *am* a Christian', he muttered quietly, 'a Christian that can allow himself make fun of this strange faith'. He then began, according to one witness, to amuse himself by playing on the word *reir* (to laugh).

Torn between pity for his suffering and anger at his defiance, Corcheno, too, began to lose patience with him.

'Call on these allies of yours then and see how they have deceived you. See how little they can do to help you now.'

'Tomorrow, you will see,' William retorted as he turned to face him, 'In here there are many figures and persons with whom I speak each hour. Tomorrow you will see.'

Outside a storm of a different nature was raging and between the rolls of thunder someone thought they heard him remark that the Devil would come to his aid. Was he hinting at a rescue attempt? The notion was surely preposterous; the man obviously deranged. Seething with exasperation, Carreño realised that he too was getting nowhere and he decided to leave William to his demons. He had done all that was humanly possible; *his* conscience, at least, was clear.

It was now well after midnight, but still they kept trying. One after another they decided to have a go; the final attempt being made by a Father Agustín de la Madre de Dios, a discalced Carmelite of a gentle disposition. Like Armentia, he too had once been a friend of Palafox and for a short time he appeared to enjoy a something approaching a civilised conversation with William. But the calm did not last for long. Each and every time he returned to the question of a confession William flew into a violent rage during which he became 'invested with such fury that darts of lightning appeared to shoot from his eyes, which were so vivid and perspicacious that it seemed the Devil had settled in his heart'. In the end even the gentle Carmelite had to admit defeat.

As his fury subsided, William stretched himself out on his bed, turned his face to the wall and pulled his blanket over his head. Numb with exhaustion and abandoned by his friends, protectors and even his God, he refused to speak any further. The pamphlets he had pasted throughout the city on the night of his escape had led to one ineluctable conclusion, and he had long since resolved to face it with courage and dignity. He had spent the best part of the last nine years preparing for this moment and knew only too well the consequences of failing to make that final confession. But he had gone beyond the fear of death. Despite the best efforts of his confessors, he appeared determined to turn this murderous charade into one final act of self-empowerment—the taking of any other course would mean that his suffering had been for nothing. And it *had* to stand for something.

As there was nothing more to be said, his confessors left him to his hallucinations and went to minister to the spiritual needs of the others. Only Armentia, deeply moved by the intensity of his suffering, remained with him . . . just in case. Elsewhere in the prison, the others who had been condemned to the stake sought small slivers of comfort in silent nostalgia or a last prolonged conversation with their confessors. No-one slept.

The Inquisitors arrived to say Mass at about 3 a.m. Three hours later, the arrangements for the procession of prisoners began. A hearty breakfast was offered to the condemned but limbs all a-tremble and hearts bursting in their chests none could face eating and the guards feasted instead. Outside, around the Plaza Mayor, hundreds of recumbent bodies rose gingerly to greet a cold, crisp and cloudy morning and the cloying aroma of hot chocolate hung like a heavy dew in first faint flowering of daybreak.

Taken from his cell under armed escort, William was forcibly dressed in a dark grey cassock emblazoned on the front with a black Cross of Saint Andrew. They called it a *sambenito* and on the back and sides were depictions of heretics being thrown into the fires of hell. A tall and conical pasteboard hat, similarly ornamented, was placed on his head and finally, when he had been bound and gagged (to prevent him escaping or repeating his 'heresy'), a small green crucifix was placed in his hands.

When the last of the prisoners had been dressed, they were taken to the Palace of the Inquisition, lined up in order of the severity of their sins and flanked on both sides by a column of musketeers. At the given signal they rolled out of the main gate of the Palace, turned left, and headed towards the Plaza Mayor. Most, like William, were silent, but a few could not help giving vent to their terror. In the distance, pregnant black clouds threatened rain.

The clergy of the dioceses led the way through the crowds in their black surplices and capes, singing the *Miserere,* and carrying the crosses of the cathedral and city parishes before them. Behind them came the thirty-two prisoners; the six facing 'relaxation' bringing up the rear. Still striving for that last minute confession, an exhausted Armentia shuffled alongside William, while behind him, in a small black coffin with painted flames, a young Dominican carried the bones of Don José Bruñón de Vértiz.

In the wake of the effigy, two liveried pages led a mule dressed from head to foot in exquisitely wrought silver armour, small silver bells and golden silk tassels. Under a caparison of red damask, the wretched beast carried a small tortoise-shell writing desk containing the list of charges and sentences. Behind him a procession of sundry scribes and officials followed, all perched astride impeccably groomed horses that were similarly rattling with silver trappings.

On reaching the Plaza Mayor, the procession marched past the Viceroy's Palace, where the Duke of Albuquerque and his family had gathered on the balcony to watch. At the corner of the plaza formed by the *Portal de Mercaderes* and the *Casa de Cabildo*, the prisoners were placed sitting on the steps of a giant dais facing a sea of hostile faces, heads bowed lest they meet the eyes of anyone they knew: the consoling gaze being as painfully lacerating as the mocking.

After the procession had passed, the Viceroy left the balcony and made his way to the Palace of the Inquisition. Here he joined a cavalcade of imperious city dignitaries, riding behind a crimson standard of the archangel Michael and flanked on both sides by the musketeers of the Viceroy's guard. Arriving at the *Casa de Cabildo* they took their seats under a plain black velvet canopy embroidered with the royal coat-of-arms and valanced with gold brocade.

When the dignitaries had been seated in accordance with their rank, a notary of the Holy Office ascended the platform, appealed for quiet, and asked the assembled public to raise their right hands and swear solemnly to defend the true faith and support the Holy Office of the Inquisition. After Mass, a Father Arellano ascended the pulpit on the right hand side of the platform to deliver a plangent sermon in which no opportunity was missed to heap revulsion upon the condemned. He was followed by a Father López, who climbed the pulpit opposite to read the Papal Bull of Pius V and finally by Father Huidrobo, Secretary of the Holy Office, who received all who were to assist in the ceremony, swore them in, and began the recitation of the charges and sentences. In order that the Viceroy might enjoy the highlights before departing for his lunch, he broke with tradition and began with the names of those facing relaxation.

When William's name was called he was marched under armed escort along a forty-five foot gangway to the pedestal where the condemned were brought to be sentenced. Still gagged, and looking pitifully emaciated and spectral, he was tied by his right wrist (the hand that had written the heresies) to a large iron ring that was bolted to an eight foot high pole. Here he was made to stand while the long list of charges against him was read to the crowd.

Throughout it all William exhibited a Daniel-like serenity and self-assurance that was totally at odds with the behaviour of the other prisoners. How much of this was pride, and how much was down to the effects of his mental illness is impossible to say at this remove; but it unnerved many of those who were close enough to witness it. During the rest breaks, when they untied him, he tormented his accusers by picking his nose and brushing his moustache with the small green cross he had been given to hold. At all other times he stood completely still— seemingly dispassionate—as though somewhere deep within him the spectre of failure or the pain of unfulfilled promise was prodding him to seize control of the arena and turn it into a theatre of vindication; to snatch a morsel of glory from the maw of his own defeat.

At 1 p.m., the Viceroy rose from his black velvet seat. Accompanied by a cortège of 530 Inquisitors, Councillors and invited guests, he left the scorching heat of the Plaza for the *Casa de Cabildo*, to enjoy the Lucullan banquet that had been prepared earlier that morning in his honour. In his absence, Father López read the lesser charges and sentences to a multitude shamelessly bathing in a heady stew of *schadenfreude* and liturgical solemnity.

The reading of the charges and sentences finally concluded at about 5 p.m., at which point the Count of Santiago rose from his seat. Resplendent in his black velvet doublet, feathered hat and diamond hatband, he swaggered with pavonine flamboyance to the steps of the main platform. Behind him his three sons looked on, their silken chests ballooning with filial pride. Overhead the sky was bruised. The rain, if it came, would be a relief to all.

Like a latter-day Caiaphas, a representative of the Holy Office approached Santiago and made the customary recommendation to mercy. Should it be found to be absolutely necessary to proceed with the execution, he requested, it should be done 'without the effusion of blood'. Forbidden by their vows from taking a direct part in the shedding of human blood, the clergy were absolved by this legal nicety from personal responsibility for what followed.

The prisoners to be 'relaxed' were now handed over to the secular authorities and marched to a platform in front of the *Portal de Mercaderes*. Here they were condemned by a civil magistrate who pronounced that, with one exception, all were to be burned alive. Sentencing complete, they were mounted on pack mules (most were too traumatised to walk) and led, surrounded by soldiers, executioners, trumpeters and a bellowing town crier through the Calle de Plateros and Calle de San Francisco to the waiting pyres in front of the Templo de San Diego (these days the Pinacoteca Virreinal) on the western side of the Alameda. A crowd of 40,000 surged forward. Not even the rain, which was now falling in torrents, could dampen their spirits: the ability to take pleasure in the suffering of heretics free from bothersome qualms of conscience being the sweetest, and most intoxicating, reward of righteousness.

Bells rang, trumpets blasted, and friars chanted all the way to the Alameda; but throughout it all William retained the steadfastness of a martyr and nailed his gaze to the sky. At the Alameda they were escorted, or in some cases carried, sobbing and shaking pitifully, to the pyre; their confessors climbing the ladders behind them, prompting even yet for that last minute confession that might save their souls.

At one point there was a flurry of activity around Sebastián Alvarez as he was hastily untied and taken back to the prison for further examination by the Inquisitors. It was to be only a brief reprieve. Back at the prison he once again reiterated his claim to be Jesus Christ and left the Inquisitors with no choice but to ratify his sentence and he was burned alive some days later.

While all this was going on the executioner climbed the ladder, fastened William's iron collar to the top of the stake and tied his legs to the bottom. Before the pyres could be ignited, however, there was one last formality to be taken care of. A rope was placed around the neck of Pedro García de Arías through which a short stick was placed. Like spittle from a wet chamois the life was unceremoniously wrung out of the heretical hermit while the more squeamish amongst the onlookers buried their heads in their programmes.

Then suddenly, and only for a moment, an extraordinary silence fell upon the crowd. The only sounds to be heard were the jingling of harnesses, the clip of hooves and the fluttering of ladies' fans. As the burning brands were brought forward, a great cheer greeted the first flame. Behind the dense smoke that rose from the damp pitch-covered woodpile, William began to writhe and struggle. Choking from the fumes and blinded by the rivulets of rain that were running into his eyes, he summoned what remained of his strength for one last effort.

Perhaps the executioner, in a moment of pity, had neglected to secure his feet; perhaps the flames had loosened his bonds; perhaps it was merely the settling of the woodpile. We may never know for certain. One eyewitness said he leapt from the pyre and hung himself from his iron collar; another merely noted that he strangled himself. But whatever the truth, their testimonies ensured that at least one of his prayers—that his story would live on—was answered. Like Hercules on Mount Oeta, he had entered immortality through a portal of fire; his courage and dignity ennobling him in a manner no title ever could.

The smell of charred flesh still hung in the air at nightfall, when a detail of municipal workers descended upon the Alameda to douse the embers and clean up the sludge before the gentry of the city came to promenade the following afternoon. With their brooms and their shovels they dumped William's ashes and bones, along with those of the other executed prisoners, into a murky stream that ran next to the high walls of the Templo de San Diego. By midnight all evidence of the day's activities had been removed and the last of the stragglers, drunk on self-congratulation and spiritually uplifted by the day's festivities, had returned to their homes to sleep the sleep of the righteous. The Inquisitors, too, had returned to their big houses, their slaves and their concubines. The Irishman was finally gone. Things could return to normal. Or could they?

Epilogue

*J*UST TEN DAYS after William's execution, His Worship Don Francisco de Estrada y Escobedo sent a brief letter to Madrid. Taking great care to absolve himself from any personal responsibility—and he stressed that he had been one of the few who had voted to seek ratification before proceeding—he informed the *Suprema* that the Irishman, Don Guillén de Lombardo, had been executed.

Since 1647 it had been required that all sentences made by local tribunals be passed to the *Suprema* for ratification. In William's case that position had been underscored, in 1655, by a letter to the Mexican Inquisitors. A strongly worded letter of reproof was sent from Madrid, demanding to know why the Irishman had been executed despite explicit orders to the contrary, and insisting that the two volumes of documents relating to his trial—lately described by the eminent Mexican psychiatrist and ethnohistorian, Dr. Ernestina Jiménez Olivares, as 'one of the largest and cruellest' of the Mexican Inquisition—be sent immediately to Madrid. Ten years later they would still be waiting for them.

In 1661, Estrada died from an apoplectic fit. The following year the *Suprema* ordered the Visitor of the Holy Office, Don Pedro de Medina Rico, to bring his investigation of the Mexican Inquisition to a conclusion. Anticipating a quick return to Spain, he set about the task with renewed venom. In fact such was the extent of the corruption he uncovered that from the Chief Inquisitor to the lowliest clerk there was not a single member of the Holy Office that he did not find guilty of some offence or other.

Juan Sáenz de Mañozca was found guilty of the theft of prisoners' belongings, of having seriously libelled Bishop Palafox and of having been responsible for the deaths of two prisoners, for all of which he was fined the sum of 1,300 pesos and barred from the Holy Office for nine and a half years. Despite his conviction, he managed to have himself preferred to the bishoprics of Havana, then Guatemala, and finally Puebla, where Palafox's ghost would haunt him for the rest of his days. The punishments meted out to the other Inquisitors, all of whom were found guilty of corruption, were equally derisory.

Palafox died shortly before William, on 1 October 1659, having just been appointed to the bishopric of Osma—one of the poorest in Castile. In 1666, following a campaign to have him canonised, his tomb was opened and his corpse found to be uncorrupted. In Mexico his former parishioners began to worship him as a saint, prompting the Inquisition, in 1691, to renew the ban on the production or possession of his portrait. Despite this, on 12 September 1767, he was beatified and his proposed elevation to sainthood led to another bitter war between the Carmelites and the Jesuits (who successfully blocked his canonisation).

As for the luckless Villena, he was exonerated, rehabilitated and once more offered the position of Viceroy of New Spain. But he had had his fill of this troublesome colony and opted instead for the relative calm of Sicily, and much later that of Navarre. He died in Pamplona on 27 February 1653 and was entombed at the monastery of Parral in Segovia. It is not known what happened to Ana or Teresa.

William's poetic tirades against slavery and corruption might well have remained amongst the minutiae of history had his story not been rescued from the teeth of eternal oblivion by the intervention, in 1872, of Vincente Riva Palacio. In much the same manner as Courtilz de Sandras' fictionalised biography of Charles de Batz-Castelmore had inspired Dumas' *Three Musketeers*, the retired Mexican army general's fictionalised account of William's life, at least according to one historian, helped to inspire the American author, Johnston McCulley, to create the fictional character of *Zorro*.

In Riva Palacio's *Memoirs of an Impostor*, Don Guillén Lombardo leads a double life as a poet and dandy by day and a swashbuckling swordsman with an eye for the ladies by night. The real Don Guillén, however, enjoyed no more a reputation as a swordsman than any other soldier of his day and only ever had confirmed relationships with two women—one of whom had seduced *him*. Despite leaving a substantial body of poetry behind him, his work has rarely been studied or properly assessed, though at least one prominent Mexican academic (Gabriel

Méndez Plancarte) has described him as a 'great religious poet' whose Latin 'for all its defects . . . contains an extraordinary energy and expressive power that is both uncommon in, and superior to, . . . the many servile imitators of the Cicero'.

Had it not been for Palacio's novel, the name of William Lamport (or *Guillén de Lampart* as he is better known in México) might have faded into obscurity. As it was, the book ensured the Irishman remained of interest to a small circle of Mexican intellectuals until 1901 when, with the centenary of the Independence struggle just nine years away and plans to erect a monument to the heroes of the Independence movement already well advanced (the foundation stone would be laid the following year), a pamphlet was published in Mexico City by one Don Alberto Lombardo.

Entitled *Historical Injustices—The forgotten man who was first to conceive of, and attempt to gain, independence for Mexico,* Lombardo's pamphlet proposed erecting a statue to William Lamport as one of the precursors of Mexican independence—a suggestion that was vehemently criticised seven years later by Luis Gonzalez Obregón in his *Indigenous Rebellions and Precursors of Mexican Independence.* Lamport, Obregón claimed, could quite legitimately be called a 'martyr', but he did not deserve the title of 'precursor', having come to Mexico as an 'adventurer'.

The statue, nevertheless, *was* commissioned and sits today, rather too controversially for some, within the mausoleum that lies beneath Alciati's 'Angel of Independence', alongside the remains of such iconic figures of the Independence movement as Miguel Hidalgo y Costilla and José María Morelos y Pavón (the fathers of modern Mexico), and Ignacio María Allende y Unzaga (the idealistic instigator of the Independence struggle of 1810). Here few see it, and fewer recognise it.

As far as William Lamport himself goes, that should have been the end of it all. His story, however, swept through the decades on the Lethean current, began to surface again in 1999 following the assertion of an Italian academic (Fabio Troncarelli of Viterbo University) that the Irishman had been the primary inspiration for the creation of the comic book character of Zorro—at that time the subject of the TriStar/Amblin film, *The Mask of Zorro,* starring Antonio Banderas and Anthony Hopkins.

Troncarelli's theory was founded upon the premise that Zorro's creator, Irish-American journalist Johnston McCulley, had based his hero on Riva Palacio's *Don Guillén Lombardo*. In his book, *La Spada e la Croce* (Rome, 1999), Troncarelli drew a direct line between McCulley and Riva Palacio on the basis that the nickname of *'el Zorro'* had already appeared in another of Riva Palacio's novels, *Martin Garatuza*.

McCulley's and Riva Palacio's heroes, Troncarelli argued, share many similarities in that they both lead double lives, are pamphleteers, ladies' men and lovers of poetry, and both are leaders of a conspiracy of noblemen whose aim is the overthrow of tyranny. They even share ties to the Franciscans. Both authors, he further asserted, were masons and the choice of the letter Z was most likely a symbolic representation of the Semitic word ziza (shining), which for masons symbolises the 'divine sparkle' that lies in all of us. The treatment of Troncarelli's theory in the popular press led to Lamport becoming popularly known as The Man Behind the Mask of Zorro, The Original Zorro, Paddy O'Zorro, Zorro the Irishman, The Irish Zorro, etc.

In his review of McCulley in *Twentieth-Century Western Writers*, however, Wade Austin had already noted an equally marked similarity between McCulley's *Zorro* and Baroness Emmuska Orczy's *The Scarlet Pimpernel*: a book first published when McCulley was twenty-one years of age and in which the Scarlet Pimpernel is called 'a cunning fox' by his adversary, Chauvelin (the Spanish word for fox is *zorro*). These similarities were further explored, one year prior to the publication of Troncarelli's book, by Sandra Curtis in her *Zorro Unmasked—the Official History*.

Wife of John Gertz (son of Mitchell Gertz to whom McCulley sold the rights to *Zorro*), Curtis allowed that the similarities were purely speculative and that the characters were differently motivated. She noted, nevertheless, that apart from their dual identities and their distinctive marks, more profound analogies exist between Zorro and the Scarlet Pimpernel. Both are introduced at an inn on a rainy night; both are wealthy and handsome young men who dress well, own fine horses and are followed by a league of gentlemen; both possess irritating social quirks such as 'sleepy yawning behaviour'; and both inspire the devotion of 'the fairest of young women, neither of whom initially knows her man's secret identity':

Both Marguerite St Just, Sir Percy Blakeney's wife, and Lolita Pulido, Diego de la Vega's love, disdain their men for being either a 'laughing stock', according to Lolita, or an 'empty headed nincompoop' from Marguerite. Yet each praises the secret identity of her hero for the strength, bravery and loyalty they enjoy from the men who follow them. Each woman's suspicions regarding the true identity of her male companion is aroused after perusing her man's private quarters. Each woman stands by her man in his darkest hour, preferring death to betrayal.

In her preface to the 1998 re-issue of *The Mark of Zorro*, Curtis further speculated that the character development of Don Diego Vega may have been influenced by the adventures of two mid-nineteenth-century Californian bandits. 'Tiburcio Vasquez,' she wrote, 'was an outlaw, but his people idealised him as a hero for refusing to submit to the Anglo conquest.' She presented an even stronger possibility in Joaquin Murieta, whose 'romantic prowess and aristocratic background, along with his concern for justice, may well have fuelled McCulley's imagination in creating Zorro.'

The identity of the real Joaquin Murieta—a bandit who terrorised California during the Gold Rush of the 1850s—is shrouded in mystery. From what little is known for certain, it is unlikely that he would have had much in common with the romantic figure of Zorro. The myths and legends that have grown up around him, however, are another matter entirely, and very much fit the prototype. A handsome Robin Hood type character, the Murieta of literary invention was driven to crime following the rape of his girlfriend and the murder of his half-brother, and was said to have avenged the injustices inflicted upon Mexicans in the mining towns of the Southern Mother Lode by killing over 300 people. At the time McCulley was writing, this image had become so ingrained in the consciousness of Californians that it was accepted by many as truth.

It may well be the case that Johnston McCulley had laid his hands on a 47-year-old work of romantic Mexican fiction. He may even have borrowed the title of *Zorro* from yet another book by the same author. But even allowing for this, it would appear that they were not his only influences. There is no doubt that in real life William Lamport displayed some very Zorro-like qualities and since his story pre-dates that of Pierre Picaud (whose life story inspired the creation of Dumas' *Count of Monte Cristo*—the literary precursor of *The Scarlet Pimpernel* and every other cloaked avenging hero of modern fiction), he may even merit being called 'the original'. But as for McCulley, the question of coincidence or influence remains open. The most one can say about William Lamport is that his story *may* have played a part in the creation of Zorro.

Perhaps the most important difference between William Lamport and Don Diego de la Vega, however, is that at the end of their respective stories Zorro becomes the quintessential American hero—a success—whereas William Lamport does not. Years of subjugation at the hands of a European colonial power, however, have led Mexicans and Irish alike to judge people less against their accomplishments than their intentions; to see more than good in victory and more than shame in defeat. Both nations love their martyrs; and their iconic heroes, more often than not, have been failures. For every Cuauhtémoc, Morelos, Madera and Zapata, there is a Cúchullain, Wolfe Tone, Emmet and Parnell; for every Hidalgo, a Father John Murphy. History has taught both nations to recognise the heroism of the struggle as much as the glory of victory; the idea as much as the act. We do not expect our heroes to be impossibly virtuous.

Had William Lamport been purely and simply a poet, his various bouts of mental illness would probably not have been so much of an issue, and his written work, much of which was written in waves of great lucidity, might well have been allowed to stand on its own merits and demerits rather than being dismissed as the ravings of a demented foreign libertine. And while it might be true to say that he would never have set off down the rocky road to revolution had he not lost everything to the drought, the fact is that he did, and we must recognise that ideas, once given a voice, have a life of their own and a value independent of their origins.

Much has also been made by the Irishman's detractors of his ambition to raise himself to the throne of an independent Mexico, and it has been touted more than once as evidence of his 'megalomaniacal' tendencies. Such retrospective judgements, however, are more than a little anachronistic; men can, after all, only be judged against the standards of their time, and at that particular juncture William's proposals for radical social upheaval could *only* have been accomplished by a ruler who enjoyed absolute power—the country being too loosely knit to be governed in any other way. William, in any case, had never known any other form of government and the writings of Suárez allowed that democracy was impracticable except in the smallest of city states, and the people should therefore be allowed to delegate power to an elected monarch.

One hundred and seventy four years later, when the Mexican Constitutionalists met to draft the 1917 Constitution, they reluctantly had to face up to this very same fact of life. Decades of failed revolutions, dictatorships and ideologies, had led them to restoring the crown in the person of a president, who effectively became the source of all power and legitimacy. After centuries of bloodshed, Mexico found itself ruled by the modern day equivalent of William's constitutional monarch; a man who made the law but remained above it. One could freely criticise the government, but both the person and the office of the president, like that of a king, were sacrosanct.

William's revolution never took place: he was arrested before his plans could be tested. But whether or not the assistance he had been promised would ever have materialised, his intent was very real indeed. Whatever his personal mix of influences and motivations, he *did* attempt to formulate a legal and moral justification for his rebellion, *did* intend to install a constitutional monarchy elected on broadly democratic principles, and *did* intend to liberate the slaves. He is also on record as stating that he would restore to the native races their ancient rights and lands, and provide 'equality of opportunities' for all, regardless of 'quality or condition'.

In many respects he was probably ahead of his time (though not uniquely so) and it is perhaps also worth noting that the caste system he so abhorred would not be legally abolished in Mexico until 1851, and chattel slavery not for another seven years after that. When viewed in this light, he is probably deserving of the accolade of 'precursor of Mexican Independence' and perhaps that is exactly how he should be remembered, and not as the 'impostor' of Vincente Riva Palacio or the 'Zorro' of Johnston McCulley.

William Lamport may well have been a mass of contradictions, but so too were Hidalgo and Morelos. He may have been motivated as much by wounded pride and disaffection as by principle, but then so too was Allende. His intended rebellion may have been tainted with more than a touch of opportunism, but no more so than that of Carranza (leader of the Constitutionalist side in the revolution). And though his plans for racial equality and land reform would almost certainly have proved unworkable at the time, they were surely no more so than those of Morelos a century and a half later. Perhaps it is time then, that the efforts of this talented, conceited, pious, disillusioned but ultimately decent man were recognised; time, perhaps, his statue saw the light of day?

Appendix A

William Lamport and Rubens' *Young Man in Armour*

*I*N DECEMBER 1634, in order to fulfil a promise he had made to the Pope to speak with Richelieu, the Marquis of Leganés left Flanders and returned to Madrid by way of Paris, most likely bringing with him his Jesuit confessor, Father Antonio Camassa. It had, after all, been at Leganés' insistence that Camassa had accompanied him on campaign in the first place; and if Camassa had left for Madrid, it seems equally likely that William, as one of his students, would have been obliged to accompany him. Nothing, however, is known for certain about the Irishman's movements at this time, but the possibility that he may have remained behind in Brussels has led to a certain amount of speculation regarding the subject of a little-known portrait by Rubens.

In recent years it has been suggested that Rubens' *Portrait of a Young Captain* (Timken Museum, San Diego, California)—a bust-length three-quarter profile that up until then had been tentatively dated to the 1620s—may in fact be a portrait of William Lamport. Throughout the latter half of the twentieth century, however, this painting was generally assumed to be a 'study head' intended by Rubens to be brought back to his atelier for subsequent elaboration into a full length portrait. It was also assumed to be the painting listed as No. 129 in the inventory of Rubens' estate, compiled after his death in 1640. Previous to this, the portrait had usually been discussed as a 'Portrait of the Duke of Mantua', Francesco IV Gonzaga, to whom the subject in truth bears little resemblance. Apart from the identity of its creator, therefore, there was little that could be said about this portrait with any degree of certainty.

A well-built young man with an aristocratic mien and a self-confident expression, the sitter betrays nothing of the insecurity and anxiety evoked in the drawing of Lamport by Van Dyck. Significantly, perhaps, the young man wears a red sash over the left shoulder of a dented cuirass; though that said, there is little in the portrait to resolve the question of costume or uniform.

The wearing of armour in 17th century portraiture was not necessarily an indication of military rank or experience and perhaps this is why the painting has often been referred to simply as the *Portrait of a Young Man in Armour*. The presence of the red sash, however, is another matter entirely: it suggests not only command, but elevated social status. In fact, in a contemporary battle painting by Sebastian Vranckx—an artist renowned for the exactitude of his military uniforms—it is only officers of the cavalry who wear cuirasses and red sashes; similar, in fact, to those that announce the Count-Duke of Olivares as captain-general of the cavalry in Rubens' allegorical portrait of 1626 (as engraved by Paul Pontius). William, however, if we accept his account of the battle for the Allbuch, had been little more than an assistant to a military tactician and, generally speaking, only the nobility could afford commissions in the cavalry.

And then there is the small matter of timing. From November of 1634, Rubens had been holed up in a house on Antwerp's Nieuwe Doelenstraat, where he had been 'so overburdened' with the preparation of the triumphal arches and stages that were to grace the ceremonial procession of Ferdinand on his official entry into the city, that he had 'time neither to live nor write'. The ceremony had originally been planned for January of 1635 but, plagued with gout and struggling to cope with the constant noise that was emanating from the renovations being undertaken at the headquarters of the Antwerp *Kloveniersdoelen* (whose shooting range backed on to his garden), he found himself unable to complete the commission on time and the ceremony had to be postponed until the following April.

In the meantime, in March of 1635 to be precise, the Spanish raided the ecclesiastical electorate of Tréves and kidnapped the Elector. Like a number of other small and predominantly Catholic Rhineland states, Tréves had originally welcomed Spanish occupation as a means of protecting them from the advancing forces of Protestantism, only in more recent years to grow resentful of the burden of maintaining Spanish troops on its soil. At the time of the Spanish raid the Elector had gone so far as to place himself under French protection, thereby presenting Richelieu with the excuse he had been waiting for to declare war on Spain. The declaration was formally announced in Brussels on 19 May 1635, just twenty-one days after Richelieu had signed a treaty of alliance with Sweden. If Jan-Karel della Faille had not returned to Madrid in December, then he was almost certainly recalled now, and William along with him.

For William to have been painted by Rubens during his first visit to Flanders, therefore, the portrait would have to have been executed sometime between the middle of April and the end of May—a time when Rubens was tormented by gout and exhausted by his efforts to complete his commission for the *Blijde Inkomst*. Indeed, such was the darkness of the Flemish master's mood at this time that many of the paintings with which he finally decorated the route were saturated with negative and depressing classical allegories: one depicting Mercury (the patron deity of art and commerce) *leaving* Antwerp; another, the doors of the Temple of Janus being opened to admit the ravages of war.

So even if William *had* been available to sit for a man universally acclaimed as the *Apelles* of the age, it seems rather implausible, does it not, that the gouty, exhausted and disillusioned master would be willing to undertake such an insignificant commission at a time when he was also under pressure to produce paintings for an increasingly impatient King of Spain, and perhaps also, even yet, considering the possibility of another secret diplomatic mission to the Dutch Republic?

What then of the sitter?

When compared to the Van Dyck sketch, the subject of the Rubens portrait exhibits both similarities and differences, not least of which are the hair (fine and straight in the Van Dyck; thick and lanate in the Rubens) and the apparent discrepancy in age (Rubens' *Young Captain* appears to be quite a few years older). If the *Young Captain* had been painted in 1635, then it could only have been a matter of months after the Van Dyck sketch was made and such appreciable differences seem unlikely in the same sitter.

Such differences, however, are far less marked when Rubens' *Young Captain* is compared to his 1604 portrait of the then ten-year-old

Vincenzo II Gonzaga (Kunsthistorisches Museum, Vienna), the youngest brother of Francesco IV Gonzaga, and later Duke of Mantua in his own right. Indeed such are the similarities that it is difficult *not* to assume that they are the same person: but then assumptions can be very dangerous things. Nevertheless, here we see the same high forehead and prominent chin, the same mop of curly hair, same full lips, large eyes and aristocratic mien.

The connection of the *Young Captain* to the Gonzaga family, in fact, has a long history; beginning with a listing in the collection of Charles I of England of a '*picture of the deceased young Duke of Mantua's brother done in armoure to the Shouldrs by Sr Peeter Paule Rubins when he was in Italie*'. The last five words of this entry appear to have led to the assumption that this was a portrait of Francesco Gonzaga. But what if those five words themselves were an assumption? What if the portrait was painted later than 1608?

In Walter Liedtke's description of the painting for the Timken Museum Catalogue, the painting is described as '*strongly reminiscent of Rubens' study heads and portraits dating from ten to fifteen years after he returned to Antwerp*', a time when *Vincenzo* Gonzaga, like the subject of the painting, would have been in his mid-twenties. Could it possibly be that Charles' art-historians had confused their Dukes of Mantua?

That is not to say that William's portrait was never painted. Indeed, having had his appetite whetted by his visit to the atelier of Van Dyck, it would be entirely consonant with his pretensions, if not his income, to seek to have himself immortalised on canvas. But even if this were so, it seems more likely to have been in Brussels or Madrid than Antwerp, and by someone other than the 'prince of painters and painter of princes'.

GLOSSARY OF NAUTICAL TERMINOLOGY

Abaft/aft In the direction of the rear of the boat.

Almiranta Spanish term for second ranked ship in fleet.

Armada Fleet of Spanish warships.

Armada de la Guardia Guard squadron assigned to protect Spanish merchant fleets.

Astrolabe Instrument used for measuring the altitude of heavenly bodies, e.g. to determine latitude.

Aviso Spanish ship or fleet carrying official mail.

Beakhead A horizontal projection of a ship's stem above water.

Bilge Part of ship below lowermost floorboards.

Binnacle Housing for a ship's compass.

Bow The forward end of a vessel.

Bowsprit Heavy spar pointing forward from the stern.

Bow wave The wave that breaks on the ship's bow.

Broadside Simultaneous firing of all guns on one side.

Cable Anchor chain or rope.

Camarada Group or clique of sailors who shared the same living space on a ship.

Capitana Spanish equivalent of 'flagship'.

Caravel Small lateen rigged vessel, smaller than a *nao*.

Carrera de Indias The sea route from Cádiz to the Indies.

Caulk To seal the gaps between planks with oakum and pitch.

Colours Flags of identification.

Close-hauled Steering as close to the wind as possible.

Dogwatch Watches between 4 and 6 p.m. or 6 and 8 p.m.

Double To sail around (a headland etc.).

Flagship Ship bearing the commander of the fleet.

Flota Spanish word for 'fleet'.

Flotilla A small fleet.

Fore Towards the bow or front of a vessel.

Galley Warship propelled by oars and sails.

Gaskets Piece of line used to lash a furled sail.

Guardia de Cuartillo Spanish term for 'dogwatch'.

Gurapas The oar deck of a galley.

Hawsehole Hole through which anchor cable passes.

Hull The main body of a vessel.

Islote Spanish term for a small barren island.

Jury-rig Improvise or set up in makeshift manner.

Landsman Person with little or no experience of the sea.

Larboard Old term for left side when facing forward.

Lead line A weight on a marked line used for sounding.

Lee The direction in which wind is blowing.

Merchantman A merchant ship.

Nao A merchant galleon, usually unarmed.

Oakum Rope fibres from old rope used for caulking.

Ordnance Cannon or artillery.

Poop deck Short deck built over aft end of quarter deck.

Prow The bows or stem of a ship.

Quarter deck The deck above the main deck.

Rigging The ropes controlling the masts and spars.

Shoal A stretch of shallow water.

Shorten sail To reduce or take in sail.

Sounding Measuring the depth of water beneath a ship.

Starboard The right hand side when facing forward.

Stem/Stempost Timber forming the centrepiece of the bow.

Stern The rear of a vessel, opposite of bow.

Sterncastle The raised decks at the rear of a vessel.

Stern sheets The part of an open boat near the stern.

Strike colours To lower flags in salute or surrender.

Tack To change course.

Topside Parts of a ship above the uppermost deck.

Trade winds Wind blowing northeast towards the equator.

Treasure fleets Fleets that carried silver bullion to Spain.

Windward The side towards the wind.

Yard Spar from which sails are hung.

GENERAL GLOSSARY

(Spanish unless otherwise specified)

Alcalde Judge/member of City Council.

Alcalde Mayor Mayor/District Governor/Magistrate.

Adíos! Goodbye!

Agnus Dei Wax medallions of the Lamb of God (Latin).

Auto de fe Penitential religious ceremony in which victims of the Inquisition were punished (the term 'auto da fe' is Portuguese).

Bastardo Bastard.

Batería Battery/fortified artillery emplacement.

Buenos Días! Good Morning!

Caballeros Knights.

Calle Street

Casta Caste.

Cerro Hill or peak.

Chirimoya Chirimoya, a fruit

Cocoliztli Sickness or epidemic (Nahuatl).

Conquista The Spanish conquest of the Aztecs (1521).

Conquistador Spanish soldier who participated in the conquest.

Converso Convert to Catholicism.

Coraza Cuirass: a piece of armour covering chest and back.

Corregidor Royal municipal administrator.

Criado Creature.

Criollo Offspring of European and Mestizo/a.

Cuarterón Offspring of European and Mulatto/a.

Encomienda A grant of Indian labour and tribute.

Gachupínes Derogatory Mexican term for peninsular-born Spaniards (literally 'spurred ones').

Habito Religious or military order.

Hacienda A large landed estate.

Hidalgo The lower levels of the nobility.

Historia Story or history.

Indio Indian.

Infanta/Infante Daughter/Son of King not heir to the throne.

Junta de Ejecución War cabinet.

Letrado Highly educated person (literally, 'lettered').

La Isla Verde The Green Island.

Licenciado Lawyer.

Limpieza de Sangre Purity of blood.

Maese de Campo Fieldmaster (honorary military title).

Mancha Stain.

Marrano Crypto–Jew; literally, swine or filth.

Memorial Petition or memorandum.

Merienda Early afternoon snack of light refreshments.

Mestizo Offspring of European and Indio/a.

Morisco Moor/North African.

Mulatto Offspring of European and Negro/a.

Nahuatl Native language of central Mexico.

Negro African (literally 'Black').

Padre Father or priest.

Paseo Promenade.

Pietà A work of art depicting the dead Christ supported by the Virgin Mary (Italian, literally 'pity')

Portal Portal or vestibule

Pundonor Dignity, honour, self-respect.

Recua A drove of beasts of burden.

Repartimiento Assignment of Indians to perform labour.

Residencia Official trial or examination of the conduct of a retiring high official.

Santiago St. James.

Solimán Biochloride of mercury.

Templo Temple

Teocalli A temple pyramid (Nahuatl: lit. 'House of God').

Teponaxtli A type of bitonal wooden xylophone (Nahuatl).

Tezatlipoca God of night and sorcery/God of War (Nahuatl).

Teatro de Grandeza Theatre of grandeur.

Tierra Land

Tierra Caliente Hot land.
Visita Inspection.
Visitador Inspector/Visitor.
Zambo Offspring of Negro/a and Mulatto/a.
Zorro Fox.

Acknowledgements

Of the many people who assisted me in the preparation of this book, there are certain individuals to whom I owe a special debt of gratitude.

Irasema Corona de Moreno and her family wandered into my life through the most bizarre of coincidences. She has given so much that has been invaluable to the completion of this book, not least of which are the photographs she has contributed. My debt to her is profound and heartfelt.

Doctor Ernestina Jiménez Olivares of the department of History and Philosphy of Medicine at the Universidad Nacional Autónoma de México, has been incredible in her generosity. Unasked, and at her own expense, she not only sent me copies of her books on psychiatry and the Inquisition, but also photocopies of the source documents of William's trial, including a copy of William's coded letter to Felipe IV of Spain.

Tom and Lois Lambert of Warragul have also been unstinting in their generosity. Their knowledge of the Lamberts/Lamports of Wexford is truly unsurpassable. They have been a fountain of useful information, invaluable suggestions and, most importantly, of encouragement and support. This book owes to them one of its greatest debts.

Professor John Richmond of University College Dublin has been of incalculable assistance to me in the translation of the more difficult Latin passages from William's process, as indeed has **Maureen Forde** with the Spanish. I am also indebted to **Fabio Troncarelli** for his co-operation in the early years of the research of this book, especially for the photocopies of Ana and Teresa's letters, and to **Lindie Naughton, Michael Kerrigan, Terry Fitzgerald** and **Steve McDonogh** for their editorial advice and suggestions. I am also indebted to Cuban historian **Marita Corrales**, who befriended me in Madrid and advised me of the existence of letters concerning William's process that up to that point I had overlooked.

There were many others who helped me along the way, to greater and lesser extents, but space does not allow for a detailed description of their contributions. I hope the following individuals and institutions will accept instead my sincerest thanks for their patience, advice and assistance: Penny Woods (Russell Library, Maynooth), Ursula Carlyle (Mercers Company/Gresham College, London), Liliane Dahlmann (Archivo Medina Sidonia, Sanlúcar de Barrameda), Orna Sommerville (Jesuit Archives, Dublin), Dr. Brendan Rooney (Centre for the Study of Irish Art), Margaret Donnelly (National Gallery of Ireland Library), Jarlath Glynn (Wexford County Library), Fergus Gillespie (Deputy Chief Herald of Ireland), Charles Van den Heuvel (Leiden University Library), István Németh (Szépmüvészeti Muzeum, Budapest), Peter O'Regan (sailing barque *Jeanie Johnston*), Elaine Carey, Brian Metcalf, Andy and Karen O'Keefe, Ciarán O'Scea, Hilary Murphy, Charlie O'Connell, Andrea Giardina, Paloma Millán, Paul McCauley, Ned and Catherine Fleming and the staff of the following libraries and archives: The National Library of Ireland (Dublin), The Royal Irish Academy (Dublin), The Instituto Cervantes (Dublin), Trinity College Library (Dublin), The Linenhall Library (Belfast), The British Library (London), The Timken Museum of Art (San Diego, California), The Archivo Histórico Nacional Museo del Ejército (Madrid), The Biblioteca Nacional (Madrid), The Museo de Bellas Artes de Sevilla (Seville), The Kunsthistorisches Museum (Vienna), The Palacio de San Lorenzo de el Escorial (San Lorenzo), The Archivo General de la Nación at the Palacio de Lecumberri, and the Chapultepec and Churubusco museums (Mexico City).

Finally, but by no means least, I am especially grateful to my wife, Cliona, for her patience, support and willingness to travel halfway round the world with me in pursuit of this story. Without her this book could never have been written.

Sources

MANUSCRIPT SOURCES

DUBLIN

A biographical dictionary of Irish Jesuits in the time of the Society's Third Irish Mission 1598–1773, by Francis Finegan S.J. Unpublished hand-written manuscript, Jesuit Archives, Dublin.

Catologus Missionis Hiberniae, by John McErlean S.J. Unpublished hand-written manuscript, Jesuit Archives, Dublin. Visitatio Seminarii Hibernorum Compostellani, 4 Iunii 1638,

Copy of MS., Arch. Coll. Hib. Salamanca, Legajo 34. Num 1. ICOL/SANT/3(1), Jesuit Archives, Dublin.

Genealogical MS., Loose Pedigrees, P162, P217, National Library of Ireland.

Genealogical MS., 49, p. 55. Marriage of Richard Stafford, National Library of Ireland.

The Heraldic Visitation of Wexford, by Sir David Molineaux, 1618, National Library of Ireland.

MAYNOOTH

Letter from the Duke of Lerma to Jesuit Provincial of Castille, Salamanca Archives, Legajo S.33/1/4, Russell Library, St. Patrick's College, Maynooth, Co. Kildare.

Depositions against Felix O'Neill, 27–28th July 1631, Salamanca Archives, Legajo S.33/1/15, Russell Library, St. Patrick's College, Maynooth, Co. Kildare.

History of St. Patrick's College, Santiago, from 1614, Salamanca Archives, Legajos S.33/1/14–15, Russell Library, St. Patrick's College, Maynooth, Co. Kildare.

LONDON (BRITISH LIBRARY)
Egerton 1509, ff. 116r–119r (Letter from Mexican Inquisitors).
MS 28,470, ff 54-57.
Hist. MSS Comm. Rep. Stuart MSS Vol. I, 1902, f.69.

NOTTINGHAM (UNIVERSITY LIBRARY)
MS. Pw A 2068, 3.1628, Letter from Jesuits of Clerkenwell, Catalogue of the Papers of (Hans) William Bentinck, Part 10: Public Miscellanea.

MADRID (ARCHIVO HISTORICO NACIONAL)
Inquisición 1065, ff. 189r, 374r–384v, 452v–456r.
Inquisición 1731, 53, 4.
Inquisición 1731, 53, 5.
Inquisición 1731, 53, 20, ff. 1r–12r.
Inquisición 1740, 10, I, ff. 1v–2r.
Inquisición 5348, 11, f. 1v.
Libro-Estado 722, no. 26, #3, a,b,c.

MADRID (BIBLIOTECA DE PALACIO)
MS. II-2225, ff. 63–64.

MADRID (PATRIMONIO NACIONAL, REAL BIBLIOTECA)
Palafox y Mendoza, Juan de, Obispo de Osma.
Cartas que el obispo de la Puebla visittador general de esta Nueva España escrivio y remitio a su magestad en el real aviso que navego a los 30 de henero de 1641. Manuscritos de América, S.XVII (1640–1642) f. 136r–137v, 138r–v, 145r–147.
Controversias del venerable Don Juan de Palafox y Mendoza con la Compañía de Jesús. Manuscritos de América (1648–1650), f. 1r–297v.
Mexico. Año de 1650. Cartas y testimonios de autos hechos sobre dos escudos de armas que estaban puestos en la Capilla Mayor de los Reyes de la yglesia de la Puebla de Los Angeles. S. XVII (1650), f. 3r–57r.

SANTIAGO DE COMPOSTELA (ARCH. CATEDRAL)
Tomo V, Varia, no. 399, 1633.

SIMANCAS (Archivo General)

MS. Estado 2559, unfoliated.

MS. Estado 2603, no. 72, ff. a–b.

MS. Estado, 2752, Negocios de partes, España (1624).

Bibl. nacional, Seccion de MSS., X, 157, Archivo de Simancas, Inquisición, Libro 31, ff. 34, 637.

ROME (VATICAN LIBRARY)

MSS. Barberini Latini, 8626, f. 23rv.

MSS. Barberini Latini, 3098, f. 184r.

MEXICO (BIBLIOTECA CERVANTINA, MONTERREY)

MSS. of Guillén Lombardo, ff. 23r–25r, 42r, 87r, 89r, 101r–v, 105r–106r, 147r, 205r–245r, 211r, 248r–249r, 324r–325v.

MEXICO (ARCHIVO GENERAL DE LA NACIÓN, MEXICO CITY)

Inquisición 2, 42, f. 76r–76v (1644).

Inquisición 3, f. 76r–77v (1650).

Inquisición 163, 9, 14, f. 20r–21v (1644).

Inquisición 163, 12, (1641).

Inquisición 165, 4, 80, f. 139–140 (1653).

Inquisición 167, 51, f. 2–5 (1642).

Inquisición 216, 1459, 1462 (1651).

Inquisición 289, 12 (1620).

Inquisición 374, 6 (1642).

Inquisición 393, 5, f. 28r f. 305r–324r (1642).

Inquisición 393, 17, f. 28r–v (1642).

Inquisición 398, 1 (1642).

Inquisición 400, 2, 392 (1643).

Inquisición 407, 12, 438 (1642).

Inquisición 409, 2, f. 305r–324r (1644).

Inquisición 415, I (1641).

Inquisición 416, 10, (1643).

Inquisición 416, 36, f. 434r–466v (1643).

Inquisición 416, 42, f. 538r–544v, 566r (1649).

Inquisición 424, 5, f. 463r (1646).
Inquisición 432, 14, f. 99r–593r (1650).
Inquisición 457, 15, f. 150r–157r (1650).
Inquisición 489, f. 97r–111r (1641).
Inquisición 503, 30, f. 9r (1650).
Inquisición 503, 63, f. 9r (1650).
Inquisición 506, 1, f. 1r–83r (1651).
Inquisición 624, 1435–1442 (1649).
Inquisición 641, 4, f. 412r–414r (1656).
Inquisición 892, 2, f. 36r–71r (1650).
Inquisición 898, 3, f. 71v (1650).
Inquisición 1496, 1, f. 1r–110r, 230r (1642).
Inquisición 1497, 1, f. 1r–288v (1642).
Inquisición 1497, 2, f. 263r–374v (1650).
Inquisición 1497, 3, f. 76r, 375r–683r (1650).
Inquisición 1498, 1, f. 1r–117r (1643)
Inquisición 1499, 1, f. 1r–244r (1650).
Inquisición 1499, 2, f. 1r–280r (1650).
Reales Cédulas, 1, 263, f. 499r.
Reales Cédulas, 2, 42, f. 76r–v.
Reales Cédulas, 4, 60, f. 141r–142r.
Reales Cédulas, 31, 178, f. 143r.
Edictos de Inquisición, 3, f. 74r.
Edictos de Inquisición, 3, f. 76r–77v.
General de Parte, 7, 390, f. 271r.
Mercedes, 39, f. 128v.
Bienes Nacionales, 531, 55.

MAPS AND ARTWORKS REFERENCED

Battle, by Sebastian Vranckx, Museo de Bellas Artes de Sevilla, Seville.

Bildnis eines Prälats und eines Edelknaben, by Antoon Van Dyck, Szépmüvészeti Múzeum, Budapest.

Cardinal Niño de Guevara, by El Greco, Metropolitan Museum of Art, New York.

The Count-Duke of Olivares, attributed to Diego de Velázquez, École des Beaux-Arts, Paris.

Forma y Levantado de la Ciudad de Mexico, by Gómez de Trasmonte (1628), Editorial Alberto Misrachi, Mexico D.F.

Jan-Karel della Faille, by Antoon Van Dyck, Museés Royeaux de Beaux-Arts de Belgique, Brussels.

Monasterio del Escorial, by Pedro Salcedo de las Heras, engraved by Pedro Peñas. Lit. de G. Ruiz, Espíritu Santo 18, 1876.

BIBLIOTECA NACIONAL, MADRID

La Villa de Madrid, Corte de los Reyes Católicos de Espanna, by Frederick de Wit (1922), Museo Municipal, Madrid.

Portrait of a Young Captain, by Peter Paul Rubens, Timken Museum, San Diego, California.

Portrait of Vincenzo II Gonzaga, by Peter Paul Rubens, Kunsthistorisches Museum, Vienna.

Retrato de Don Gaspar de Guzmán, conde-duque de Olivares, by P. Pontius and P.P. Rubens, Biblioteca Nacional, Madrid.

Topografía de la Villa de Madrid descrita por Don Pedro de Texeira, año de 1656, full scale facsimile reproduction, Madrid: Ayuntamiento de Madrid, n.d., ca. 1960.

PRINTED SOURCES

IRELAND

'Beyond Faith and Fatherland: The Appeal of the Catholics of Ireland c. 1623', by Glyn Redworth, in *Archivium Hibernicum,* Vol. LII. Maynooth: Catholic Record Society, 1998.

Calendar of Inquisitions Formerly in the Office of the Chief Remembrancer of the Exchequer, by Margaret C. Griffith. Dublin: Stationery Office for Irish Manuscripts Commission, 1991.

Calendar of Material relating to Ireland from the High Court of Admiralty Examinations 1536–1641, A; ed. John C. Appleby. Dublin: Irish Manuscripts Commission, 1992.

Calendar of State Papers, Ireland, 1601–1603, 1606–8, 1625–32. London: Public Record Office, H.M. Stationery Office, 1860.

'Catastrophic Dimensions: The Rupture of English and Irish Identities in Early Modern Ireland, 1534–1615', by D. W. Cunnane, in

Essays in History, vol. 36. Virginia: Corcoran Dept. of History, University of Virginia, 1994.

'Catholic Families of the Pale', by John Kingston, in *Reportorium Novum*, vol. I, Dublin Diocesan Historical Record. Dublin: Browne and Nolan, 1956.

Civil Survey, The; (1654–1656), IX, County of Wexford, ed. Robert C. Simmington. Dublin: Stationery Office for the Irish Manuscripts Commission, 1953.

Commentarius Rinuccinianus vols I–V, eds. B. O'Farrell, D. O'Connell, and J. Kavanagh. Dublin: Catholic Church, 1949.

Crown Surveys of Lands 1500–1541 with the Kildare Rental Begun in 1518, ed. Gearóid Mac Niocaill. Text I, London Public Record Office, SC11/935. Dublin: Irish Manuscripts Commission, 1992.

Dialect of Forth and Bargy, The; by T.P. Dolan and Diarmuid Ó Muirithe. Dublin: Four Courts Press, 1996.

Distinguished Irishmen of the 16th Century, by Edmund Hogan, S.J. London: Burns & Oates, 1894.

'Dublin Residence of the Society of Jesus 1598–1832, The'; by Rev. John McErlean S.J., in *Irish Jesuit Directory and Year Book*. Dublin: Irish Messenger Office, 1933.

'Dunkirk of Ireland: Wexford Privateers during the 1640s, The'; by Jane Ohlmeyer, in the *Journal of the Wexford Historical Society*, 12. Wexford: Wexford Historical Society, 1988.

'English Language in Early Modern Ireland, The'; by Alan Bliss, in *A New History of Ireland*, vol. 3, eds. T. W. Moody, F. X. Martin and F. J. Byrne. Oxford: Oxford University Press, 1999.

Exile of Ireland: Hugh O'Neill, Prince of Ulster, An; by Micheline Kerney Walsh. Dublin: Four Courts Press, 1996.

'"Firm Catholics" or "Loyal Subjects": Religious and Political Allegiance in Seventeenth-Century Ireland', by Alan Ford, in *Political Discourse in Seventeenth and Eighteenth-Century Ireland*, eds. David G. Boyce, Robert Eccleshall and Vincent Geoghegan. Basingstoke: Palgrave, 2001.

Georgian Society Records of Eighteenth-Century Domestic Architecture and Decoration in Dublin (1912), The; Georgian Society (Dublin, Ireland). Shannon: Irish University Press, 1969.

'Guide to Material for a Biography of Father Luke Wadding', by Benignus Millet, in *Father Luke Wadding: A Commemorative Volume*, ed. Franciscan Fathers. Dublin: Clonmore and Reynolds, 1957.

'Henry O'Neill and the Formation of the Irish Regiment in the Netherlands, 1605', by Jerrold Casway, in *Irish Historical Studies*, vol. 17, Irish Historical Society. Dublin: Hodges Figgis & Co., 1972–73.

History of Enniscorthy, by William H. Grattan-Flood. Enniscorthy: Echo Printing Works, 1920.

History of the Catholic Diocese of Dublin; eds. J. Kelly and D. Keogh. Dublin: Four Courts Press, 1999.

History of the County Dublin, A; by Francis Erlington Ball, vols I–VI. (Reproduced by photolithography from the first impression of 1902). Dublin: Gill and Macmillan, 1979.

History of the Diocese of Ferns, by W. H. Grattan-Flood. Waterford: Downey, 1915.

History of the Town and County of Wexford, vols 1–6, ed. Philip Herbert Hore, London, 1906 (Reprint). Dublin: W.A. Hennessy esq., 1978.

'Immensity Confined: Luke Wadding, Bishop of Ferns', by Celestine Murphy, *Journal of the Wexford Historical Society, no. 12*. Wexford: Wexford Historical Society, 1988–89.

Indexes of Irish Wills, by W.P.W. Phillimore and Gertrude Thrift. Baltimore: Baltimore Genealogical Publishing Co., 1970.

'Irish Abroad, The'; by Father John J. Silke, in *A New History of Ireland* vol. 3, eds. T. W. Moody, F. X. Martin and F. J. Byrne. Oxford: Oxford University Press, 1999.

'Irish Economy 1600–60, The'; by Aidan Clarke, in *A New History of Ireland*, vol. 3, eds. T. W. Moody, F. X. Martin and F. J. Byrne. Oxford: Oxford University Press, 1999.

Irish Military Community in Spanish Flanders, The; by Gráinne Henry. Dublin: Irish Academic Press, 1992.

'Irish Names in the Malines Ordination Registers 1602–1749', by B. Jennings, in *The Irish Ecclesiastical Record*, February 1951–May 1952. Dublin: Browne and Nolan, 1952.

Jesuits in Dublin, The; by Edward Eugene O'Donnell S.J. Dublin: Wolfhound Press, 1999.

'Lambert of Wexford', by Hubert A. Lambert, in *The Past*, vol. 11. Enniscorthy: Iris Chumann Seanchais Uí Cinsealaigh, 1921.

Medieval Religious Houses: Ireland: with an appendix to early sites, by Aubry Gwyn and R. Neville Hadcock. Harlow: Longmans, 1970.

'Pacification, Plantation and the Catholic Question, 1603–23', by A. Clarke and R. Dudley Edwards, in *A New History of Ireland*, vol. 3, eds. T. W. Moody, F. X. Martin and F. J. Byrne. Oxford: Oxford University Press, 1999.

'Religious Life in Old Dublin', by the Rev. Myles V. Ronan, in *Dublin Historical Record*, vol. II, 1939–40. Dublin: Old Dublin Society, 1940.

'Selling Royal Favours, 1624–32', by Aidan Clarke, in *A New History of Ireland*, vol. 3, eds. T. W. Moody, F. X. Martin and F. J. Byrne. Oxford: Oxford University Press, 1999.

State Policy in Irish Education, A.D. 1536 to 1816, exemplified in documents collected for lectures to post graduate classes, by Rev. Timothy Corcoran S.J. Dublin: Fallon Brothers, 1916.

Old English in Ireland, The; by A. Clarke. Dublin: Four Courts Press, 2000.

Peerage of Ireland, The; by John Lodge esq., vol. VI. Dublin: printed for J. Leathley, G. and A. Ewing, W. Smith, J. Smith, G. Faulkner, A. Bradley, and A. Moore, 1754.

Social History of Ireland, A; by P.W. Joyce. London: Longman, Green & Co., 1903.

'Superiors of the Irish Mission of the Society of Jesus 1598–1774, The'; by Rev. John McErlean S.J., in the *Irish Jesuit Directory and Year Book*. Dublin: Irish Messenger Office, Dublin, 1929.

To the Greater Glory: A History of the Irish Jesuits, by Louis McRedmond. Dublin: Gill and Macmillan, 1991.

Was Wexford Betrayed to Cromwell?, by Kathleen Browne. Wexford: 1940.

Wexford: History and Society, eds. K. Whelan and W. Nolan. Dublin: Geography Publications, 1987.

Wild Geese in Spanish Flanders 1582–1700, by Brendan Jennings. Dublin: Stationery Office for the Irish Manuscripts Commission, 1964.

'Wild Goose Tradition, The'; by Micheline Kerney Walsh, in *The Irish Sword*, vol. 17, 1987–90. Dublin: Military History Society of Ireland, 1990.

ENGLAND

Art of Memory, The; by Frances A. Yates. London: Routledge & Kegan Paul, 1966.

Brief History of Gresham College 1597–1997, A; by Richard Chartres and David Vermont. London: Gresham College, 1998.

Clongowes Record, The; by Timothy Corcoran S.J. Dublin: Browne and Nolan, 1932.

General History of the Pyrates, A; by Daniel Defoe (1724), ed. Manuel Schonhorn. London: J.M. Dent & Sons, 1972. (The authorship of this volume has been wrongly attributed to Defoe. The author is now generally accepted to have been a Captain Charles Johnson.)

History of Britain: The British Wars 1603–1776, A; by Simon Schama. London: BBC Worldwide, 2001.

Defensio fidei Catholicae, et apostolicae adversus Anglicanae sectae errores, by Francisco de Suárez (Coimbra, 1613). Paris: Vives, 1878.

Dictionary of National Biographies, vols I–XXIII, ed. Leslie Stephens and Stephen Lee. London: Smith, Elder & Co, 1890.

Divine Right and Democracy: An Anthology of Political Writing in Stuart England, ed. David Wootton. Harmondsworth: Penguin, 1986.

English Dictionaries 800–1700: The Topical Tradition, by Werner Hüllen. Oxford: Clarendon Press, 1999.

'Gresham College: Precursor of the Royal Society', by Francis R. Johnson, in *Journal of the History of Ideas*, vol. I, issue 4. Baltimore and London: Johns Hopkins University Press, 1940.

Life Among the Pirates, by David Cordingly. London: Little Brown & Company, 1995.

London: A Social History, by Roy Porter. London: Hamish Hamilton, 1994.

On the Composition of Images, Signs and Ideas, by Giordano Bruno, ed. Dick Higgins. New York: Willis, Locker & Owens, 1991.

Records of the English Province of the Society of Jesus, series I, vol. I, by Henry Foley S.J. London: Roehampton [printed], 1877.

Safeguard of the Sea: A Naval History of Britain, The; vol. I, 660–1649; by N.A.M. Rodger. London: HarperCollins, 1997.

Selections from Three Works of Francisco Suárez . . . De legibus, ac Deo legislatore, 1612; Defensio fidei Catholicae, et apostolicae adversus angli-

canae sectae errores, 1613: De triplice virtute theologica, fide, spe, et charitate, 1621. (Vol. I. The photographic reproduction of the selections from the original editions. Vol. II. The translation). Prepared by Gwladys L. Williams, Ammi Brown and John Waldron. Oxford: Clarendon Press, 1944.

Studies in the History of Classical Teaching, by Timothy Corcoran S.J. Dublin: Educational Company of Ireland, 1911.

William Bathe S.J., 1564–1614, A Pioneer in Linguistics, by Seán P. Ó Mathúna. Philadelphia: J. Benjamins Pub. Co., 1986.

'William Bathe S.J., Recusant Scholar, 1564–1614: "Weary of the Heresy" ', by Seán P. Ó Mathúna, in *Recusant History*, vol. 19, no. 1, May 1988.

FLANDERS

Age of Rubens, The; by Peter C. Sutton. Ghent and Boston: Museum of Fine Arts, Boston, in association with Ludion Press, 1993.

Anthony Van Dyck: A Life, by Robin Blake. London: Constable, 1999.

Armada of Flanders, The; by R.A. Stradling. Cambridge: Cambridge University Press, 1992.

Battles of the Thirty Years War, by William P. Guthrie. Westport CT: Greenwood Press, 2002.

Bibliothèque de la Compagnie de Jésus, ed. Carlos Sommervogel. Paris-Brussels: 1891.

De Pavía a Rocroi, Los Tercios de la Infantería Española, by Julio Albi de la Cuesta. Madrid: Balkan Editores, 1999.

Ein Söldnerleben im Dreißigjährigen Krieg, by Jan Peters. Berlin: Eine Quelle zur Sozialgeschichte, 1993.

Flandes y el Mar del Norte (1618–1639), (second edition), by José Alcalá Zamora. Madrid: Centro de Estudios Constitucionales, 2001.

Flandes y La Monarquía Hispánica 1500–1713, by Miguel Ángel Echevarría. Bacigalupe: Editores Silex, 1998.

Galicia en el Camino de Flandes: Actividad Militar, Economía y Sociedad en la España Noratlántica, by María del Carmen Saavedra Vázquez. La Coruña: Ediciós do Castro, 1996.

Hall's Dictionary of Subjects and Symbols in Art (revised edition). London: John Murray, 1974.

Katalog der Galerie Alter Meister, Vol I, by Anton Pigler. Budapest: Akadémiai Kiadó, 1967.

Letters of Peter Paul Rubens, The; trans. and ed. Ruth Saunders Magurn. Cambridge: Harvard University Press, 1971.

Memorable y glorioso viaje del Infante Cardenal Don Fernando de Austria desde 12. de Abril 1632. que salió de Madrid con su Magestad Don Felipe IV. su hermano para la ciudad de Barcelona, hasta 4. De Novembre de 1634. Que entró en la de Bruselas, by Diego de Aedo y Gallart. Antwerp: 1635.

Militaris disciplina. kritische Ausgabe. herausgegeben von Bodo Gotzkowsky, by Hans Wilhelm Kirchhof. Stuttgart: Hiersemann, 1976.

'Peter Paul Rubens', by Walter Liedtke, in *Timken Museum of Art* (Catalog). San Diego: Timken Museum, 1999.

R.P. Jean Charles della Faille, de la Compagnie de Jesus Precepteur de Don Juan d'Austriche, Le; by H.P. van der Speeten. Brussels: *Collection de Precis Historiques*, 3, 1874.

Rubens: Paintings, Drawings, Prints, in the Prince's Gate Collection, by Helen Braham. London: The Trustees of the Home House Society for the Courtauld Institute of Art, 1988.

Söldner im Nordwestdeutschland des 16. und 17. Jahrhunderts, by Peter Burschel. Göttingen: Sozialgeschichtliche Studien, 1994.

Thirty Years War, The; by C.V. Wedgwood. London: Pimlico, 1938.

Van Dyck: Paintings and Drawings, by James Lawson. Munich and London: Prestel, 1999.

War and Society in Early-Modern Europe, 1495–1715, by Frank Tallett. London: Routledge, 1992.

Wild Geese of the Antrim MacDonnells, The; by Hector McDonnell. Dublin: Irish Academic Press, 1999.

FRANCE

Cardinal Richelieu and the Making of France, by Anthony Levi. London: Carroll & Graf, 2001.

Henry de Rohan, son rôle politique et militaire sous Louis XIII 1579–1638, by Auguste Laugel. Paris: Firmin-Didot, 1889.

History of the French Navy from Its Beginnings to the Present Day, A; by Ernest H. Jenkins. Annapolis: Naval Institute Press, 1973.

Louis XIII: Roi Cornélien, by Pierre Chevallier. Paris: Fayard, 1979.

Richelieu and Olivares, by J. H. Elliott. Cambridge: Cambridge University Press, 1984.

SPAIN

Anales de la Nobleza de España, by D. Francisco F. de Béthancourt. Madrid: Imprenta de José Garcia a cargo de J. Peña, 1880.

Así vivían en el Siglo de Oro, by José Calvo. Madrid: Grupo Anaya, 2000.

Bibliothèque de la Compania de Jesús, vol. VI, eds. Agustin de Backer, Aloys de Backer, Aguste Carayon and Carlos Sommervogel. Brussels-Paris: Schepens, A. Picard, 1895.

'Companhia de Jesus e a Restaurção de Portugal 1640, A'; by Padre Francisco Rodrigues, in *Anais de Academía Portuguesa da História*, vol. I, no. 4. Lisbon: Academia Portuguesa da História, 1942.

Contributo alla storia feudale della Calabria nel sec. XVII, by J. Mazzoleni. Naples: Ed. Fiorentino, 1963.

Count-Duke of Olivares: The Statesman in an Age of Decline, The; by J. H. Elliott. New Haven and London: Yale Univesrity Press, 1986.

'Devotional World of the Irish Catholic Exile in Early-Modern Galicia 1598-1666, The'; by Ciarán O'Shea, in *The Irish in Europe 1580–1815*, ed. Thomas O'Connor. Dublin: Four Courts Press, 2001.

Diccionario Histórico Biográfico del Perú, by Manuel de Mendiburu, Lima: Editorial Universitaria, 1933.

Diccionario Historico de la Ciencia Moderna en España, by José Maria Lopez Piñero et al. Barcelona: Edicions 62, 1983.

'Early-Modern Irish College Network in Iberia 1590–1800, The'; by Patricia O'Connell, in *The Irish in Europe 1580–1815*, ed. Thomas O'Connor. Dublin: Four Courts Press, 2001.

'El Colegio de Irlandeses de Santiago de Compostela', by José Couselo Bouzas, Santiago: Seminario Conciliar 1935.

Elenco de Grandezas y Titulos Nobiliaros Españoles. Recopilado y redactado por don Ampelio Alonso de Cadenas y López, & don Vincente de Cadenas y Vicent. Madrid: Instituto Salazar y Castro, 1995.

El Escorial: Royal Monastery of San Lorenzo, by Juan Losada and José Manuel Tornero. León: Everest, 1991.

Enciclopedia Universal Ilustrada Europeo-Americana. Barcelona: Hijos de J.Espasa, 1925.

Gazeta y Nuevas de la Corte de España desde el año 1600 en adelante, by G. Gascón de Torquemada. Madrid: Ed. Marqués de la Floresta, 1991.

'Geometric Analysis of the Design of Stones and Arches in the Architectural Treatise of Jean Charles de La Faille', by I. Vázquez Paredes in Publicacions Mathematiques de la Seccio de Universitat Autonoma de Barcelona (Journal), *Publ. Sec. Mat. Univ. Aut. Barcelona* 20. Barcelona: Universitat Autonoma. 1980.

Histoire de la Marine, vol. I, by Philippe Masson. Paris: Lavauzelle, 1992.

Historia de la Caída del Conde-Duque de Olivares, Anon. Madrid: Editorial Algazara, 1992.

Historia de la Filosofía en España hasta el Siglo XX, by Mario Méndez Bejarano. Madrid: Imprenta Renacimiento, 1927.

Historia de la Santa A.M. Iglesia de Santiago de Compostela, vol. IX, by Antonio Lopez Ferreiro, Facsimile edition. Santiago de Compostela: Seminario Conciliar Central, 1999.

Historia del Colegio Viejo de San Bartolomé Mayor de la Célebre Universidad de Salamanca, by F. Ruiz de Vergara y Álava, ed. J. de Rojas y Contreras (Marqués de Alventós). Madrid: Andrés Ortega, 1766–1770.

Historia de Úbeda en sus Documentos, vol. II, *Linajes y Hombres ilustres*, by Ginés de la Jara Torres Navarrete. Úbeda: Gráficas Minerva. 1997.

Historia de una Conjura, by Louisa Isabel Alvarez de Toledo. Cádiz: Ed. Diputación de Cádiz, 1985.

Historiae Catholicae Iberniae Compendium, by Philip O'Sullivan (Lisbon, 1621). Cork: Centre for Neo-Latin Studies, UCC, 2001.

Iglesias y Conventos del Antiguo Madrid, by Ramón Guerra de la Vega, Madrid: 1996.

'Irish College, Santiago de Compostela: 1605–1767, The'; by Pat O'Connell, in *Archivium Hibernicum*, vol. L. Maynooth: Catholic Record Society, 1996.

'Las relaciones sobre el sitio de Fuenterrabía (1638–1639): la construccíon de un acontecimiento en la España de los Austrias', by Javier Díaz Noci, in *Euskonews y Media*, no. 149, 4–11 de Enero. San Sebastián: Sociedad de Estudios Vascos, 2002.

'Not Only Seminaries: The Political Role of the Irish Colleges in Seventeenth-Century Spain', by Oscar Recio Morales, in *History Ireland*, vol 9, no. 3, Dublin: 2001.

O'Neills in Spain, The; by Micheline Walsh. Dublin: Belgrove University, 1957.

'O'Sullivan Beare in Spain: Some Unpublished Documents', by Micheline Kearney Walsh, in *Archivium Hibernicum*, vol. XLV. Maynooth: Catholic Record Society, 1990.

Palace for a King: The Buen Retiro and the Court of Philip IV, A; by J. Brown and J. H. Elliott. New Haven and London: Yale University Press, 1980.

Política Internacional de Felipe IV, La; by Francisco Martín Sanz, edición electronica. Segovia: Libros en red, 2003.

Selections from the Zoilomastix of Philip O'Sullivan Beare (1624–1667), ed. Thomas J. O'Donnell, S.J., M.A. Dublin: Stationery Office for the Irish Manuscripts Commission, 1960.

Sitio y Socorro de Fuenterrabía y Sucesos del Año de 1638 by Juan de Palafox y Mendoza. (quarta imp.), Madrid: La oficina de don Gerónimo Ortega y Herederos de Ibarra, 1793.

Spain and its World 1500–1700, by J. H. Elliott. New Haven and London: Yale University Press, 1997.

Spain in the Seventeenth-Century, by Graham Darby. New York and London: Longman, 1994.

Spanish Monarchy and Irish Mercenaries: The Wild Geese in Spain 1618–68, The; by R.A. Stradling. Dublin: Irish Academic Press, 1994.

Spanish Seaborne Empire, The; by J. H. Parry. California: University of California Press, 1990.

Students and Society in Early Modern Spain, by Richard L. Kagan. Baltimore and London: Johns Hopkins University Press, 1975.

'Students of the Irish College Salamanca (1595–1619)', by D. O'Doherty, in *Archivium Hibernicum*, vol. II. Maynooth: Catholic Record Society, 1913.

'Will of John O'Neill, Third Earl of Tyrone, The'; by Micheline Walsh, in *Seanchas Ard Mhacha*, vol. 7, no. 2. Armagh: Armagh Diocesan Historical Society, 1974.

THE JOURNEY FROM ESCALONA TO MEXICO CITY

'Apuntamientos en torno de la administración pública y gobierno civil y ecclesiástico en el siglo XVII', by Ernesto de la Torre Villar, in *Estudios de Historia Novohispana*, vol. 8. Mexico: Instuto de Investigaciones Históricas, Universidad Nacional Autónoma de México. 1985.

Arco triunfal: emblas, geroglificos y poesías con que la cuidad de la Puebla recibío al Virrey de Nueva España, Marqués de Villena, by P. Mateo Salcedo. Puebla de los Angeles: 1640.

Introducción al Estudio de los Virreyes de Nueva España, 1535–1746, vol. 1, by J. Ignacio Rubio Mañé. Mexico: Ediciones Selectas. 1955.

Régimen Jurídico de las Armadas de la Carrera de Indias, Siglos XVI y XVII, El; by José Antonio Caballero Juárez. Mexico: Instituto de Investigacion Jurídicas, U.N.A.M. 2001.

Sátiras Políticas de la España Moderna, by Teófanes Egido. Madrid: Alianza Editorial. 1973.

Six Galleons for the King of Spain: Imperial Defence in the Early Seventeenth-Century, by Carla Rahn Phillips. Baltimore & London: Johns Hopkins University Press, 1986.

Spain's Men of the Sea: Daily Life on the Indies Fleets in the Sixteenth Century, by Pablo Emilio Pérez-Mallaina, trans. Carla Rahn Phillips. Baltimore and London: Johns Hopkins University Press, 1998.

Viaje del Virrey Marqués de Villena, by Cristóbal Gutiérrez de Medina (1640), con introducción y notas de Don Manuel Romero de Terreros. Mexico: Imprenta Universitaria, 1947.

MEXICO

Anecdotario de Viajeros Extranjeros en Mexico en Siglos XVI–XX, by José Iturriaga de la Fuente. Mexico: Fondo de Cultura Económica, 1988.

'Apologia de la Carta Pastoral del Sr. Obispo . . . Por D. Antonuio Belvis, 1642; Lo que pasó en Méjico dejando de ser virey el marqués de

Villena y entrando P. en un interim, 20. Juli 1642', in *Memorial Histórico Español*, vol. XVI. Madrid: 1862.

Audiencia de México Según Los Visitadores (Siglos XVI Y XVII), La; by Pilar Arregui Zamorano. Mexico: UNAM, Instituto de Investigaciones Jurídicas, 1985.

Aztecs Under Spanish Rule, The; by Charles Gibson. California: Stanford University Press, 1964.

'Barroquismo y Criollismo en los recibimientos hechos a don Diego López Pacheco Cabrera y Bobadilla, virrey de Nueva España 1640: un estudio preliminar', by Solange Alberro, in *Colonial Latin American Historical Review*, vol. 8, no. 4. New Mexico: 1999.

Blacks in Colonial Veracruz: Race, Ethnicity and Regional Development, by Patrick J. Carroll. Austin: University of Texas Press, 2001.

'Borja y Velasco, Gaspar', by Q. Aldea Vaquero, in *Diccionario de Historia Eclesiástica de España*, vol. I. Madrid: Instituto Enrique Flórez, 1972.

Capital, La; by Jonathan Kandell. New York: Henry Holt & Co., 1988.

'Cartas de Jesuitas', in *Memorial Histórico Español*, vol. VII. Madrid: 1854.

Castas Mexicanas, Las; by María Concepción García Sáiz. Milan: Olivetti, 1989.

Catalogo de los Textos Marginados Novohispano, Inquisición: Siglo XVII, ed. María Argueda Méndez et al. México: Archivo General de la Nación, 1997.

Church in Colonial Latin America, The; ed. John F. Schwaller. Wilmington: SR Books, 2000.

'Ciencia Española bajo la Inquisición, La'; by Marcelino Menéndez Pelayo, ed. J. Rodríguez, in *Azogue*, no. 2, July–December. Barcelona: 1999.

Codex Telleriano-Remensis, trans. and ed. by Eloise Quiñones Keber. Austin: University of Texas Press, 1992.

Crime and Punishment in Late Colonial Mexico City, 1692–1810, by Gabriel Haslip-Viera. Albuquerque: University of New Mexico Press, 1999.

Critical Passions: Selected Essays, by Jean Franco. Durham: Duke University Press, 1999.

'Cronologia de las Epidemias y Crisis Agricolas de la Epoca Colonial', by E. Malvido, in *Historia Mexicana.* Mexico: 1973.

'Crypto-Jews and the Inquisition in New Spain in the 17th Century', by Pinhas Bibelnik in *SISCA Report* No. 7. Jerusalem: The Vidal Sassoon International Centre for the Study of Anti-semitism, the Hebrew University of Jerusalem. 1992.

Datos para la Historia de la Iglesia en Guatemala, vols I and II., by Agustín Estrada Monroy. Guatemala: Sociedad de Geografía e Historia de Guatemala, 1973.

Description of the Indies, c. *1620*, by Antonio Vázquez de Espinosa. Washington: Smithsonian Institution Press, 1968.

Devastation of the Indies: A Brief Account, The (reprint edition); by Bartolomé de las Casas, Herma Briffault and Bill M. Donovan. Baltimore: Johns Hopkins University Press, 1992.

Diario 1648–1664, vol. I, by Gregorio M. de Guijo. Mexico: Ed. Porrua, 1953.

Diccionario Bio-Bibliografico de la Compañia de Jésus en Mexico, vol. XIII. Mexico: Editorial Tradición, 1967.

'Don Guillén de Lamport y su "Regio Salterio"', by Gabriel Méndez Plancarte, in *Ábside*, vol. XII. Mexico: 1948.

Don Guillén De Lampart, La Inquisición y la Independencia en el Siglo XVII, by Luis González Obregón. Mexico: Librería de la Vda. De C. Bouret, 1908.

Don Juan de Palafox y Mendoza: Obispo de Puebla y Osma, Visatador y Virrey de la Nueva España, by Genaro García. Mexico: 1918.

Early History of Greater Mexico, The; by Ida Altman, Sarah Cline and Juan Javier Pecador. New Jersey: Prentice Hall, 2002.

'Encyclopedia de Mexico; Los Gobernantes de Mexico' in *Don Juan de Palafox y Mendoza*, by Genaro García. Mexico: Secretaria de Education Publica, 1918.

Escudo de Armas de Mexico: celestial proteccion de esta nobilissima ciudad, de la Nueva-Espana, y de casi todo el nuevo mundo, Maria Santissima, en su portentosa imagen del Mexicano Guadalupe, milagrosamente apparecida en el palacio arzobispal el año de 1531, by Cayetano de Cabrera y Quintero (edición facsímil). Alicante: Biblioteca Virtual Miguel de Cervantes, 2004

Fire and Blood: A History of Mexico, by T. R. Fehrenbach. New York: Da Capo Press, 1995.

'Frecuencia y Duración de Sequías en la Cuenca de México de Fines del Siglo XVI a Mediados del XIX', by Gustavo Garza Merodio, in *Investigaciones Geográficas Boletín del Instituto de Geografía*, no. 48. Mexico: U.N.A.M., 2002.

Gobernantes de México: desde la Época Prehispánica hasta Nuestros Días, by Fernando Orozco Linares. Mexico: Panorama Editorial, 1985.

'Hernán Cortés en la Obra del Cronista Sepúlveda', by Ramón Iglesia, in *Revista de Indias*, vol. 9. Madrid: Consejo Superior de Investigaciones Científicas, 1948.

Hierarchia Catholica medii et recentoris aevi sive Summorum Pontificum, S.R.E. cardinalium ecclesiarum antistitum series, eds. Guilelmus van Gulik, Conradus Eubel, Ludovicus Schmitz-Kallenberg, Remigius Ritzler, and Pirminus Sefrin, vols V and VI. Munich: Librariae Regensbergianae, 1913–1978 (reprint edition). Padua: Il Messaggero di S. Antonio, 1968.

Historia de la Inquisición en España y America: Obra Dirigida por Joaquin Pérez Villanueva y Bartolomé Escandell Bonet, vol. I., *El Conocimiento Científico y el Proceso Histórico de la Institución (1478–1834)*. Madrid: Patrimonio Nacional, 1984.

Historia del Colegio Imperial de Madrid, vol. I, by José Simón-Díaz. Madrid: Instituto de Estudios Madrileños/CSIC, 1952.

Historia del Hospital San Francisco de Paula, by Jorge LeRoy y Cassá. Havana: El Siglo XX, 1958.

Historia del Nuevo Reino de Leon (1577–1723), by Eugenio del Hoya. Mexico: Ediciones Al Voleo, 1979.

Historia del Tribunal del Santo Officio de la Inquisicíon en México, by José Toribio Medina. Mexico: Ed. J.J. Rueda, 1952.

Historia Documental de Mexico, ed. M. León Portilla et al. Mexico: U.N.A.M., Instituto de Investigaciones Históricas, 1964.

Historia Verdadera de la Conquista de Nueva España, by Bernal Díaz del Castillo (prologue by J. Ramírez Cabañas). Mexico: Editorial Porrúa, 1966.

History of Puebla, The; by Malitón Salazar Monroy. Puebla: Salazar Monroy, 1945.

History of the Inquisition in Spain, A; vols I–IV, by Henry C. Lea. New York: Macmillan, 1922.

'Impresores Libreros en Nueva España del Siglo XVII, Los'; by Luisa Martínez Leal, in *Casa del Tiempo*. Mexico: Universidad Autónoma Metropolitana, May 2002.

In Defence of the Indians, by Bartolomé de las Casas, trans. Stafford Poole. Illinois: Northern Illinois University Press, 1992.

Inquisición y Sociedad en Mexico 1571–1700, by Solange Alberro. Mexico: Fondo de Cultura Económica, 1988.

Inquisition, The; by Michael Baigent and Richard Leigh. London: Penguin Books, 1999.

Irish Flora, An; by D.A. Webb, J. Parnell, and D. Doogul. Dundalk: Dundalgan Press, 1996.

Jews in New Spain: Faith, Flame and Inquisition, The; by C. Gables. Miami: University of Miami Press, 1970.

Juan de Palafox y Mendoza: Ideas Politicas, ed. José Rojas Garciadueñas, Mexico: Ediciones de UNAM, 1946.

Justice by Insurance: The General Indian Court of Colonial Mexico and the Legal Aides of the Half-Real, by Woodrow W. Borah. Berkeley: University of California Press, 1983.

Herbolaria en Mexico, La; by Xavier Lozoya. Mexico: Tercer Milenio, 1998.

'Lucha contra el Oscurantismo, La'; by Javier Flores, in *La Jornada*. Mexico: 26 May 1997.

Land and Society in Colonial Mexico: The Great Hacienda, by Francois Chevalier. Berkeley: University of California Press, 1952.

Lieutenant Nun: Memoir of a Basque Transvestite in the New World, trans. Michele and Gabriel Stepto. Boston: Beacon Press, 1996.

Médicos en el Santo Oficio, Los; by Ernestina Jiménez Olivares. Mexico: Departmento de Historia y Filosofía de la Medicina, U.N.A.M., 2003.

'Megadrought and Megadeath in 16th Century Mexico', by Rodolfo Acuna-Soto, David W. Stahle, Malcolm K. Cleaveland, and Matthew D. Therrell, in *Emerging Infectious Diseases*, vol. 8, no. 4. Atlanta: Centre for Disease Control, April 2002.

Mexico's Merchant Elite, 1590–1660: Silver, State and Society, by Louisa Schell Hoberman. London: Duke University Press, 1991.

'Mobilario del Siglo XVII', by María Paz Aguiló Alonso, in *El Mueble Español: Estrado y Dormitorio*. Madrid: Museo Español de Arte Contemporáneo, Communidad de Madrid, Consejería Cultural, Dirección General de Patrimonio Cultural, 1990.

Orígenes de la Ciensa Moderna en México (1630–1680), Los; by Elias Trabulse. Mexico: Fondo de Cultura Económica, 1994.

Poblacion Negra de Mexico: estudios etnohistóricos, La; by Gonzalo Aguirre Beltrán. Mexico: Fondo de Cultura Económica, 1972.

'Presence of People from Jewish Origin and Their Activities in New Spain', by Eva Alexandra Uchmany, in *Reunir*, vol. III. Mexico: January 1998.

Property and Permissiveness in Bourbon Mexico, by Juan Pedro Viqueira Albán, translated by Sonya Lipsett-Rivera and Sergio Rivera Ayala. Wilmington: Scholarly Resources Inc., 2000.

Psiquiatría y Inquisición: Procesos a Enfermos Mentales, by Ernestina Jiménez Olivares. Mexico: Departmento de Historia y Filosofia, Facultad de Medicina, U.N.A.M., 2003.

Race, Class and Politics in Colonial Mexico 1610–1670, by J.I. Israel. Oxford: Oxford University Press, 1975.

Rebeliones Indigenas y Precursores de la Independencia Méxicana en los Siglos XVI, XVII, y XVIII, by L. Gonzalez Obregón. Paris and Mexico: Fuente Cultural, 1908.

'Simón Váez Sevilla', by Eva Alexandra Uchmany, in *Estudios de Novo-Hispana*, vol. 9. Mexico: 1987.

Singular Proceso de Salomón Machorro (Juan de Léon), by Boleslao Lewin. Buenos Aires: 1977.

Spada e la Croce, La; by Fabio Troncarelli. Rome: Salerno Editrice, 1999.

Spanish Inquisition, The; by Cecil Roth. London: W.W. Norton, 1964.

Tratado de las Supersticiones y Costumbres Gentílicas que Hoy Viven entre los Indios Naturales desta Nueva España, vol. I., by Hernando Ruiz de Alarcón, México, 1629. Alicante: Biblioteca Virtual Miguel de Cervantes, 1999.

Travels in the New World, by Thomas Gage, ed. J. Eric S. Thompson. Norman: University of Oklahoma Press, 1958.

Urban Images of the Hispanic World, 1493–1793, by Richard L. Kagan. New Haven and London: Yale University Press, 2000.

'Virreinatos Americanos, Los'; by Pedro A. Vives, in *Cuadernos Historia* vol. 16, no. 83. Madrid: 1997.

'Was the Huey Cocoliztli a Haemorrhagic Fever?', by John S. Marr and James B. Kiracoffe, in *Medical History*, vol. 44, no. 3. London: July 2000.

ZORRO ETC.

Bandits (revised edition), by Eric J. Hobsbawm. New York: New Press, 2000.

Count of Monte Cristo, The; by Alexander Dumas. Hertfordshire: Wordsworth Edition, 1997.

'Death of Zorro', article in *New Ross Echo*, 12 September 2001.

'Inquisition Unmasks Zorro the Irishman', article by Richard Owen, in *The Times*, 29 January 1999.

'Johnston McCulley', by Wade Austin, in *Twentieth Century Western Writers*, ed. Geoff Sadler. Detroit: 1983.

Life and Adventures of Joaquin Murieta, by John Rollin Ridge. Oklahoma: University of Oklahoma Press, 1977.

Man Behind the Mask of Zorro, The; by Fabio Troncarelli, in *History Ireland*, vol. 9, no. 3. Dublin: Autumn 2001.

Mark of Zorro, The; by Johnston McCulley. New York: Tor, 1998.

Martín Garatuza: Memorias de la Inquisición, by Vincente Riva Palacio (Edición digital basada en la edición de Manuel C. de Villegas, 1868). Alicante: Biblioteca Virtual Miguel de Cervantes, 2000.

Memorias de un Impostor: Don Guillén de Lampart, Rey de Mexico, by Vincente Riva Palacio (1872). Mexico: Ed. V. Castro Leal, 1994.

'Paddy O'Zorro', by Karl Brophy, article in *The Mirror*, Dublin, 30 January 1999.

Robin Hood of El Dorado, The; by Walter Noble Burns. New Mexico: University of New Mexico Press, 1999.

Scarlet Pimpernel, The; by Baroness Emmuska Orczy. Thirsk: House of Stratus, 2002.

Searching for Joaquin: Myth, Murieta and History in California, by Bruce Thornton. San Francisco: Encounter Books, 2003.

'Tiburcio Vasques: A Chicano Perspective', by J.A. Burciago, in *The Californians*, May/June 1985.

True Stories of Immortal Crimes, by Henry Ashton-Wolfe. New York: E.P. Dutton & Company, 1931.

Zorro Unmasked: The Official History, by Sandra Curtis. New York: Hyperion, 1997.

Index

O'Sullivan Beare, Donal, 22
Ovid, 260, 261

Pacheco, Father Hernando, 179
Palafox, Jaime de, 94
Palafox y Mendoza, Juan de, 89, 93–4, 95,
    110, 111, 116, 123–6, 128, 150, 153,
    158, 160, 162, 166, 167, 173, 183, 191,
    197, 211, 217, 219, 257, 258, 278, 284,
    285
  appointed Archbishop of Mexico, 146,
    148–9, 150–1
  dispute with the Holy Office, 204, 205–6,
    214–15, 276
  dispute with Jesuits over tithes, 193, 254
  dispute with Salvatierra, 207, 208–9, 210
  dispute with Villena, 134–5, 136–8
  extends system of debt-peonage, 154–5
  Puebla Cathedral, 216, 218–19
  recalled to Madrid, 216
  refuses to take charge of investigation of
    Lamport, 177–8
Palatino, Juan, 52
Paris, 38, 69, 292
  parlement of, 30
Pedrosa y Tapia, Manuel de, 120, 160, 167
Peralta, Matías de, 219
  Mathías, 256
Pereira, Inés, 196
Pérez, Esperanza María, 108
Pérez, Francisco, 108
Pérez, Ignacio Fernando, 140–2, 143–4,
    155, 156, 157, 159, 161, 173, 176, 191,
    202
Pérez, Juan, 246, 248
Perote, 114, 115
Peru, ban on trade with New Spain, 91, 93
Pinto Bravo, Diego, 71, 72, 229–30, 231,
    232–4, 240, 241–2, 243, 246, 275
  death of, 253, 267
  plans escape with Lamport, 234–6,
    237–9
  recaptured, 253
pirates, 32–8, 181–2
Pluma, Mos de la, 52
Plunkett, Henry, 20, 88
Plunkett, Robert, 43, 45
Portuguese rebellion, 128, 136
Poza, Juan Bautista, 53, 55
Prada, Fray Juan de, 149
'Proclamation of Independence', 163–6
Propaganda Committee, 74, 75
psalms of David, 260, 265

Puebla de Los Angeles, 115–16, 123, 124,
    125, 132, 133, 134, 135, 136, 142, 145,
    146, 149, 162, 172, 191, 205, 211, 214,
    215, 230
  Palafox's cathedral in, 216, 218–19
Puerto Rico, 109

Quevedo, Francisco, 74
Quin, Thomas, 20
Quiroga y Moya, Pedro, 92

Ravaschiera, Ettore, 95
Ravaschiera, Geronimo, 152
Reformation, 46
repartimiento, 154, 193
Reyes, Inés de los, 247, 249
Ricarde, Claudio, 53
Riccardi, Niccolò, 169
Richelieu, Cardinal, 36, 37, 49, 74, 78, 149,
    292, 294
Riva Palacio, Vincente, 285, 286, 287, 290
Rivera, Blanca, 146, 220
Rivera, Clara, 146–7
Rivera, Isabel de, 146, 210
Rivera, María, 146–7
Roales, Francisco de, 53, 121
Roche, John, Bishop of Ferns, 42
rogation ceremonies, 130
Rome, 46, 60
Romero, Josefa, 229–31, 232
Romero, Juan, 102
Romero, María, 229–31, 232, 238, 275
Romero, Nicolasa, 229–31, 232
Romero, Teresa, 229–32, 232
Romero Zapata, Juan, 229, 230–1
Roth, Cecil, 8
Rothe, David (Bishop of Ossory), 179
Rothenburg, 66
Royal Academy of Sciences, 86
Royal Psalter see William Lamport
royal surveyors, 140
Rozas, Andrés de, 51
Rubens, Peter Paul, 68, 292–4
  Portrait of a Young Man in Armour
    (Young Captain), 292–5
Ruiz de Contreras, Fernando, 89

Saavedra, Fajardo Diego de, 74
Saboyano, 121, 162, 191
Sáenz de Mañozca y Murillo, Juan, 210,
    214, 215, 238, 239, 241, 244, 245, 247,
    249, 252, 254, 269, 273, 274, 284–5
Saint Laurence the Martyr, 52

330